HEGEL'S DIALECTIC
AND ITS CRITICISM

HEGEL'S DIALECTIC AND ITS CRITICISM

MICHAEL ROSEN

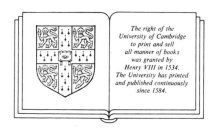

The right of the
University of Cambridge
to print and sell
all manner of books
was granted by
Henry VIII in 1534.
The University has printed
and published continuously
since 1584.

CAMBRIDGE UNIVERSITY PRESS
Cambridge
London   New York   New Rochelle
Melbourne   Sydney

Published by the Press Syndicate of the University of Cambridge
The Pitt Building, Trumpington Street, Cambridge CB2 1RP
32 East 57th Street, New York, NY 10022, USA
10 Stamford Road, Oakleigh, Melbourne 3166, Australia

First published 1982
First paperback edition 1984

Printed in Great Britain at the University Press, Cambridge

Library of Congress catalogue card number: 81–2424

British Library Cataloguing in Publication Data

Rosen, Michael
Hegel's dialectic and its criticism.
1. Hegel, Georg Wilhelm Friedrich – Logic
I. Title
160 B2949.D5
ISBN 0 521 24484 6 hard covers
ISBN 0 521 31860 2 paperback

To the memory of Achim Günther

Si comprendis non est Deus
Augustine

Contents

Preface

'Dialectic', Alexander Herzen once wrote, 'is the algebra of revolution.' More often, though, its function has been alchemical: a source of incantations by which revolutionaries have transmuted defeats into victories – or at least into vindications of the 'dialectical worldview'. This book is written in the belief that the best safeguard against such exploitation is to examine the notion of dialectic at its modern point of origin, in Hegel's theoretical philosophy. It operates there, I believe, as part of a thorough-going, consistently applied, conception of philosophical rationality, centred on the 'speculative discourse' of the *Science of Logic*. That previous commentators have failed to identify this conception has been due, as much as anything, to a concern to separate out an acceptable, independent 'kernel' from this original context. My own interpretation, however, can make no such claim; the rationality of Hegel's dialectic is, I shall argue, inextricably linked to Hegel's Absolute Idealism.

Before embarking on the interpretation which occupies the central chapters of the book, I offer, in Chapter 1, a more general account of the issues involved in the interpretation of philosophical texts; this will illuminate, I hope, my interpretative strategy. Subsequently, in Chapter 7, I discuss a modern philosopher, Theodor Adorno, whose work is based on a critical appropriation of Hegel. My aim is to illustrate, in the light of the interpretation previously developed, the way in which Hegel's categories continue to exercise a hold even outside their original context.

I have received too much help and encouragement in my work on this book to acknowledge adequately. However, I would like to express my gratitude to my teachers Rüdiger Bubner, Alan Montefiore, and Charles Taylor, to my D. Phil. examiners, Istvàn Mészáros and Alan Ryan, and to those friends from whose comments on different parts of the manuscript I have profited greatly: Graham Burchell; Josef Buscher; Alex Callinicos; Eckart Förster; Colin Gordon; Kurt Hilgenberg; Joanna Hodge; Tim Mitchell; Mary Tiles; Gavin Williams.

I also offer my sincere thanks to the Stiftung FVS, Hamburg and the Fritz Thyssen Stiftung, Cologne whose generous financial support made possible my graduate studies in Germany.

A note on texts and translations

There is no universally accepted German edition of Hegel. However, for the English reader, the new Suhrkamp edition is the most accessible, not least because of its modern script and orthography. I have used this edition with the exception of the *Science of Logic*, the *Phenomenology of Spirit*, and the *Jenenser Realphilosophie*, where the editions of Lasson and Hoffmeister are standard.

I have noted only where translations are not my own, except for Kemp Smith's translation of Kant's *Critique of Pure Reason*. Inevitably, they reflect the interpretations which the book argues for, to some extent, and I have therefore given the original German in parentheses where this seemed helpful.

In translating Hegel the most difficult problem is not that of finding equivalents for individual technical terms, but that Hegel uses many non-technical terms in a sense specific to his philosophy, while retaining − and often playing on − their non-technical associations. To signal this I have made a good deal of use of a device not available in German and capitalized such terms as 'Idea', 'Logic', 'Thought', 'Science', whenever it was necessary to make clear that Hegel was using the terms in this way. For *Begriff* and *Geist*, on the other hand, I have used the translations 'notion' and 'Spirit'. Their direct translations as 'concept' and 'mind' should not, however, be forgotten. The most difficult of Hegel's technical terms and the one which is, perhaps, the most crucial to my argument is *Vorstellung*. There is some temptation to follow Kemp Smith's translation of Kant and render it as 'representation', but the latter's associations with 'standing in the place of' and 'bringing to presence' would be utterly misleading. Similarly, if less so, the Miller and Wallace translations of 'figurative consciousness', 'general image' etc.; *Vorstellungen* are not images, although (the book will argue) they share essential features with images. I have adopted no unique translation, but have frequently rendered it as 'common' or 'everyday consciousness'.

Abbreviations of works referred to

Adorno, *Negative Dialektik* (=*Negative Dialectics*): N. D.
Hegel, *Enzyklopädie der Philosophischen Wissenschaften*, I-III (=*Encyclopedia Logic, Philosophy of Nature, Philosophy of Mind*): Enz.
Hegel, *Grundlinien der Philosophie des Rechts* (=*Philosophy of Right*): Rechtsphil.
Hegel, *Phänomenologie des Geistes* (=*Phenomenology of Spirit*): P. d. G.
Hegel, *Vorlesungen über die Ästhetik*, I—III (= *Aesthetics*): Ästh. I—III
Hegel, *Vorlesungen über die Geschichte der Philosophie*, I—III (=*Lectures on the History of Philosophy*): Gesch. der Phil. I—III

Hegel, *Vorlesungen über die Philosophie der Geschichte* (=*Lectures on the Philosophy of History*): Phil. der Gesch.
Hegel, *Wissenschaft der Logik*, I, II (=*Science of Logic*): W. d. L. I, II
Kant, *Kritik der reinen Vernunft* (=*Critique of Pure Reason*): K. r. V.
Kant, *Kritik der Urteilskraft* (=*Critique of Judgement*): K.Uk.

1

The Interpretation of Philosophy

Lorsque nous écoutons quelqu'un parler, notre oreille entend ce qu'il dit; mais nous savons aussi entendre ce qu'il ne dit pas, et ce qu'il dit quand même.

Lacan

Although problems of interpretation and meaning have taken a central place in both Anglo-Saxon and continental philosophy in recent years, little attempt has been made to apply these considerations to the interpretation of philosophy's own past. In this chapter I intend to give the outlines of such an account. I do not mean, however, to claim that without it the practice of writing history of philosophy is impossible; to the contrary I want to claim that the interpretation of philosophy is a *craft*, in the sense that it has been practised very well in the absence of an explicit theory of its operation. Conversely, one might add, the possession of such an explicit account is no guarantee of skilful or sensitive interpretative practice. However, philosophical account and interpretative practice are not entirely divorced from one another. Misconceptions about the interpretative process can lead one to draw misleading consequences from the following presumed alternative.

The dilemma for interpretation is usually seen as whether one should interpret 'intentionally' or 'anachronistically'. Although this opposition is not always clearly analysed by those who operate with it, it often appears to be based on the intuition that there is a 'text itself' whose basic meaning is independent of the intentions of the author. This text is conceived on the basis of what I shall call the language—chess *analogy*. Briefly, the language—chess analogy is the doctrine that language is a rule-governed system in which the utterances we make, like moves in a game of chess, can be specified and identified without *either* knowledge of the mental state of the player making the move *or* full knowledge of the consequences which the move has in the game. But I shall argue that this analogy, although Anglo-Saxon philosophers influenced by Frege have been inclined to accept it as a matter of course, does not hold, and that, consequently, there may be a problem of establishing the identity of concepts used meaningfully in a text in a way that could not arise in identifying a valid move in chess.

Not that the concern to separate the 'text itself' from the consciousness and intentions of speakers is confined to the Anglo-Saxon tradition. The concern to find a model to express the independence of an action's meaning from the psychological state of the agent performing it is also vital to the French 'structuralist' tradition. This is the clear implication, for example, of the following statement by Jonathan Culler:

> Structuralism is based, in the first instance, on the realization that if human actions or productions have a meaning there must be an underlying system of conventions which makes this meaning possible.[1]

This concern explains why De Saussure's conception of language was so profoundly influential for the structuralists − to the extent, notoriously, of being taken as a paradigm for anything and everything. De Saussure makes the subject-independence of meaning − via the distinction which he draws between the timeless system of *langue* and the act of utterance, *parole* − the starting point of his enterprise. In this context, too, we can understand the enormous impact of Marcel Mauss's analysis of the gift (Lévi-Strauss compared its effect on him to that which reading Descartes had on Malebranche); in Mauss's work the structuralists found the classic analysis of the separation between the *systematic significance* of a social activity and the *intentions* of those engaged in it.

There is, however, one major contemporary school of thought about language which is fundamentally opposed to this separation between author and text − the hermeneutic tradition, which developed in Germany drawing on the writings of Dilthey and Heidegger. But this is not because the hermeneutic tradition thinks of meaning as the product of the intentions of some Cartesian subject. The conception of meaning with which it works, rather, is one which is neither *reducible to* nor *separable from* its literal embodiment in a text. Its historical model is the biblical opposition between 'spirit' and 'letter'. Significance is always the product of the union of the

---

1   Culler, 'The Linguistic Basis of Structuralism', p. 21.

two. Despite this, the hermeneutic tradition is led, as a consequence of its basic model, to misconceive the problem of interpretation in another way, by seeing it primarily as a problem of *translation*. Against this view – common to both hermeneutics and the language–chess analogy – I want to claim that when we ask the basic interpretative question, 'what does X mean by …?', the sort of answer we are looking for is an *elucidation*, but not a *translation*, of the utterance in question. So the problem is not one of giving an equivalent, as it is when moving from one language to another, but of identifying the concepts used meaningfully in texts (even within a single language). The notion that meanings are fixed by 'underlying conventions' blinds us to the existence of this problem and leads to the assimilation of *interpretation* to *translation*.

When we ask what Hegel meant when he wrote 'das Wahre ist das Ganze' or what Bradley meant when he wrote that 'the Absolute participates in but does not partake of change'[2] we should not see this as a request for translation. For, evidently, in the former case the translation is trivial ('the true is the whole') whilst, in the latter, a satisfying one may not be possible at all. The request is really for an elucidation of the concept or concepts involved, which involves conveying the *point* of the concept. In trying to convey this point we are returned, I will argue, to the consideration of the author and of his intentions. But these intentions play a role in meaning quite different from the intentions attacked by 'anti-intentionalism' – the picture that meanings are referred back to the transparent awareness of a Cartesian consciousness. If we are in a position to answer the question 'how do we convey the point of a linguistic action?' we shall be able to understand, I hope, the interplay of 'intentional' and 'objective', 'historical' and 'anachronistic' components in interpretation.

Against the Cartesian picture of consciousness I want to maintain that the object of investigation – what I am calling, somewhat inelegantly, the point of the concepts we use – is not an item simply present and available to consciousness. The point of a concept is something the user may well not be aware of; indeed, the very notion

2   This example is borrowed from a seminar of Michael Dummett's. Dummett used it as an example of a sentence falling outside the capacity of a theory of meaning, of the sort he advocates, to account for. If so, and such sentences must be counted unintelligible by Dummett's systematic theory of meaning, then – whatever its other uses – such a theory will have no application to the interpretation of philosophical texts: it is sentences just like Bradley's that the interpretation of philosophy has to deal with.

of a sharp alternative between 'being aware' and 'not being aware' is out of place.

An important feature of the role of philosophical concepts in particular (although even 'descriptive' empirical concepts also encompass this role to some extent) is that they function to *organize* discourse. Thus where the evidence for someone's having a particular empirical concept may consist primarily in the fact that he[3] picks out objects in a particular way, the evidence for someone having a particular philosophical concept consists in the existence of a particular organization of discourse. So, for example, someone with a Cartesian concept of consciousness will believe that mental contents can always be contemplated without existential commitment. Thus, for such an author, 'I am conscious of X' or 'It seems to me that there is an X' is not incompatible with the proposition 'It is possible that there are no Xs'. There is a consequence here for the practice of interpretation: by connecting the possession of a concept to this idea of 'discursive organization' the approach that I am advocating ought to lead us to rethink what is at stake when interpreters argue about whether authors held a particular belief or not.

On my approach this question typically folds out into two. First, there is the question 'can the discourse be seen as falling under the pattern of organization that such a belief implies?' and, second, 'does it make sense to attribute this as a *deliberate* piece of organization on the author's part?' Now it should be apparent that the question of the deliberateness with which an organization of discourse comes about, although a question about intentions, is quite different from the psychological question 'did X ever entertain such-and-such a sentence — or a sentence which is a translation of it?' The deliberateness of our discourse ranges between two extremes. Minimally, we might say that everything that an author is prepared to stand by — every pattern that he would not see as a reason to revise what he says if it were pointed out to him — is deliberate. At the other extreme we would have a maximum degree of deliberateness were we in a position to say that not only *is* there a certain pattern in the text which the author would stand by, but also that the author *consciously organized* his text according to just this pattern. However, the interpreter of philosophy's interests do not lie at either of these extremes; the one is too broad and the other too narrow to be appropriate. On the for-

---

3   In this book — purely for familiarity's sake — I follow the convention that the philosophical subject is masculine

mer, lax, criterion all anachronism is permissible; we can talk about the classical empiricists believing in 'private languages' or the scholastics believing in 'the isomorphism of logical and linguistic structure'. So long as we are aware of what we are doing in making such identifications — interrogating an author's texts in terms of *our* discernment of its organization — this seems to me a legitimate occupation and to this extent 'anti-intentionalism' is justified; it draws our attention to the fact that what counts primarily in a text is the pattern or organization which we find in it, not the psychological intention under which it comes to be constructed. Anti-intentionalism becomes pernicious, however, when the anachronistic interpreter takes it that the right according to which the text is read in this way is that he stands at the end of philosophical history, in possession of the 'true' problems of philosophy, and that the philosopher being interpreted must (in essence at least) be aspiring to a treatment of these true problems.

Quentin Skinner — whose attempts to bring considerations from the theory of meaning to bear on the history of ideas are the outstanding exception to analytical philosophy's general neglect — would call such anachronism an example of the *myth of doctrine*. Against it Skinner believes that, even if we concede to anti-intentionalism the autonomy of language at the level of individual signs, reference must be made to intentions in order to identify the *illocutionary acts* performed in authors' texts.[4] Although I dispute Skinner's assumption that anachronistic interpretation is always the result of belief in the myth of doctrine, his demolition of that myth is devastating.

Thus I think Michael Ayers is right to take exception to Russell's treatment of Leibniz:

As Russell sees it, Leibniz's philosophy 'begins' like 'all sound philosophy', 'with an analysis of propositions'.[5]

The objections to Russell are twofold. In the first place, by making it a condition of 'sound philosophy' that an author should share his own starting point, Russell completely eliminates the historical question of the way in which the author went about organizing his text to produce the pattern which we discern in it (and, as Ayers points out, Leibniz certainly did not 'begin', in this sense, with an analysis of propositions). Although Russell's approach to interpretation

4   See Skinner 'Meaning and Understanding in the History of Ideas', pp. 4–22, for the *myth of doctrine*, and 'Motives, Intentions and the Interpretation of Texts' for his views on the subject-independence of language.

5   Ayers, 'Analytical Philosophy and the History of Philosophy', p. 44.

is an absolutist one it is easy to see how, with very little modification, his assumptions lead to scepticism about the possibility of objective interpretation. Lacking Russell's high opinion of his ability to identify the true problems, we come to a position of tragic pessimism; each generation makes the heroic, doomed assumption that it stands at the end of historical time, knowing, all the while, that its own approach is bound to be superseded. This relativist position is as unattractive as Russell's complementary absolutist one.

The second objection is that we are led by an approach like Russell's towards a false assumption about the pattern of philosophical discourse itself. If we read the great texts of the past as reaching out 'in essence' towards our standards of what 'sound philosophy' is, we are not, even in principle, able to countenance the possibility that there are discontinuities at a fundamental level in the concepts and standards of philosophical discourse. Yet, unless we realize that aspects of philosophy as fundamental as the understanding of what it is to *explain* a phenomenon, or what is to count as a standard of proof, have in fact changed radically in the course of history, we are bound to give a distorted account of it. In generalizing our own standards we risk simply eliminating from discussion texts which cannot be construed according to those standards, as fundamentally 'unsound'. No more striking case than the Anglo-Saxon treatment of Hegel could surely be imagined. Alternatively, which is more insidious, philosophers who can be construed to some extent on current standards (Hume or Kant, for example) are dealt with only in terms of their agreement with those standards, their divergences being treated as aberrations. The result is to pull the history of philosophy towards a 'Whig' view of the past.

However, restricting oneself to the alternative, narrow pole of deliberateness is no better stratagem. According to this we should aim at the intention under which the author generated the pattern of the text. But such information will be less and less informative the more traditions diverge. The interpreter of philosophy is especially concerned with those basic concepts — for example, of *experience*, *proof*, *subjectivity*, *argument* etc. — which set standards for discourse but which a tradition applies more or less unreflectively. It may perhaps be informative for a reader operating *within* the Idealist tradition to be told, say, that Hegel wrote with the intention of introducing mediation into Schelling's concept of the Absolute. But such information, which is the sort of thing that we might learn if we had access to Hegel's inner life, is too superficial for ourselves, standing outside that tradition. We want to know the function of the concept of the Absolute itself; indeed, we *need* to know it before we can make sense of the change that is introduced. Although such concepts as the Absolute, *Geist*, and the like, which form, as it were, the basic structure of German Idealism, were not applied entirely unreflectively, in studying a philosopher we need to go beyond his own reflection. For the concepts which will stand most in need of interpretation will be those background or basic concepts in terms of which Hegel's conscious discursive intentions are formed. These concepts will organize discourse in much the same way as a rule of grammar. That is to say 'having' a standard of what counts as an argument may mean having a systematic intuition as to what does and what does not meet that standard. But it need not mean having an explicit formulation of the standard.

Furthermore, what we are trying to do is to convey the point of Hegel's concept; the aim is to express this in such a way that we, the readers, can grasp what he, the author, is trying to do. This deserves emphasis because, when properly understood, it provides a key to the understanding of the role of 'anachronistic' explanation. Consider what is involved in interpreting the point of an action in a very simple case: when, for example, we observe a dog chasing a cat into a tree and sitting down at the bottom. We say that the dog *believes* that the cat is in the tree; that it is *waiting* for it to come down; that it *expects* that it will come down. Now all of these are 'mentalist' interpretations of the dog's behaviour. But, in my view, it is a misconstruction to think that our ability and entitlement to make such interpretations rests on our ability to 'get inside' the dog's mind. We do not have to answer the question 'what is it like to be a dog?' in order to make such attributions. But the reason that we do not have to is not because we, in some sense, project *our own* mental make-up onto the dog's behaviour. This suggestion shares with the initial one the view that knowledge of 'mental life' is necessary in order to make the interpretation and only differs whether it is the dog's or our own. Against that I want to claim (in a Wittgensteinian spirit) that the *behaviour* we observe is quite sufficient to make such interpretations. To do this we use *our* language to characterize *its* behaviour. But there is no sense in which this is a 'second best'; what seems to be the ideal (using *its* language to characterize *its* behaviour) is really no ideal at all. So, similarly, when we characterize a philosopher's enterprise as, say, providing a derivation of the structure of reality from self-evident principles, what counts is whether this accurately captures his enterprise — specifically, the structure of his discourse — rather than whether he would have acknowledged the statement 'philosophy derives the structure of reality from self-evident principles' were it (hypothetically, of course) put to him.

In the light of this the significance of such questions as 'what does Hegel mean by "das Wahre ist das Ganze"?' will, I hope, emerge. Such statements use concepts (in this case the concept of *truth*) which organize discourse at the most fundamental level. Unless we have some conception of the organizing standards provided by such fundamental concepts it is evident that discerning patterns at a more explicit level will be next to impossible. One consequence of the approach being argued here is to lead to a particular understanding of the terms of the interpreter's vocabulary — the 'problems', 'fundamental questions', 'traditions' and 'enterprises' we talk about. Serious practitioners have always known that these terms are vital to their activity. Nevertheless they have regarded them as philosophically dubious. They have been reluctant to commit themselves to the full-blooded neo-Idealism that would make such ideas as 'milieu' or 'basic question' epistemologically fundamental,[6] and so have tended to use the concepts without explicit justification, or else to salve their materialist consciences by renaming them (as *epistemes* or *problématiques*, for example). The neo-Idealist justifies the use of the interpreter's vocabulary in terms of an account of meaning which takes meaning as an 'emergence' against a background or horizon of tradition. It is this context, then, at which the interpreter aims.[7] But the rejection of such an epistemology need not mean the rejection of the terms of the interpreter's vocabulary as part of the Idealist miasma. If my approach has merit they can be accommodated in a way that should be unobjectionable to any disciple of Wittgenstein (or, for that matter, of Donald Davidson). The true function of the interpreter's technical terms is to try to elucidate the pattern of discourse with reference to the concepts operating in it at the most fundamental — for the author, frequently, least reflective — level.

This does not, of course, mean that we always *can* fit texts into the Idealist's overriding systematic structures of 'movements', 'ques-

6   R. G. Collingwood mounts a famous defence of such a position in his *Autobiography* (see especially Chapters 5 and 7).
7   See Gadamer, *Truth and Method*, especially Part 2, Chapter 2.

tions of the age' and so on. I am not defending a concept of *Geist* by which such interpretation is always guaranteed to be possible. My claim is the modest one that, insofar as 'anti-historicists' see a necessary connection between the use of these terms and an Idealist picture of cultural meaning, their objection can be met.

It seems to me that the approach according to which the business of interpretation revolves around the elucidation of fundamental concepts accords well with what interpreters of philosophy in fact do.

For example, Gerd Buchdahl has unified his ambitious attempt to read the great philosophers from Descartes to Kant by the assertion that, running through their work, is an attempt to find a solution to the problem of the 'propositional link'. To this end he constructs a set of ideal 'models' of answers to the problem, posed in his own terms.[8] But his aim in doing so is not to discuss the problem *sub specie aeternitatis*. Rather, each model represents a general structure, a set of rules of organization, according to which texts can be classified: those who answer the problem in terms of 'substance'; those who answer it in terms of 'laws'; etc. Thus we have an illuminating pattern under which we can examine texts, and the fact that the authors themselves could never have constructed such ideal models should not lead us to say that Buchdahl's interpretation is a projection of anachronistic concerns; the question whether they could have constructed the interpretative model themselves is quite irrelevant to its value.

To take another example, which will figure prominently in the main body of the book: Charles Taylor (following Isaiah Berlin) has proposed that we understand the late eighteenth and early nineteenth centuries in Germany as developing a doctrine which he calls 'expressivism'.[9] This doctrine incorporates the aspiration to return to the view of the cosmos as a meaningful order, but to do so in such a way as to accommodate the 'modern conception of subjectivity'. To this end it develops a doctrine of meaning which sees significance as always a 'tension in unity' between an expressing subjectivity and a medium of expression. Here again the interpreter gives us a model for 'what the author is doing' which can be tested against an author's texts. But the test is *not* whether the author would ever have assented to an account in these words of what he is doing. The test is: can this

8   Buchdahl, *Metaphysics and the Philosophy of Science*, Chapter 2.
9   Taylor, *Hegel*, especially Chapter 1.

pattern be found embodied in the text? Do the authors of the time indeed have the modern conception of subjectivity, account of meaning, etc., which 'expressivism' implies? Furthermore, does it make sense to see this as something novel, an 'aim of a new epoch'?

To sum up: if we admit that there may be a difficulty in identifying the basic concepts in a text, then it is reasonable to see the activity of interpretation as concerned with an elucidation of these concepts. Thus we want to know what Locke means by 'idea', or Kant means by 'transcendental', or Hegel by '*Geist*'. The role of philosophical concepts is such that their elucidation consists in showing the way in which they regulate the organization of texts. From this point of view the 'psychological'/'objectivistic' alternatives for interpretation will be, I hope, decisively realigned.

The Language—Chess Analogy

I now want to turn to an examination in more detail of the language—chess analogy. The interpreter of language wants to know what the utterer meant, *what his utterance said*. The language—chess analogy suggests that we can illuminate the question by comparing it with the way in which we go about answering the corresponding question in the game of chess: 'what move did he make?'. Generally, if we ask this question, the answer we receive is something like 'P—K4'. What is involved in understanding it? The first point is that, for the person who understands it, 'P—K4' will *include* a specification of the changed physical disposition of the piece. But it is not just a physical specification. It is a specification in terms of the *move of a piece*, and the person who understands it will understand *what* the piece is in the game, that is to say, what its movement rights are. Such understanding of the movement rights of the piece goes beyond just knowing if the movement specified by 'P—K4' is legitimate. To understand it as a move in chess is also to know something about the consequences of moves. The person who makes a move knows that each legitimate move stands at what we might think of as the apex of a pyramid of possible legitimate game dispositions. He knows that, if the move is valid, it must allow either a following valid move or a resolution of the game. Provided that only valid moves are made the game will not break down.

Now this feature of chess — the certainty that each move has its place in a closed system — gives our understanding of the moves a very important characteristic. We can distinguish between what a chess move *is*, what it *implies*, and what the agent *foresees* of the move's consequences. Chess is a closed system and so even unforeseen consequences can be said to be determinately implicit. Thus we can differentiate the objective consequences of a move from the dispositions and intentions of agents and allow that a move 'has' possible consequences which no player of the game may ever foresee; and, of course, it is this feature which makes chess a worthwhile game to play (in a way in which, for the moderately farsighted, noughts and crosses is not).

Now, neither the objective consequences of the move nor the agent's subjective awareness of those consequences seem to be what is involved in the act of identifying the move. For the objective consequences will be unknown to the agent and therefore − although one might concede that they were part of its 'ultimate identity' in some sense − they could certainly not be what is involved in the identification of the move; they could not be what the agent knows when he knows what the move is. On the other hand, agents differ radically in their ability to foresee consequences. Yet, although a champion has a far superior ability to play the game to win than a novice, the two do not identify the moves differently. So what enables us to identify and specify the moves of chess if it is neither their ultimate consequences nor the agent's foresight?

For the modern Anglo-Saxon philosopher, at least, the automatic answer is that someone who identifies a move in chess does so by virtue of 'knowing the rules' of chess. What does this involve? One thing that knowing the rules of chess *need not* involve is that the agent entertains a specific set of propositions. Rather, someone knows the rules if they can recognize, in any circumstances, what is and what is not a legitimate move. Of course the proviso 'in any circumstances' makes the state of knowledge quite unlike a physical state in that it is impossible conclusively to verify its conditions. Thus we frequently concede that the fact that agents make moves correctly is more than a coincidence only in the light of statements by means of which they express their grasp of the rules. But the fact that they give us a satisfactory explicit reason for what they do is not a necessary part of their grasp of the rules itself.

Given the closure of the chess system it makes perfect sense to talk of someone knowing the rules without knowing the full consequences of the moves. What the agent must, however, be able to do is to distinguish *at each stage* what are legitimate and what are illegitimate continuations. And this knowledge — 'synchronic' knowledge, one might call it — is complete, whereas 'diachronic' knowledge (of consequences) is not. This part of the agent's total chess knowledge is what guarantees the closure of the game and, hence, may be separated from knowledge about future situations as being sufficient to allow the game (in some impoverished form) to be played. People (or computers) who had no other knowledge than this would play chess indescribably badly; but they would play chess.

The important feature is that in any situation we know all the moves that are immediately licensed. We have complete knowledge of immediate consequences. Provided that the game is in a legitimate disposition the person who knows chess is *never* at a loss whether a single transfer of a piece on the board is or is not a valid move. It is this feature, I suggest, which allows us to separate out our grasp of the identities of moves (which is perfect) from our, decidedly imperfect, awareness of their consequences. The question, then, is, is there some knowledge — the knowledge of meanings — which plays an equivalent role in determining 'what was said' in natural languages as knowledge of the rules does in determining the move made in chess?

Apparently, the obvious analogy in language to the knowledge of the licensed continuations in chess is the knowledge of valid inferences, truths in virtue of the *meaning* of words. In virtue of our knowledge of the meaning of 'bachelor' we know that bachelors are unmarried. The question then becomes: do speakers who use words meaningfully always have complete knowledge of such immediately licensed continuations? The thought that they do is supported by an equivocation in the word 'meaning'. On one sense of 'meaning' it is no more than a tautology to say that someone who can use a word meaningfully knows its meaning. Yet, on the other hand, truths such as that John, being a bachelor, is unmarried, are traditionally said to be true in virtue of the meaning of the words. Now we should not be misled by the fact that in this simple case 'knowing the meaning' in these two senses — having the ability to use a word meaningfully, and knowing the inference it licenses — probably coincides. We would never be likely to admit that someone could use a word as basic as 'bachelor' meaningfully without knowing that it licenses the ascription of the predicate 'unmarried' to whatever it refers to. But this is certainly not so in more sophisticated cases. Specifically, it seems absurd to suggest that such knowledge of inferences can be assumed in the case of the words which we find used in texts of philosophy. A simple consideration demonstrates this. Consider two philosophers disagreeing about the concept of causality. Their disagreement is likely to involve a disagreement as to whether some proposition — say 'causal relations obtain only between separately identifiable events' — is or is not a conceptual truth. But if 'knowing the meaning' in the two senses distinguished above coincide, then one or the other of them (the one whose grasp of the semantic properties was incorrect) would be failing to use the word meaningfully, in which case it is hard to see how a rational disagreement could be taking place at all. If we believe that philosophy (at least some of the time) aims at conceptual truth, and is capable (at least some of the time) of rational disagreement, then we must accept that knowing how to use a word meaningfully does not entail a complete knowledge of immediately licensed inferences. But this, if accepted, amounts to a striking disanalogy with 'knowing the move' in chess.

It is important that we should not ignore this disanalogy because of what, superficially, is an analogy: the ignorance of the chess player of the further consequences of his moves, and the ignorance of the philosopher about conceptual truths. In fact the analogy is not a true one. Conceptual truths license inferences *directly*. But what the chess player is ignorant of are not directly licensed continuations (these, indeed, he must know completely in order to identify the move) but more distant, future ones.

This disanalogy leaves us with a number of questions. First of all: what does a speaker know who knows how to use a word meaningfully (let me call this meaning$_1$)? Second, what is it that enables us to go beyond meaning$_1$ to arrive at superior understanding of a word's inference-licensing force, its semantic power (let me call this meaning$_2$)? Third, what is it that the interpreter of philosophy should be interested in? Should he try to elucidate meaning$_1$ or meaning$_2$? Or must he, indeed, aim at both?

To take the first question: may we, if we restrict ourselves to meaning$_1$, not nevertheless salvage the idea of grasp of meaning as grasp of rules? May we not take the position (which also seems to be that which Jonathan Culler attributes to structuralism) that, as Gilbert Ryle says: 'If I know the meaning of a word or phrase I know something like a body of unwritten rules, or something like an unwritten code or general recipe'?[10] The answer is, surely, 'no', if we think that for every word there must be the unique rule or set of rules

10   Ryle, 'Use and Usage', p. 52.

which enables us to use it meaningfully. For it is evident that in the case of a great many words there is more than one set of features knowledge of which would be sufficient to allow us to pick out the referent of a word systematically. Thus we may know that a triangle is a three-sided figure and discover (with some surprise) that it also has, necessarily, three angles. Or else vice versa; there is no single recipe.

I have already suggested the answer to the second question: what allows us to make discoveries about the inferences which our concepts license? It is the fact that we grasp their point. Thus it may be an actual discovery for a seventeenth-century philosopher that it is part of his concept of consciousness as immediate awareness that it entails that the existence of the external world is not certain on the basis of perception alone. Not all concepts in language, of course, are sufficiently complicated to have such undiscovered points. Some may be (this will be particularly so of technical concepts) 'well-defined' in the way that the logical positivists once hoped to make all language. But a great many are not. The attempt to grasp the full implications of concepts, to bridge the gap between meaning$_1$ and meaning$_2$ is a crucial part of human discursive endeavour.[11] Moreover, it is an activity which forms a central part of philosophy. Hence the texts which the interpreter of philosophy has to deal with are, typically, ones where this gap is crucial.

The third question was: what should the interpreter aim at elucidating? This seems to offer another chance of saving the 'objectivist' thesis. It is meaning$_2$, the objectivist might say, which is *really* ('*de re*', as it were) the meaning expressed by what the speaker utters — not his own awareness of what he says. Thus what is said is what the words, ultimately, mean. A consequence is that *we*, the speakers of the language, may never know this ultimate meaning (for we do not stand at the end of philosophical time). But, at any rate, the ultimate meaning is a goal, a *telos* by which our interpretation should guide itself.

There is certainly something to this suggestion. When a philosopher says, for example, 'reasons are causes' he does not mean to say 'reasons 'in my sense of the term' are causes, as I understand

11   Ronald Dworkin, for example, argues that a proper understanding of the relationship between the *concepts* of jurisprudence and subjects' *conceptions* of those concepts is indispensable to constitutional construction. See *Taking Rights Seriously*, especially Chapter 5.

them' but to say something about the concepts *as they will turn out to be*. Of course it is only sensible to think that one is in a position to make such statements if one has grounds for believing that one's understanding of the concepts does, in fact, correspond to what they will turn out to be. However, it would distort the enterprise of interpretation to see it as aiming in this way solely at the concepts as they will turn out to be at the end of time. For we are not just interested in *the* concept of the subject but in *Hegel's* (or Kant's, or Hume's) concept of the subject. Let us concede that these are competing attempts to elaborate what is ultimately the same concept. Nevertheless it would be absurd to take them as *meaning the same thing*. These differences in authors' grasp of the concepts they employ are just what interpretation is about. Moreover this will show up concretely. A text guided by, for example, a Cartesian concept of the subject will have a particular organization, and this organization will be systematically present, even if we concede that ultimately there 'is' no such concept of the subject. Even the fact that concepts which philosophers employ are self-contradictory does not mean that they cannot impose a systematic pattern on a text. This important point is often neglected by philosophers eager to 'reconstruct' the texts of the past. Even if we conclude that Kant's concept of synthesis involves the self-contradictory notion of a 'timeless process', this is no reason for the interpreter (if he really is interested in giving an account of Kant's text) to leave it out of account.

Philosophical Concepts

If we are returned, then, to the speaker's own grasp of his concepts, this must be to the grasp which he shows in the way that he uses the word. For, as I have argued, there need not *be* anything — a unique recipe — which constitutes the speaker's ability to use a word meaningfully. Indeed, even if we *had* such a recipe, this would not be what we are interested in; the object of interpretation is how words function in texts. We are not interested in the way in which this comes about, except as it specifies this functioning. This is why the Wittgensteinian starting point is in order here, the doctrine that in order to establish what concepts a speaker has we should look at his behaviour, not in the reduced sense of 'behaviour' employed by *behaviourists* but at the *use* he makes of words.

Thus we establish that someone has the concept 'brown' not by looking into his head to discover his 'state of mind' but by establishing that he classifies objects in the appropriate way, that he uses the word as a general term to characterize a subject-term, that he realizes that the application of 'brown' excludes the simultaneous application of 'green', 'blue' or 'black' etc. In short we establish that he is following (in Wittgenstein's sense) the 'grammar' of the word.

How is this picture applicable to the concepts of philosophy? It seems to me that two special features of philosophical concepts — their function in organizing discourse and their complexity — are important. In the first place, philosophical concepts are, typically, discursive. That is to say that their role is not to govern observation (although there are exceptions — the concept of 'cause', for example) but to organize the ways in which we talk about the world. How, for example, does it show up whether an author does or does not have the seventeenth-century concept of 'idea'? Since this is a concept which aims to account for what people are doing in perceiving and judging, one cannot expect it to show up in empirical behaviour — as a philosophical concept it aims to capture the way we all judge, not just those who employ the concept. Where it will show up is that someone who has this concept will believe in certain inferences: that it makes sense, for example, to separate thoughts from the words that embody them; that our experience contains itself no commitment to the existence of a reality from which it originates; etc. Now the point that I want to make is that the fact that the evidence for the possession of a philosophical concept is typically discursive does not alter the stress on behaviour as the use made of words. It does not mean that we are establishing what concepts an author possesses 'psychologically' or attempting to look into his mind. When we say, as part of our evidence for someone holding the seventeenth-century conception of 'idea', that they *believe* that words and thoughts can be separated we ought to understand this as analogous to the claim that it is evidence for someone having the concept 'brown' that they systematically pick out brown things. It is a belief, then, *not* in the sense of a mental state but as a propensity to organize discourse in a certain way.

This sense of belief, as the propensity to organize texts in a particular pattern, goes against the understanding, common among philosophers, which seeks to tie the concept of belief to the body of sentences a speaker assents to. (Of course, they have their reasons for doing so, which I am not out to object to. My point is only that this understanding is misleading for the use of *belief* in the interpretation of historical texts.) Thus Dummett writes:

Roughly speaking, a person believes something to be the case if an expression of that belief can fairly easily be elicited from him by prompting him appropriately.[12]

As Dummett points out, this notion of 'appropriate prompting' is a loose one. But it is indispensable because people's beliefs are not always fully present to them. However, not any prompting is automatically 'appropriate'. If we do not make any restriction and 'count a person as believing something provided that he would assent to it in some context which did not involve the production of new evidence'[13] we shall have opened the concept of belief so far as to count a person as believing anything which can be proved from what he consciously assents to. For what else, as Dummett says, is *proof* but the production of contexts without new external evidence? Without some constraint on what is 'appropriate' prompting we shall all be said to believe all the provable truths of logic and arithmetic, and philosophers will be credited with all the logical consequences of their texts. Of course it is absurd to suggest that we live in this Leibnizian utopia. An idea of appropriate prompting is thus indispensable. In consequence, belief becomes, Dummett says, an 'ineradicably vague' notion.

My approach escapes the dilemma of having to decide what would be 'appropriate' prompting of long departed philosophers by claiming that, when interpreters are arguing, say, about whether Locke believed in private languages, they are *not* arguing about whether there are conceivable circumstances in which the statement 'there are private languages' might be elicited from him. The argument is about whether it is reasonable to see him as having organized his text in this way. An explicit statement is no more part of the conditions for this being so than giving an explicit formulation of a grammatical rule is a condition for saying that someone is following it. The connection between sentences such as 'there are private languages' and the pattern of the text is only that if someone *did* assent to this explicit sentence then it would also entail organizing the text in this pattern; explicit assent to a sentence expressing a philosophical belief is not a necessary condition of the pattern which that belief leads to being ascribable.

It may be useful, at this stage, to compare this approach to 'an author's beliefs' to the tradition of hermeneutics. According to

12   Dummett, *Frege*, p. 285.
13   Dummett, *Frege*, p. 288.

Charles Taylor the aim of hermeneutic interpretation is:

> to make clear, to make sense of an object of study. This object must ... be a text, or a text-analogue, which in some way is confused, incomplete, cloudy, seemingly contradictory – in one way or another, unclear. The interpretation aims to bring to light an underlying coherence or sense.[14]

The means by which this clarification is achieved is, according to Taylor, a re-expression – one which illuminates the subject matter:

> The interpretation appeals throughout to our understanding of the 'language' of expression, which understanding allows us to see that this expression is puzzling, that it is in contradiction to that other, etc., and that these difficulties are cleared up when the meaning is expressed in a new way.[15]

In order to avoid the restriction that such re-expressions are only legitimate if they are 'reasonably attributable' to the mental state of the author, the hermeneuticists, like structuralism and the language –chess analogy, create their own doctrine of the independence of meaning. But their picture is not that of words as counters, with values fixed by 'underlying conventions'. Their doctrine is of a 'space of meaning', successor to Husserl's noematic realm and surrogate of the Idealist conception of *Geist*. Significance flows and eddies in a fluid medium of 'historicity', and it is this, rather than the author's state of mind that gives the text its identity. But this is a solution (however metaphysically 'charming' we might find it as a vision of culture and history) to a problem, the legitimacy of non-contemporaneous ascriptions, which arises from a false starting point: namely, the view that interpretation is *translation* or *re-expression*.

The position argued for here corresponds to Kant's idea that we can 'understand an author better than he has understood himself '; the reason being, in Kant's view, that 'as he has not sufficiently determined his concept, he has sometimes spoken, or even thought, in opposition to his own intention'.[16] For Gadamer, making the possibility of understanding an author in a way that he himself could not a matter of 'determining concepts' is unacceptable because essentially *rationalistic*[17] – a label that neither Kant nor I would object to.

---

14 Taylor, 'Interpretation and the Science of Man', p. 153. Essentially similar positions are argued in Gadamer, *Truth and Method* and Ricoeur, *Freud and Philosophy*.
15 Taylor, 'Interpretation and the Science of Man', p. 155.
16 *K. r. V.*, B370.
17 Gadamer, *Truth and Method*, p. 172.

Characteristically *hermeneutic* views of meaning, however, such as Schleiermacher's or Gadamer's own, see texts as the outcome of a creative, productive activity.

The second feature of philosophical concepts that should be stressed is their complexity. As I suggested above, this is no accident but actually part of the reason why they *become* philosophical concepts. In the case of an empirical concept we say that someone has grasped it when they have 'seen the point' of the classification principle, when they have reached a state when they feel that they can go on. They need not, however, be able to make this principle explicit. Nor is there necessarily a hard and fast line dividing 'grasp' from 'lack of grasp'. This will be true of philosophical concepts especially; interesting concepts such as 'self', 'law', 'game', will not have definite boundaries, but are open-textured, their application governed by no single, determinate underlying principle. However, the Wittgensteinian idea that there may only be 'family resemblances' between items falling under a concept should not be misconstrued. It denies, to be sure, that there must always be a determinate 'essence' governing the application of words. On the other hand this does not mean that our use of words is completely heterogeneous, arbitrary, nominalist, and that it never makes sense to ask what it is about games that makes us call them 'games' or about legal systems that makes us call them systems of 'law'.

In interpreting we are concerned with the *points* of concepts, and this means knowing not just the way in which, actually, the author *does* use the concept to organize his text, but also, normatively, the way in which it *should*, ideally, govern all texts in which it *might* be used. In this way knowing the point of a concept leads us towards knowledge of meaning₂, knowledge of its semantic power. What we are aiming at — the point of the concept — is not the sort of thing which *could* be fully revealed to an ideal observer. This is why I have adopted the word point; unlike a rule or a recipe, it cannot be thought of as something determinate underlying the use of a word. The notion of a point is always relative to a context of explanation; it is not an object or state of affairs which one *encounters* but something one *shows* to other people or even to oneself. But this is not to say that the notion is therefore purely subjective. We can avoid confusion by thinking of the explanation of linguistic behaviour (as Wittgenstein advocated) by relating the idea of *explaining* to that of *teaching*. In explaining the point of a concept we are involved in trying to put the person taught in a position to use the concept himself.

Interpretation as a Craft

This is why interpretation must be a craft. There cannot be canonical rules for showing someone the point of an action. In practice the business of elucidating the point of a concept is often extremely complicated. The interpreter tries to judge how a word actually functions in a text, how it ought to function, and the extent to which the author was aware of the tension between the two. The interpreter's craft consists, as much as anything, in reducing this complexity to manageable dimensions.

One practical consequence of the account of interpretation outlined in this chapter, which seems to me of outstanding importance, is the element of choice which it implies. Were interpretation primarily concerned with translation the interpreter would have a clear goal: to give a translation of the text. If, on the other hand, interpretation is crucially about the elucidation of problematic concepts the interpreter must make a choice. Conceptions of the philosophical enterprise which are a matter of course to philosophers within one tradition may require explanation and justification for readers from another, and the sort of explanation that might have been counted satisfactory within that tradition may be insufficient for those outside it.

Commonly this problem of selection is 'solved' by the tradition in which the work is preserved and discussed. The history of such traditions resembles strikingly the picture advanced by Thomas Kuhn of the structure of scientific revolutions. At first the work strikes the philosophical community as revolutionary; banners are raised, for and against. But, with time, we find that it gains the accretions of academic normalcy — archives, congresses, centenary symposia, international societies. The effect is that the work is handed down to those standing at the end of a tradition carrying with it a set of 'classic' problems, a series of authoritative questions under which the text has been interrogated, and which provide a context for further investigation. Thus, like the creatures of the coral reef, each reading contributes its lifeless carapace to the body of tradition on which its successors will move.

This process is, no doubt, inevitable, but there are dangers. As the body of interpretation grows the pressures increase to 'normalize' the questions interpreters ask; to substitute for those questions which evaluate the work as a whole more restricted and 'scholarly' ones, which can be answered in the context of the academic division of labour without threatening the continued validity of the enterprise. There is, then, perhaps some advantage for the interpreter, who does not find himself satisfied with the received answers to these 'revolutionary' questions, in standing outside such a tradition.

On the other hand the problem of the choice of an interpretative strategy is more starkly posed as the limitations of two conventional approaches become apparent — that of commentary and of intellectual biography.

In a commentary the development of the interpretation is expected to correspond to the sequence of the text. It suggests that the interpreter's task is to 'build up the argument' with (one hopes) the same structure as the text itself. This may be possible where the concepts used in the text are familiar, or where new concepts are introduced step-by-step. But where unfamiliar concepts are not introduced explicitly; where they are enmeshed with other novel concepts through the whole of a text — or, indeed, the whole of an author's work — then an overall perspective may be necessary before we can even identify the individual 'steps' in the argument.

One familiar way of gaining an overall perspective is by tracing the development of the author's key ideas. The limitation here is that the concepts which need interpretation are not necessarily those which presented difficulties for the author. The concepts which readers outside the tradition find problematic are very often those which the author himself took for granted. How else should one choose the questions in terms of which to interrogate a text?

Although it is a choice which only the interpretation itself can justify let me now give some anticipation of the questions which I will use to guide interpretation.

The question which I ask in Chapter 2 is 'is dialectic open to rational criticism?'. There is a construction of Hegel's enterprise according to which it is not; the totalizing movement of dialectic being taken to be such as to absorb all criticism within its own self. I argue that, if this is so, this is a serious objection, for the dialectical movement contains features which the philosopher standing outside it would feel no compulsion to grant. The construction is, however, a mistaken one, and from this two important consequences will follow; first, that the characteristic feature of Hegel's dialectic — *determinate negation* — is not a feature of rationality in general but is a characteristic of the speculative movement, only displayed and developed freely in the *Science of Logic*. Only from this point can we justify the claim that dialectic is the 'underlying truth' of ordinary reasoning. Second, dialectical proof is ineliminably *experiential*; it has a necessary first-hand character which means that it cannot be substituted for, resumed or criticized by ordinary, non-Scientific discourse.

Thus the aim of interpretation cannot be to *reconstruct*, in the sense of re-express in common discourse, dialectical argument. Rather, I attempt, in Chapter 4, to *characterize* the nature of the experience of Thought as an answer to the question 'what is rational experience like?'. The foregoing parts of this chapter will have justified, I hope, interrogating texts in terms of such questions, which it is no part of my case to say that Hegel could ever have formulated to himself. I identify three traditional answers to this question — rational experience as the 'presence' of a *quasi-image*, rational experience as the *subsumption* of what is given under a *classificatory concept*, and rational experience as *manifestation*, the *showing forth* of the true and universal in the particular. Hegel's 'rational experience' is, I claim, an untraditional version of the third answer.

Using these conclusions I illustrate my approach in Chapters 5 and 6 in relation to two key topics — Hegel's understanding of language, and the beginning of the *Logic* — and try to show that it gives readings superior to prevailing interpretations of Hegel. Finally, in Chapter 7, I consider the most ambitious and, in my opinion, the most interesting, attempt to formulate a neo-Marxist conception of dialectic — Theodor Adorno's, as embodied in his final major work on philosophy, *Negative Dialektik*. I try to show how the challenge which Adorno makes to two key features of Hegel's philosophy systematically transforms the conception of the philosophical enterprise.

2

Determinate Negation and Immanent Critique

It is the *ways in* to philosophy that are the most interesting part of the
subject; for it is the course taken at the outset — in the first steps taken
from ordinary ways of speaking to the extraordinary things which
philosophers habitually say — that determines the whole of a thinker's
theories.

R. M. Hare

The question which is to initiate the interpretation of Hegel is: can
Hegel's speculative dialectic be criticized rationally? The question is
of evident concern to the interpreter. But why should its openness to
criticism be a special problem for the discussion of Hegel's system?
What seems a forceful consideration presents itself: 'The true', Hegel
writes,

is the whole. But the whole is only the essence which completes itself
through its development. It is to be said of the Absolute that it is essentially
result, that only at the end is it that which it is in truth.

(*P. d. G.*, p. 21)

And further:

The true form in which the truth exists can only be as its Scientific system.

(*P. d. G.*, p. 12)

If the truth requires a system, then it only properly exists at the
point of completion of the system; what precedes it is only partial,
but not adequate. As critics, however, what should interest us is *how*
that point of completion is obtained, and whether we have arrived at
it legitimately or not. But, on one obvious interpretation of the
quotations above, what they say is that, except as we attain this point
of completion, we are not at the standpoint of truth, and that,
therefore, we are not in a position fully to comprehend (and hence to
justify or criticize) the method by which it was reached. In this way
we have the paradox: to criticize Hegel is to claim that the system

does not attain validly its point of completion. But to criticize from any point other than the point of completion violates a crucial presupposition of the system itself, namely, that only someone who has really attained its final point can perceive the rationality of its attainment. I shall call this the *post festum* paradox.

If one acknowledges that the conception of rationality which Hegel offers is sufficiently plausible to make it worthwhile at least *entering* his system, then the *post festum* paradox, together with Hegel's claim that his system contains all previous philosophical standpoints as subsidiary components of itself, ensures that the question of Hegel becomes the question of philosophical rationality itself. The *post festum* paradox in this strengthened form has had considerable historical force.

There is no clearer example of its effect than in the writings of Marx and Engels. The consequence which they drew from the paradox led to the rejection of philosophy as an autonomous enterprise in favour of a science which was to move, as they put it, 'from earth to heaven'; that is to say one which would not operate immanently within the sphere of philosophical validity, but would give a scientific, causal account of that sphere itself. But, although Marxism drove philosophy out with a pitch-fork, it soon found its way back; if historical materialism is the science which accounts for philosophy, philosophy itself can hardly claim the right to call it to epistemological account. Does this leave historical materialism, then, as a science whose methodological and conceptual apparatus is beyond criticism? If so, on what basis does it claim to be *scientific*? But, if not, from where are the standards derived according to which criticism can be made?

This dilemma explains why Marxism, its commitment to causal science notwithstanding, has undergone periodic waves of sympathy with explicitly anti-rationalist doctrines which faced up to the *post festum* paradox. The greatest of these, in the nineteenth century, were the philosophies of Kierkegaard and Nietzsche. For Kierkegaard the dilemma of the *post festum* paradox implies a transfer of attention from theology as a universal rational activity to the *experience* of Christianity, which does not seek rational grounds to vindicate itself, but whose particularity can resist philosophy's universalizing efforts to capture it. Nietzsche's response to the same dilemma is expressed in the provocative sub-title of *Götzendammerung: Twilight of the Idols*, or *How to Philosophize with a Hammer*. Philosophical rationality, we are to understand, is not be *refuted* (for in its own terms it is irrefutable) but to be *overcome* by a resolute, destructive will.

The consequences of the *post festum* paradox are, then, to call the conception of rationality itself into question and to challenge the continued existence of philosophy as an autonomous discipline. Yet, if the consequences are anti-rationalist, it is not enough to dismiss them as *irrational*. For if it really is the case that reason, when pressed to the limit, becomes an enclosed, self-supporting system, then the decision for or against reason is not one that it itself can help us take.

The power of the *post festum* paradox continues to be felt in contemporary continental philosophy. Thus Hans-Georg Gadamer, the most distinguished contemporary exponent of philosophical hermeneutics, writes:

Polemics against an absolute thinker has itself no starting point. The Archimedean point from where Hegel's philosophy could be toppled can never be found through reflection. This is precisely the formal quality of reflective philosophy, that there cannot be a position that is not drawn into the reflective movement of consciousness coming to itself.

Gadamer is unsympathetic, however, to those, like Marx and the explicit anti-rationalists, who try to refute Hegel by what he calls an 'appeal to immediacy'. This, he says, is self-refuting:

The appeal to immediacy – whether of bodily nature, or of the 'Thou' making claims on us, or of the impenetrable factualness of historical change, or of the reality of the relations of production – has always been self-refuting, in that it is not itself an immediate attitude but a reflective activity.[1]

Here, then, we have the *post festum* paradox clearly expressed: Hegel's philosophy is taken to embody a conception of rationality (the reflective movement of consciousness) sufficiently persuasive to make entry into the system inevitable. Even historical materialism is a 'reflective activity'. Yet, on the other hand, there is no point from which the process itself may be criticized.

In order to disarm the paradox Gadamer himself has recourse to the Heideggerian thesis that, in the progress of thought, 'revelation' or 'disclosure', and 'concealment' go together. Heidegger himself expresses this claim as follows:

The nature of truth, that is of unconcealedness [*Unverborgenheit*] is dominated throughout by a denial. Yet this denial is not a defect or a fault, as

---

1   Gadamer, *Truth and Method*, p. 308.

though truth were unalloyed unconcealedness that has rid itself of everything concealed. If truth could accomplish this it would no longer be itself...
denial in the manner of concealment belongs to unconcealedness as clearing.[2]

This amounts to a rejection of the possibility of attaining the point
of completion; ever-new concealments renew the task of the reflective movement. Each *dis-closure* brings with it a new *fore-closure*: the
history of thought is not a univocal progress of enlightenment but an
unceasing ebb and flow.

The *post festum* paradox is of particular relevance to Critical
Theory (the group of authors also known as the Frankfurt School) in
relation to its enterprise of *Ideologiekritik* (the criticism of ideology).
Critical Theory, unlike the 'orthodox' Marxism it separates itself
from, aims at more than a 'reading' of intellectual phenomena which
refers them back to the economic forces and class antagonisms in
which they originate. Can it arrive at its account of them — in
particular, its account of Hegel — by a process of immanent critique?
    This, certainly, is the claim:

Nothing other leads out of the dialectical context of immanence [*Immanenz-
zusammenhang*] than its own self.

(N. D., p. 145)

Thus the possibility of Adorno's Critical Theory depends upon a
resolution of the *post festum* paradox. I want to consider now various
ways in which this might be achieved.

Method and System

One way in which to escape the paradox would be if we could draw a
distinction between Hegel's dialectical *method* and the speculative
system in which it is lodged. If that were possible, then the question of
the rationality of the method could be separated from the question of
the attainment of the ultimate standpoint, which is the truth of the
system. In this way we could reject Hegelianism while retaining a
dialectical conception of rationality.
    This distinction between method and system was given canonical
authority for Marxism by Engels himself in his *Ludwig Feuerbach*:

[Hegel] was compelled to make a system, and, in accordance with all the
traditional requirements, a system of philosophy must conclude with some
sort of Absolute Truth ... In this way, however, the whole dogmatic content
of the Hegelian system is declared to be Absolute Truth, in contradiction to

<hr>

2   Heidegger, 'The Origin of the Work of Art', p. 680.

his dialectical method, which dissolves all dogmatism. Thus the revolutionary side becomes smothered beneath the overgrowth of the conservative side.[3]

Despite Engels's authority the distinction between 'acceptable' Hegelian method and 'unacceptable' system has been attacked within the Marxist tradition by Louis Althusser. In a famous essay he claims that:

It is inconceivable that the essence of the dialectic in Hegel's work should not be contaminated by Hegelian ideology, or, since such a 'contamination' presupposes the fiction of a pure pre-'contamination' dialectic, *that the Hegelian dialectic should cease to be Hegelian and become Marxist by a simple, miraculous 'extraction'.*[4]

In other words, the dialectic which is extracted from Hegel's system remains a Hegelian dialectic and so unsuitable for Marxism. But, one may ask, is it even possible that a Hegelian dialectic could, in fact, be 'extracted'? It is possible, if at all, only by violating Hegel's own conception of dialectic. This can be made clear from the Introduction to the *Science of Logic:*

In every other [science] the object of which it treats and the scientific method are different from one another.

(*W. d. L.* I, p. 23)

The object of Hegel's Science is the system of truth; the identity of method and content which Hegel makes its identifying characteristic means that, just as the truth of the content is the system's final result, so too is the Science's own identity:

Not only the communication of the Scientific method, but even the notion [*Begriff*] of the Science itself belongs to [the *Logic's*] content, and constitutes indeed its final result; thus it cannot say in advance what it is, but its whole treatment brings out this knowledge from itself as its last element and its completion.

(*W. d. L.* I, p. 23)

Thus the attempt to isolate a dialectical method takes us out of the *post festum* paradox only at the price of abandoning its common ground with Hegel. For the very impossibility of separating out a dialectical method is a differentiating feature of philosophical procedure as Hegel understands it. It is what guarantees his undertaking as true and scientific:

3   Engels, *Ludwig Feuerbach*, p. 23.
4   Althusser, 'Contradiction and Overdetermination', p. 91.

How could I fail to be of the opinion that the method which I follow in this system of Logic — or which, rather, this system follows in its own self — is capable of being much further completed and of much improvement in individual cases? But yet, at the same time, I know that it is the only true one. This becomes apparent from the fact that it is nothing different from its object and its content; for it is the content in itself which moves it forward. It is clear that no presentations [*Darstellungen*] could count as Scientific which do not follow the step of this method and are not in accordance with its simple rhythm, for it is the step of the subject-matter itself [*Gang der Sache selbst*].

(W. d. L. i, p. 36)

The search for a dialectical method as the key to the rationality of Hegel's dialectic leads, then, to a dead end, inasmuch as the unity of method and content means that an account of the methodological aspects of his philosophy involves exactly the same problems as those facing an account of the philosophy taken as a whole.

Immanent Critique

A second attempt to deal with the *post festum* paradox starts from the understanding of dialectic as *immanent critique*. This appears to offer a way of defusing the paradox's destructive implications without, thereby, violating the principle of the identity of method and content. The defender of such an approach would argue as follows: dialectic does not possess — he might concede — a *method*, in the sense of a procedure, presupposed and intersubjectively acknowledged prior to the commencement of its investigation, or in the sense of privileged access to a sphere of self-evidence, according to which its transitions could be justified. Dialectic is, indeed, a 'law unto itself '; but the pejorative implication which this carries is misplaced. Being a 'law unto itself ' dialectic is *autonomous*, which is not the same thing as being *arbitrary*. Dialectic can escape this charge of arbitrariness not by calling on a single method, whose standards it treats as absolute, but by returning to its roots in the sense of *discussion, dialogue, debate*. Dialectic is legitimated, therefore, not with reference to absolute (or Absolute) principles, but by the ability which it has to deal with objections and to satisfy them *on their own terms*.

This understanding of dialectic as a critical movement through presuppositions has affinities, evidently, with Gadamer's description of it as a 'reflective movement' and it has, indeed, been defended vigorously by a former student of Gadamer's, Rüdiger Bubner, in his book *Dialektik und Wissenschaft*. His view that the rationality of dialectic consists in the willingness to engage alternatives on their own terms is clearly articulated in the following two paragraphs:

The strength of dialectic consists in critically entering into contrary positions in order to uncover the irrational, dogmatic elements [*Momente*] in them. But this it has only thanks to an aspiration towards reason which it recognizes as binding on itself and which it cannot lay claim to one-sidedly. The engagement aims to uncover irrationality and limitation in order to strengthen rationality.

and

the method shows its autonomy in determining itself through a structure whose determinacy in its turn is determined by nothing further. Thus what gives the method its character as method does not depend on something given − a posited goal of knowledge or dogmatic concept of truth − to which the procedure would be simply subordinated, without allowing of being turned upon it in turn.[5]

On this view dialectic is methodologically *open* (it takes the ground-rules on which it operates only insofar as these can be justified in the course of debate with the alternative conceptions of philosophy it criticizes) and *autonomous* (in aiming to generate binding principles from its own resources).

It is possible to establish strong support in Hegel's text for this understanding of dialectic as immanent critique. Hegel gives his most explicit discussion of the matter in the introductory remarks to the chapter on the notion (*Begriff*) in the *Science of Logic*. He reviews there his treatment of Spinoza's philosophy, taking it as an example of the proper way for philosophy to deal with alternative systems. True philosophy, Hegel says, cannot simply *reject* those systems which diverge from its own conception of the truth:

The general remark has already been made elsewhere with regard to the refutation of a philosophical system, that the erroneous conception must be excluded, by which the system is to be presented as entirely false and as if the true system by contrast was merely opposed to the false one.

(*W. d. L.* II, p. 217)

Opposing systems are not just worthless illusions. They are rational enterprises − albeit imperfect ones − and, as such, are more than merely subjective:

Such a standpoint [as Spinoza's] is thus not to be regarded as an opinion [*Meinung*], as the arbitrary, subjective way of conceiving [*Vorstellungsweise*]

5   Bubner, *Dialektik und Wissenschaft*, pp. 130, 171.

or way of Thinking of an individual, as a deviation of speculation. The latter, rather, finds itself necessarily transferred to it on its journey and to that
extent the system is entirely true. But it is not the highest standpoint.

(*W. d. L.* II, p. 217)

The true system develops and vindicates itself by including these
lower standpoints within itself. But it must not, Hegel says, do that
'externally' (as Marxists do, for example, when they treat other systems merely as symptoms of ideological history). It must establish
common ground with them, and this means participating in their
assumptions. Only then can criticism have force:

The refutation must not come from outside, that is, it must not proceed
from assumptions which lie outside that system and which do not accord
with it. The system merely need not recognize those assumptions; the deficiency is only a deficiency for someone who proceeds from the needs and
demands which are based upon them.

(*W. d. L.* II, p. 217)

Further:

The true refutation must enter into the power of the opponent and place
itself in the compass of his strength.

(*W. d. L.* II, p. 218)

Determinate Negation

So far, then, the text strongly supports Bubner's account. Yet there
remains a crucial question for this reading of Hegel's dialectic as
argumentative engagement and immanent critique. The reading
needs to account for the characteristic Hegelian doctrine that immin-
ent critique yields a *positive* result — the doctrine of *determinate negation*. Examination of the text demonstrates that it is precisely this
feature of leading to a positive result which is, for Hegel, the distinguishing feature of his *speculative* dialectic, in contrast with those
forms of dialectic which he calls 'formal', 'negative' or 'sophistic'.
The first aspect of dialectic (the aspect which is negative and critical
of the subject-matter under investigation) is all that 'formal philosophy' can grasp:

Formal philosophy cannot look at dialectic in any other way than as being
the art of confusing ordinary conceptions or even notions [*Begriffe*] and de-
monstrating their nullity, thus making the result merely negative.

(*Gesch. der Phil.* II, p. 62)

But this understanding of the result of criticism as negative makes formal philosophy the ally of scepticism:

> The dialectical principle as employed by the understanding separately and independently — especially as set forth in scientific concepts — constitutes scepticism; the result of the dialectic is mere negation.
>
> (*Enz.*, para. 81)

True philosophy is to avoid this by producing a positive result:

> [True philosophy] includes the sceptical principle as a subordinate function of its own in the shape of dialectic. In contradistinction to scepticism, however, philosophy does not remain content with the purely negative result of dialectic. Scepticism mistakes the true value of its result when it holds fast to it as mere, that is to say, abstract negation. The negative, as the result of dialectic, is, because a result, at the same time the positive; it contains what it results from, absorbed [*aufgehoben*] into itself, and does not exist without it.
>
> (*Enz.*, para. 81, *Zusatz* 2)

Here, then, is the doctrine of *determinate negation*. It amounts to the claim that negation in the course of dialectic is positive. This claim, which Hegel calls a 'logical proposition' is, he says, a 'tautology'; yet it is *the* fundamental feature of true philosophical procedure:

> The only requisite for the acquisition of the *Scientific* progression — and the very simple insight into this is what essentially concerns us — is the cognition of the logical proposition that the negative is equally positive, or that that which contradicts itself does not dissolve into Zero [*Null*] but essentially only into the negation of its particular content, or that such a negation is not all negation but the negation of the determinate subject-matter [*Sache*] which dissolves and is thus *determinate* negation, so that that from which it results is essentially contained in the result — which actually is a tautology, for otherwise it would be something immediate and not a result.
>
> (*W. d. L.* I, p. 35)

Clearly this thesis about the nature of immanent critique — that it leads to a positive result — is fundamental to Hegel's understanding of the nature of his enterprise. Yet how is it to be established? Does it, perhaps, even *need* establishment? Hegel has, indeed, claimed that it is 'actually a tautology' that to negate is to produce a negated something, not nothing. Yet very little examination shows the doctrine of determinate negation to be in fact anything but a tautology, in the sense of being trivially true.

We can separate two quite different claims in this doctrine of determinate negation. The first is the claim that

(1) negation is not all negation but the negation of a determinate matter which dissolves

and the second the claim that

(2) that from which it results is essentially contained in the result.

These are fundamentally different claims, and, if the 'so that' with which Hegel connects the two were to be taken to mean that the former claim entails the latter, this is certainly wrong.

One can explain the first claim by means of an analogy. To think of negation as 'all negation' would be to think of it as a procedure which is in no way adapted to its objects. The act of negation would then be like the 'wiping clean' of a blackboard; whatever is inscribed on the 'mental slate' is wiped off, *no matter what its intrinsic character, by one and the same action*. Against this analogy the first claim says that we should see negation as a process which must adapt itself to the *contours* of whatever it is that is to be negated.

In pursuit of this first claim we might substitute another metaphor for that of negation as a 'wiping clean'; we might say that negation is an *operation*. Does this new metaphor also establish the second claim? It seems that it *does* only if we build a further assumption into the metaphor of the negating operation. This is the assumption that negation is an activity performed upon a thing-like object as its material. Conceived in this way it might indeed be tautologous that what the negated material 'dissolves into' is not Zero but that there is a residual product which is 'the negation of its particular content'. But why should we make such an assumption? Certainly, as Ernst Tugendhat has pointed out, the assumption that *thinking* and other mental activities referred to by propositional attitude verbs are really operations performed upon some material is a traditional one.[6] Indeed, when someone is thinking, asserting or negating then our language entitles us to say that there is *something* that he thinks, asserts, or negates. This 'something' is the 'object' of the thinking, asserting, or negating activity. But, encouraged by the surface structure of our language, philosophers have assumed that these objects are like 'things' and share their status as entities. So they are drawn into a metaphysical quest for 'propositional objects'. Students of philosophical history are familiar with typical answers: they are 'entities which have being without existence', they are 'intentional objects' etc. If we follow Tugendhat it looks as if Hegel is making the traditional, but paralogistic, assumption of equating negation with an

6   See Tugendhat, *Traditional and Analytical Philosophy*, and 'Das Sein und das Nichts'. Tugendhat's views are discussed in Chapter 6.

ordinary transitive verb of action. Yet, if we do not assimilate negation to action in this illegitimate way, then the second claim does not follow from the first one; even if we concede that negation is a process which must adapt itself to the contours of its object, why should this be like moulding a piece of wax or chiselling a block of marble (which always leaves a new shape), rather than like unravelling a knot in a piece of string (which by no means leaves a new knot when we have finished)?

This *positive* aspect which dialectic claims for the process of immanent critique is indispensable to Bubner's attempt to vindicate a dialectical conception of rationality against what he sees as the irrationalism of modern science. According to his conception of dialectic:

> The overcoming of contradiction means the design of a new theory according to that inadequacy which led the old theory into contradiction ... The new theory does not present a different theory in which by chance the contradiction is not present but is determined with respect to the previous one as the better theory, i.e. the theory which better fulfils its own aspirations. The new theory is superior *as regards its status as theory*.[7]

However, this claim that theories do have such progressive aspirations – and that there are common standards between theories according to which they can be judged – is exactly what the sceptical trend in modern philosophy of science, pioneered by writers such as Kuhn and Feyerabend, denies. Moreover, even if we concede the existence of common standards, this does not itself amount to Hegel's claim. For, as Sir Karl Popper (who does defend the existence of common standards) has pointed out, it is one thing to give refutation a heuristic role in the establishment of new theories but quite another to give it a *logical* one. In the absence of an independent justification of determinate negation the assumption that theories inherently develop towards higher standards looks like a reintroduction of 'the cunning of reason'.

The arguments given above aimed to show that immanent critique does not lead to a positive result as a 'mere tautology' and that the claim that it does stands in need of justification. I have, furthermore, suggested that the process of philosophical justification is, for Hegel, a process of immanent critique. And yet this conception of immanent critique itself contains a claim standing in need of justification. Is the claim that immanent critique leads to positive results *itself* supposed to be the positive result of an immanent critique? If so then it

7   Bubner, *Dialektik und Wissenschaft*, p. 173.

appears that Hegel's dialectic is self-supporting in an unacceptable
sense, for (the commitment to dialogue and debate notwithstanding)
it would have established itself by means of an assumption which would
be denied, to give an obvious example, by any consistent Kantian.

My point can be illustrated by consideration of the comparison
which Hegel makes between his own conception of dialectic as a
process of determinate negation and Kant's. Hegel expresses the
contrast between the two as follows:

Kant's dialectical presentations in the *Antinomies of Pure Reason* do not merit
great praise when scrutinized as they will be in this work. But the general
idea which he took as his basis and defended is that of the objectivity of
illusory appearance [*Schein*], and the necessity of contradiction, which belongs to the nature of the determinations of thought ... This result, comprehended in its positive side, is nothing other than their inner negativity, as
their self-moving soul, the principle of all natural and spiritual vitality. But
as it comes to rest at the abstract negative side of the dialectic, the result is
only the familiar one that Reason is incapable of knowing the infinite.
(*W. d. L.* I, p. 38)

Yet this passage shows no argument for the superiority of Hegel's
conception of dialectic which the Kantian need acknowledge as
rationally compelling. Despite his own strictures on refutation,
quoted above, Hegel appears to be adopting standards quite at
variance with the Kantian system, for it is Kant's whole point that
the positive results, the speculative truths which Hegel wants, are,
by the limitations of human beings' cognitive constitutions, un-
attainable.

To make this clear let us look at the structure of the argument
which Kant uses in the Antinomies. In outline, this is as follows:

(a) If a genuine empirical property is intelligibly applicable to an object then either the object in fact has that property or it does not.
(b) In the case of certain intelligibly applicable properties there are
objects of which it can be establlished that they must both have
and lack the property (the denial of either can be shown to entail
an absurdity).
(c) Such properties are therefore of a special kind – they are *cosmical*,
rather than empirical, Kant says (*K. r. V.*, B 4 34) – and are not
applicable in the standard way.

Now the requirement of immanent critique says that an author must be challenged on the basis of his own assumptions. If we accept this as a fair reconstruction of Kant's argument, which of Kant's assumptions could Hegel challenge? Hegel advances no reasoned objection to this structure of argument. His criticism, as we saw above, is that it is insufficiently strong to reach the positive, speculative conclusions he sees dialectic as requiring. But if we were, for example, to grant, as defenders of dialectic have sometimes claimed, that the Law of Excluded Middle is a 'dogmatic presupposition' then we would be entitled to reject (a), which logically depends on it. However, if we do this, the conclusion we are left with actually becomes *weaker*. For the basis of even the weak result of the Kantian argument (the distinction in kind between empirical and cosmical concepts) is removed. The procedure of immanent critique itself gives us no clue as to what stronger version of (a) could justifiably be substituted for it by speculative philosophy in order to lead to the desired stronger outcome than (c).

'Knowledge and Human Interests'

The difficulty which this concept of determinate negation represents for Critical Theory is apparent in the first chapter of Jürgen Habermas's *Knowledge and Human Interests*. Habermas is concerned to argue in that chapter against the claim that Hegel succeeds in establishing his philosophical position against Kant by a procedure of immanent critique. To argue this he focuses on the way in which Hegel rejects the Kantian enterprise of epistemology. Hegel, Habermas says, rightly denied that the critique of knowledge which epistemologists practise could ever attain the sort of radical presuppositionlessness required by a *prima philosophia*. But rather than accommodating himself to the more modest role that this implies for philosophy and accepting 'the circle in which epistemology inevitably ensnares itself' Hegel can, Habermas says, only radicalize 'the mistrust expressed by the critical philosophy, which is the modern form of scepticism'.[8]

Only the radical aspirations of traditional philosphy could make Hegel's rejection of the epistemological enterprise compelling. But these standards are not intrinsic to epistemology in all forms and at all times. Because Hegel assumes that they are, as Habermas puts it:

what starts out as immanent critique covertly turns into abstract negation.[9]

8   Habermas, *Knowledge and Human Interests*, pp. 8, 9.
9   Habermas, *Knowledge and Human Interests*, p. 9.

This last sentence indicates the problem Habermas is left by his rejection of Hegel's critique of Kant. For to say that Hegel's claim to establish his discipline of speculative knowledge by a process of immanent critique rests on an 'abstract' negation shows that Habermas himself wants to retain the conception of *determinate negation* for his Critical Theory. But what sense can he give to the contrast? If Habermas is dissatisfied with Hegel's critique of the Kantian enterprise of epistemology, he cannot, one would think, endorse the speculative claim which, as we saw above, Hegel makes against Kant, that immanent critique leads to positive results. Yet, remarkably, Habermas does indeed think that what he is taking over is Hegel's conception of determinate negation and that he is justified in doing so. I shall argue, however, that he is mistaken in his account of Hegel.

Habermas's account of determinate negation identifies it with the *phenomenological* path taken by the self-development of consciousness. Such progress is to be contrasted both with strictly *logical* relations between antecedent and consequent and with *causal* relations:

This figure of determinate negation applies not to an immanent logical connection but to the mechanism of the progress of a mode of reflection in which theoretical and practical reason are one ... A *form of life* that has become an abstraction cannot be negated without leaving a trace, or overthrown without practical consequences. The revolutionized situation contains the one that has been surpassed, because the insight of the new consists precisely in the experience of revolutionary release from the old consciousness. Because the relation between successive states of a system is brought about by what is in this sense determinate negation and not by either a logical or a causal relation, we speak of a self-formative process [*Bildungsprozess*].[10]

This account of determinate negation, however, cannot correspond to Hegel's own understanding of it. On Habermas's account it is a necessary feature of determinate negation that it involves the progress through *forms of life*. Only where there is a unity of the theoretical and the practical can the continuity between antecedent and successive states be guaranteed, so that the latter are really the 'outcome' of the former. But if this restriction of determinate negation to a progress through forms of life is to be applicable to Hegel we have to accept one or other of the following two consequences for his system. Either the concept of determinate negation is inapplicable to the *Science of Logic* or the determinations of thought dealt with in that work are themselves to be taken as embodied in 'forms of life'.

10 Habernas, *Knowledge and Human Interests*, p. 18

The former option is absurd; as we have seen, determinate negation is the identifying characteristic of Scientific philosophy for Hegel and the *Science of Logic* is philosophical Science in its purest form. Yet, against the other option, Hegel clearly states that the dynamic development of the *Logic* depends not on the fact that what it deals with are 'forms of life' but, to the contrary, on the fact that what it deals with has left the 'externality' of consciousness behind. Indeed even the '*Bildungsprozess*' of consciousness itself depends on this formal, Logical development:

Consciousness is Spirit as concrete knowledge, caught up in externality. But the progressive movement of this object rests solely – as does the development of all natural and spiritual life – on the nature of the pure essentialities which constitute the content of the *Logic*. Consciousness, being Spirit in appearance which has freed itself from its immediacy and external concretion, becomes pure knowledge which gives itself as its object those pure essentialities as they are in and for themselves.

(*W. d. L.* I, p. 7)

Habermas is, in fact, elaborating his own conception of determinate negation. But he is doing so in a process of what hermeneuticists call the 'productive misunderstanding' of another text – Hegel's. It should be assessed therefore in its own right. As such it is open, I suggest, to strong objections.

The point of Habermas's making determinate negation a matter in which 'theoretical and practical reason are one' is to defend it from the sort of objections I made above to Hegel's own account – in particular, to guarantee that immanent critique should produce a determinate result. The fact that determinate negation is taken to be a movement between forms of consciousness guarantees that it does not lead to a complete dissolution, like the unravelling of the knot in a piece of string. So long as there is continuity of consciousness determinate negation will always lead on to a new form. My objection is not to the claim that this movement produces a result, but to the claim that it represents a model of rational progress. This, it seems to me, goes beyond what the model licenses. Habermas uses Hegelian language to express the claim that the succession of forms of consciousness represents progress: 'The revolutionized situation', he writes, 'contains the one that has been surpassed.'[11]

In explaining it, however, he makes an analogy between the path of determinate negation and the progressive dissolution of illusions

11   Habermas, *Knowledge and Human Interests*, p. 18.

characteristic of psychoanalysis:

The reversal of consciousness means the dissolution of identifications, the breaking of fixations and the destruction of projections. The failure of the state of consciousness that has been overcome turns at the same time into a new reflected attitude in which the situation comes to consciousness in an undistorted manner just as it is.[12]

Yet this analogy between rational progress in theoretical development and the psychoanalytic process is quite misleading. Essentially, psychoanalytic enlightenment is a process of *disillusionment*. The subject is brought face to face with his (false) beliefs in the hope that in challenging them he will become free to pursue his goals effectively, rather than continuing to pursue them in a way distorted by persistent (because unconscious) illusions. In this case the analogy with the knot in a piece of string is appropriate; as his illusions are dissolved the subject becomes freer to pursue whatever goals may be truly his because the path to their realization is no longer tangled and twisted.

But this process of disillusionment is quite unlike any reasonable model of the progress of knowledge. Whereas the removal of an illusion in the psychoanalytic context brings the subject nearer to being able to realize his own goals and is, therefore, progress, this is not the case with the rejection of a false piece of theoretical knowledge. Cognitive progress does not consist in rejecting false theories only, but in *extending* knowledge by means of better ones. This point holds whether one is a 'realist' or an 'instrumentalist' about the status of scientific theories (whether one thinks they can properly be treated as 'true' or 'false' or just ranked as 'better' or 'worse'). The analogy with psychoanalysis diverts attention from the fact that Habermas's picture of determinate negation fails to provide an account of the generation of this new and better content. Even if there is continuity between the initial form of life in which an agent holds a false theory and a subsequent one in which he has abandoned it this is not sufficient to speak of progress. Common sense would say – more acurately, surely – that the person who has done no more than reject a theory as false has ended up back where he started. The psychoanalytic analogy smuggles a notion of progress into the critical procedure without which Habermas's conception of determinate negation is weak, indeed trivial.

12   Habermas, *Knowledge and Human Interests*, p. 18.

It is worth reiterating that an objection to this claim that there exist logical means for generating new content in the course of the process of refutation is at the heart of Sir Karl Popper's attack on Hegel's dialectic. Refutation, Popper claims, consists in confronting a theory with a logically incompatible observation. But, he points out, from a body of sentences (theory and observation) which contains a contradiction *anything* can be deduced. In consequence, he suggests, refutation can at best be a *heuristic* device for suggesting better theories, but not a logical one for inferring them.[13] If determinate negation is to be defended against Popper then some way needs to be found to show how this 'heuristic' process could, in fact, be internally rigorous without making use of the inferential omnipotence of self-contradictory bodies of sentences.

On the positive side, then, the definition of dialectic as a process of immanent critique has met certain of the requirements for a rational understanding of dialectic. In making rationality a matter of 'entering into the strength' of one's opponent it gives a definition of rationality which is *prima facie* plausible enough to make entering the system reasonable. Furthermore it is strongly supported by Hegel's own text. At the same time it accomodates the requirement that method and system should not be separate from one another, for immanent critique is itself not so much a method as a commitment to take one's philosophical method from the exigencies of the particular critical situation. Finally, it gives an explanation of why those who make this commitment to the Hegelian system should be led into the *post festum* paradox. The dialectical process of criticizing presuppositions is not open to criticism itself before the point of its completion; criticism of the system can always be shown to fall back into criticism *within* the enterprise of the system itself.

Against this one must set the difficulty with the most characteristic feature of immanent critique as Hegel understands it − the claim that immanent critique produces a positive result. This claim, I have argued, is not a 'mere tautology', but yet it is not established as the outcome of an immanent critique of alternative conceptions of immanent critique. Hegel merely proclaims the evident superiority of his conception of an immanent critique producing a positive result over Kant's, rather than taking the latter's conception seriously in its own terms as his official doctrine prescribes.

13 Popper, 'What is Dialectic?', especially pp. 403−10.

The 'Phenomenology'

If Hegel's conception of immanent critique is not established directly by an immanent critique of Kant's conception is it, perhaps, established independently elsewhere in his writings? The obvious place to expect such a justification is in the *Phenomenology of Spirit*. If determinate negation is, as Hegel claims, characteristic of Science then it is reasonable to expect a justification of it from the *Phenomenology*, whose role, Hegel says, is to provide a deduction of the conception of Science in the form of Absolute Knowledge:

I presented in the *Phenomenology of Spirit* ... consciousness in its forward movement from the first immediate opposition to Absolute Knowledge. This way leads through all the forms of the relationship of consciousness to the object and has as its result the notion of Science [*Begriff der Wissenschaft*]. This notion needs therefore (apart from the fact that it emerges itself within the *Logic*) no justification here, and it is capable of no other justification than this its production by consciousness, whose own forms all dissolve and resolve themselves into it as the truth.

(*W. d. L.* i, p. 29)

But, in deriving his notion of Science by means of the *Phenomenology*, Hegel appears to be operating inside a vicious circle. The forms of consciousness which lead to Absolute Knowledge are to be shown to be a rational, necessary sequence. Each form must show itself to be the result of the previous one until the final, completed form is reached:

The necessary progression and interconnection of the forms of the unreal consciousness will by itself bring to pass the completion of the series.

(*P. d. G.*, p. 68)

Yet by what right is each form to be taken to be the *result* of the previous one? John Plamenatz develops this charge. He accuses Hegel of providing no explanation why the progressive development he claims comes about:

[Hegel's reason for the development] amounts to saying that something must develop merely to acquire a property which it lacks. And what is meant by its lacking a property? No more than its not having it; If that is all that is meant, the argument is absurd. No doubt, if something is to acquire a property it does not have it must change; but its not having it is not a reason for its changing. Is the lack here in question a felt want? Who, then, feels it? Not the members of the community, for they as yet have no inkling of what it is they lack.[14]

What Plamenatz completely misses is the point that for Hegel the

14   Plamenatz, *Man and Society*, ii, p. 182.

logical exigencies of the development of consciousness *do* make themselves felt in the minds of the members of the community. The deficiency of a stage of consciousness makes itself felt directly; however, its true significance and progressive role is not apparent. The questions which Plamenatz should have asked instead are: what right has Hegel to adopt a perspective according to which the breakdowns of forms of consciousness do not constitute an adventitious sequence but go together to make a single, progressive movement? What right have we to say that the deficiency experienced by the members of a community relates to the new form of life which replaces it in such a way as to make this later stage into a *fulfilment* of the former one?

Hegel does, however, provide an answer to these questions. He makes a contrast between the movement which is presented in the *Phenomenology* and the 'one-sidedness' and 'scepticism' of 'natural consciousness'. The point of view of the *Phenomenology,* he says, is to grasp the underlying unity of the movement as a process of *determinate negation:*

> The exposition of the untrue consciousness in its untruth is not a merely *negative* procedure. The natural consciousness itself normally takes this one-sided view of it; and a knowledge which makes this one-sidedness its very essence is itself one of the patterns of incomplete consciousness which occurs on the road itself, and will manifest itself in due course. This is just the scepticism which only ever sees pure nothingness in its result ... When, on the other hand, the result is conceived as it is in truth, namely as a *determinate* negation, a new form has thereby immediately arisen, and in the negation the transition is made through which the progress through the complete series of forms comes about of itself.
>
> (*P. d. G.*, p. 68, Miller trans.)

But clearly such an argument from determinate negation is less than the sort of presuppositionless derivation of determinate negation one might hope for. The 'scepticism' (as Hegel calls it) of the natural consciousness, which denies the possibility of there being a positive result for immanent critique, is to be displayed as 'one of the patterns of incomplete consciousness which occurs on the road itself'. But the condition of the possibility of such a display, laying out the forms of consciousness as a sequence of determinate negations, is that the stage of 'natural consciousness' has already been left behind. The sequence of determinate negations is only intelligible to this later, higher stage. Hegel himself is under no illusions about this presupposition. He explicity draws the distinction between the experience of the consciousness whose development the *Phenomeno-logy* charts and the consciousness of author and reader to whom it is displayed, observing that consciousness's progress is intelligible 'for us' in a way that it cannot be for itself while undergoing the process. The 'reversal of consciousness' involved in development and the standpoint from which it becomes apparent (which Plamenatz accuses Hegel of attributing without justification to the subjects under examination) involve, as Hegel puts it, 'going behind the back of consciousness':

> The new object shows itself to have come about through a *reversal of consciousness itself*. This way of looking at the matter is something contributed by *us*, by means of which the succession of experiences through which consciousness passes is raised into a scientific progression − but it is not known to the consciousness that we are observing ... *For it*, what has thus arisen exists only as an object; for us it appears at the same time as movement and a process of becoming. Because of this necessity, the way to Science is itself already *Science*, and hence, in virtue of its content, is the Science of the *experience of consciousness*.
>
> (*P. d. G.*, p. 74, Miller trans.)

The deduction of the Scientific stage of consciousness in the *Phenomenology* appears to have exactly the same structure as we saw in the earlier discussion of immanent critique; the belief that the negation of forms of consciousness − their breakdown − leads to a positive result is not demonstrated within the conceptual framework of someone who denies it − the form of consciousness which is in fact undergoing the process − in such a way as to win him over rationally. The 'sceptical' position finds itself, rather, integrated into the course of an exposition which presupposes determinate negation for its very possibility.

The way to Science, the *Phenomenology*, is itself, Hegel grants, already Science and, were it the task of its 'deduction' of Science to provide a universally acceptable, presuppositionless derivation of dialectical rationality, then this circularity would be − talk of the 'Münchausenism' of Hegel's philosophy, notwithstanding − a fatal objection. The *Phenomenology* cannot dislodge the resolute sceptic about determinate negation with a compelling argument that his own principles force him to accept. Yet, surely, the fact that Hegel himself articulates this circularity strongly suggests that he did not, in fact, see this as the *Phenomenology's* task. But then if, as Hegel claims, the *Phenomenology* is Science which provides the derivation of the *notion* of Science, by what right does it operate itself ? Logically (for it is the only possibility) Hegel must believe that what brings consciousness to Science is not the possession (in conscious form) of the notion of Science. The *Phenomenology* can be written only because the development by means of which the natural consciousness comes to Science has, Hegel believes:

already been implicitly [*an sich*] accomplished; the content is already the actuality reduced to a possibility, its immediacy overcome, and the embodied shape reduced to abbreviated, simple determinations of Thought.

(*P. d. G.*, p. 28)

The *Phenomenology* is written at the end of a process of cultural development (of *Bildung*) by which Spirit, the individual's 'inorganic nature', in which he participates as a member of the community, has come to itself. The individual must appropriate this achievement:

This past existence is the already acquired property of universal Spirit, which constitutes the substance of the individual and hence appears externally to him as his inorganic nature. In this respect formative education [*Bildung*] consists in his acquiring what thus lies at hand, absorbing his inorganic nature and taking possession of it for himself.

(*P. d. G.*, p. 27)

The *Phenomenology* is in fact concerned with a *double* process of development; on the one side there is the development of the consciousness under observation, and this must be distinguished from the observing consciousness for which alone its progress can really be apparent as *progress*. But this observing consciousness itself is not static. In the process of observing the development which has been implicitly [*an sich*] accomplished it becomes transformed itself. What is familiar to it, in the form of *Vorstellung* (common consciousness, figurative representation) is *comprehended*, and made a matter of genuine knowledge:

Hence this acquired property [of no longer needing a 'sublation of existence'] still has the same character of uncomprehended [*unbegriffner*] immediacy, of passive indifference, as existence itself; existence has thus merely passed over into figurative representation [*Vorstellung*]. At the same time it is thus something *familiar* [*Bekanntes*], something with which the existent Spirit is finished and done, so that it is no longer active or really interested in it. Although the activity that has finished with existence is itself only the movement of the particular Spirit, the Spirit that does not comprehend itself [*sich nicht begreifenden Geistes*], genuine knowing [*Wissen*], on the other hand, is directed against the representation thus formed, against this mere familiarity; knowing is the activity of the *universal self* [*des allgemeinen Selbsts*] and is the concern of Thought [*des Denkens*].

(*P. d. G.*, p. 28)

This transition undergone by the observing consciousness is not a transition from ignorance to knowledge. We have to have already implicitly acquired the Scientific consciousness which the *Phenomenology* is out to deduce. But we are not yet fully aware *that* we have acquired it. It is not a matter of comprehension [*Begreifen*] or Thought [*Denken*]; we merely have a figurative representation [*Vorstellung*] of it. The task of the *Phenomenology* is to bring this unconscious knowledge to full knowledge, to raise consciousness to the level of the activity of the 'universal self', to enable us to move from Science in the form of *Vorstellung* to Science proper, Absolute Knowledge or (simply) Thought. But it is itself Science in the form of *Vorstellung*. What allows it to presuppose this is a fact of history, namely, that the formative process of Spirit is completed. This is, of course, a fact of *rational history* in Hegel's sense — not an event whose date could be ascertained by empirical investigation but one whose very existence could only be shown within the perspective of 'rational history' established by the system.

. It might seem that the dependence of Hegel's enterprise on this historical presupposition, which can only be demonstrated inside the framework of the system, makes it unacceptably self-supporting. This *would* be the case, I think, were we to require a demonstration, in terms of a commonly acceptable framework of argument, that the standpoint from which the *Phenomenology* claims to operate had been achieved *before* we were prepared to embark on it. But consider the following defence of Hegel: if Hegel is right, and Spirit really has come to the end of its journey, then this is not something that can be demonstrated to the satisfaction of the sceptic *before* the commencement of the *Phenomenology* itself. Yet we should not let this deter us from undertaking its progress. For if we *do* have, implicitly, the Scientific consciousness, then this will show itself as the *practical* ability to follow the *Phenomenology*'s path. Specifically, it ought to give us the ability to carry out the operation of determinate negation and to reason in such a way that immanent critique produces positive results. Rather than giving a rational, discursive demonstration in which we try to establish in advance that such reasoning patterns are plausible, for the benefit of sceptics, the intelligibility of the *Phenomenology* will give their justification, as it were, *in use*. It is wrong to treat the problem of the rationality of Hegel's system as if it were a matter of finding a point of entry into the system, or of establishing common argumentative ground between Hegel's system and those — Kantians, for example — whose philosophical doctrine puts them, officially, outside the system, in order to rationally compel them into it. If Hegel is right *we are already inside*. Philosophy permeates our rational lives:

Whatever truth there may be in the content of any discipline or science, it can only deserve the name if such truth has been engendered by philosophy.
(*P. d. G.*, p. 55)

Let us explore the consequences of this defence. The most important one is to remove the distinction between *understanding* and *assent*; if the justification for Hegel's procedure lies in our practical ability to make use of it, then to follow the discourse of the *Phenomenology* is to assent implicitly to the rationality of its procedures. There is no point from which we can rationally criticize the discourse; we can only fail to understand it.

Such an identification of understanding and assent gives a very plausible textual explanation for the prohibition which Hegel makes of 'external' criticism of his system. The 'recounting' which, Hegel says, is characteristic of the introduction to a work of philosophy is not the truth of the work — but nor, on the other hand, is criticism made at that point entitled to challenge that truth:

[The truth of speculative philosophy] does not lie in this in part merely *recounting* exposition, and is for that reason as little refuted if it be asserted against it that something is not so but rather some other way, if accustomed conceptions [*Vorstellungen*] are recollected and recounted as accomplished and well-known truths, or else if something new gets dished up with the assurance that it comes from the shrine of inward 'divine intuition'.
(*P. d. G.*, p. 47)

But what makes it rational to embark on the path of the *Phenomenology* at all? What conception of rationality, if not that of meeting alternative conceptions of philosophy within a commonly agreed framework of argument, justifies it? Clearly, the resolute sceptic cannot be provided in advance with compelling grounds, but the following considerations are plausible. The issue between us, the Hegelian might say to the sceptic, is between two forms of consciousness, the one of which denies, whereas the other affirms, the possibility of determinate negation. There exists between the two no neutral, common framework within which the issue might be decided. However, he might claim, it remains rational to prefer the affirmation to the denial for the following reason: the standpoint of the *Phenomenology* is able to comprehend that of the sceptic and display it within its own progress, whereas, by his own admission, the sceptic cannot comprehend the *Phenomenology*. In this sense the *Phenomenology's* standpoint may fairly be claimed to be a higher one, for it offers those who adopt it a superior range of understanding to those who do not.

Yet counter-arguments are available to the sceptic about determinate negation. In the first place one might ask — this is an objection which would be appropriate coming from a disciple of David Hume — why it is always rational to prefer an increase in 'understanding'. It is clear why we should prefer to increase our *knowledge* and so, where understanding is tied to knowledge in such a way that genuine understanding can be said to be a type of knowledge, it is evident that, for this reason, we should prefer to increase understanding. But where understanding is actually its own justification — to think that one understands is to understand — as it is in this case, we have no standards to establish its genuine, cognitive character. There is, then, every possibility that what presents itself subjectively as a superior level of understanding is not a higher form of consciousness at all but an instance of the human mind's tendency to spread itself beyond its proper confines and to invest the phenomena which it is confronted with with significance. Such 'understanding' might be as spurious as the voices heard in church bells. For such a Humean objector the rational presumption lies in the direction of austerity.

There is a second, even stronger, objection with which the first one may be supplemented. According to this objection the issue is not just one of a choice between standpoints offering different degrees of understanding. What is really at issue here are two fundamentally different conceptions of philosophical rationality. On the one hand there is the Kantian conception, as embodied in the metaphor of the 'court-house of reason'. Philosophy, like a court, has the task of deciding claims — in this case claims to knowledge — that are brought before it, sorting out the legitimate from the illegitimate on the basis of rational, intersubjective procedure (a framework of philosophical 'jurisprudence'). Yet, on the other hand, Hegel appears to have a conception of rationality which rejects this enterprise of separating the sound from the unsound entirely:

To know something falsely means that there is a disparity between knowledge and its substance. But this very disparity is the process of distinguishing in general, which is an essential moment [in knowing]. Out of this distinguishing, of course, comes their identity, and this resultant identity is the truth. But it is not truth as if the disparity had been thrown away like dross from pure metal, not even like the tool which remains separate from the finished vessel; disparity, rather, as the negative, the self, is directly present in the true as such.

(P. d. G., p. 34, Miller trans.)

The objection to this is: is it rational to give up the Kantian enterprise of sorting and validating in favour of a 'higher' understanding in which the false comes to be reintegrated as a 'moment' of the true? Surely philosophy's function in deciding disputed claims to knowledge is too important to be eliminated in this way.

The implication of these objections is that, even if we *do* have the ability to participate in the Hegelian Science, then this understanding (which is neither open to explicit justification or challenge) amounts to less than the plausible definition of rationality which went with the *post festum* paradox.

Practical Understanding

I now want to look at what is involved in this practical ability. So far the issue between Hegelian and anti-Hegelian philosophical discourse has been treated as a difference with respect to the claim that immanent critique can be made to yield positive results. This claim, as we have seen, goes beyond what common logic sanctions. But it must be emphasized that Hegel's conception of determinate negation is expected to do more than *supplement* reasoning within the ordinary framework of discourse, under the rules of natural deduction, to arrive at stronger conclusions. As I pointed out with respect to Hegel's criticism of the Kantian antinomies, it is not clear what stronger premises would enable him to provide such conclusions. In fact, determinate negation has to be seen as part of an attempt to do more than provide a new, stronger than normal set of principles of inference.

Hegel distinguishes his Scientific discourse from reasoning in the common acceptance of the word, which he calls '*Räsonnieren*'. '*Räsonnieren*' treats propositions in isolation:

The *dogmatic* style of thought in knowledge [*Wissen*] and in the study of philosophy is nothing other than the opinion that the true consists in a proposition which is a firm result or which is known immediately.

(P. d. G., p. 34)

The claim that Hegel is making here is stronger than the common-place that propositions must be presented in contexts which justify them. He envisages a movement between propositions which makes the earlier ones in some sense intrinsic to those which follow. They are more than just evidence for the later propositions, as means to an end, but, taken together, form part of a single semantic whole, which Hegel describes as a self-movement:

It is not difficult to see that the way of asserting a proposition, adducing reasons for it, and in the same way refuting its opposite by reasons, is not the form in which truth can appear. Truth is its own self-movement, whereas the method just described is the mode of cognition that remains external to its material. Hence it is peculiar to mathematics ... and must be left to that science.

(P. d. G., p. 40, Miller trans.)

Deductive relations are, Hegel says, 'external' and the validity of the conclusions derived by their means is relative to the validity of the initial premises. This, he thinks, is a deficiency which the truly Scientific discourse must eliminate:

The grounds of which [deductive reasoning] makes use, are themselves in turn in need of being grounded and so to infinity. This form of grounding and conditioning belongs however to that proof which differs from the dialectical movement and thus belongs to external cognition.

(P. d. G., p. 53)

The relation between the propositions involved in philosophical Science is therefore different in principle from the deductive relations of natural logic. Where formal logic is concerned to represent valid structures of inference holding between semantically uninterpreted units, the dialectical movement actually enters into the propositions themselves and, Hegel says, undermines their 'normal' comprehensibility:

The philosophical proposition, because it is proposition, awakens the belief [*Meinung*] in the normal relationship between subject and predicate and of the accustomed attitude of knowledge. This attitude and the belief associated with it destroys its philosophical content ... only that philosophical exposition would succeed in being plastic [*plastisch*] which were rigorously to exclude the form of the normal relationship between subject and predicate.

(P. d. G., p. 52)

Although we are not used to treating propositions in this way, the text of the Scientific discourse should be comprehensible to the reader

nonetheless, for the formative process of *Bildung* has provided the
necessary condition for its difficulty to be overcome:

> The complaints about the incomprehensibility of philosophical writings rest
> for the most part on this unaccustomed inhibition [in the relation between
> the parts of a proposition] even if the other conditions of the formative pro-
> cess for their understanding are present in the individual.
>
> (*P. d. G.*, p. 52)

We are faced, then, with the problem of understanding a discourse
which differs from the common conception of rational argument,
not just in making use of stronger than normal principles of connection, but which actually *undermines* their normal individuation into
semantic atoms.

The examination of the *Phenomenology*'s role has, in effect,
broadened the problem from that which I started with. The initial
problem was: can we, assuming that we can understand the propositions involved, justify patterns of inference by which the procedure
of immanent critique can be made to yield positive results? It can
now be seen that this problem is part of a wider one — that of the
intelligibility of a discourse which differs radically from argument in
the normal sense. Despite appearances to the contrary, Hegel's commitment to immanent critique does not amount to a commitment on
the part of dialectical philosophy to operate in a common framework
of argument with its non-dialectical opponents. The conception of
immanent critique as leading to a positive result only operates within
the distinctive discourse of Hegelian Science.

The claim that we are led to enter the Hegelian system because it
offers an immediately plausible conception of rationality is, then,
refuted. The claim that immanent critique yields positive results is
only plausible from within a system which Hegel, however, claims
that even non-dialectical philosophy is implicitly, unconsciously inside. What then of the *post festum* paradox, and the prohibition which
it implied on criticism before the attainment of the final result of the
system?

It will be recalled that the claim was that criticism of the system
before its point of completion was illegitimate, insofar as the act of
criticism actually *falls into* the reflective movement of the system itself. This claim provides an interpretation of two features of Hegel's
text, namely, the thesis that 'the true is the whole' and the prohibition on 'external' criticism as practised in prefaces and introductions.

The argument against criticism before the completion of the

system presents us with the following picture: to criticize a particular transition means to accuse it of lacking justification. But what is it for a transition to be *justified*? In ordinary discourse it is the assurance that the pattern which it follows is in conformity with the rules laid down as the axioms of the system of inference, and is supported by what is agreed to be evidence. However, as we have seen, it is an identifying characteristic of dialectic that it has no methodological principles which could be specified in advance. If the transitions of the Science are to be justifiable, then, it would appear that this justification will have to be a retrospective one. 'Allez et la foi vous viendra', said d'Alembert, faced with scepticism about mathematical proof; Hegel's statement that the 'notion of Science' is itself Science's final result suggests that the validity of the transitions which we are invited to make in the Science can only be known *ex post*, with the wisdom of hindsight.

Ex post *Justification*

Yet it is extremely important to realize that this picture is wrong and that Hegel explicitly differentiates his enterprise from it. He rejects, on more than one occasion, the idea of a Science which only has *ex post* perspicuity. The following passage is quite unambiguous:

> But the forward progress of this cognition is not for this reason – because only the result emerges as the absolute ground – something provisional. Nor is it problematic or hypothetical, but must be determined by the nature of the subject-matter [*Sache*] and of its content. The beginning is neither something arbitrary and only temporarily accepted nor something which appears arbitrary and is accepted on sufferance but which shows subsequently that one was right to start from it. It is not like the constructions which one is directed to make for the purpose of providing geometrical propositions where it only emerges afterwards in the proofs that it was correct to draw just these lines and then to begin the proofs themselves by comparison of these lines and angles.
>
> (*W. d. L.* I, p. 56)

This by no means conflicts with the famous assertion in the Preface to the *Philosophy of Right* that the owl of Minerva only spreads its wings with the falling of the dusk. Properly understood, that aphorism deals with the relationship of philosophical Science to the broader processes of historical development which must have been completed for its possibility. But this does *not* mean that the Science is not rigorously *ex ante*.

Proof procedures which only yield full perspicuity *ex post* are, in

Hegel's view, characteristic of the mathematical sciences. But this is the very reason why the mathematical method is insufficiently rigorous for the purposes of philosophy. It, by contrast, is to be an entirely immanent, self-constructing movement from simplicity, and this is what gives it its rigour:

This movement of Spirit, which gives itself its determinacy in its simplicity and its equality with itself in its determinacy, is thus the immanent development of the notion. It is the absolute method of cognition and at the same time the immanent soul of the content itself. I assert that only along this self-constructing path is philosophy capable of being objective, demonstrated Science.

(W. d. L. I, p. 7)

Logically we must concede that conscious awareness of the 'notion' of Science is *not* the method by which Science is practised. However, in refuting the picture of Hegel's Science as having a retrospective justification we are depriving ourselves of an interpretation of the thesis that 'the true is the whole' and of the prohibition on external criticism.

The original question of the openness of the speculative dialectic to rational criticism has led us to the wider problem of giving an account of what is involved in the intelligibility of the Scientific discourse. Such an account will have to deal with those features which supported the original suggestion of dialectic as immanent critique, namely:

(1) *The thesis that 'the true is the whole'* — if this, as I have argued, does not mean that the rationality of the system can only be known perspicuously from its point of completion, what else does it mean?

(2) *The unity of method and system*, which prohibits the isolation of a 'dialectical method' or of 'laws of dialectic'.

(3) *The prohibition on external criticism*. Why, if not because the justification of the move made must await the completion of the system, are criticisms in introductions and prefaces illegitimate?

(4) *The claim that the method of philosophical refutation is immanent critique.* Even if this does not fully justify the dialectical procedure itself it remains an explicit feature of Hegel's text.

and also those which proved a stumbling-block for the understanding of dialectic as immanent critique. These were:

(5) *Determinate negation* — the thesis that immanent critique can lead to positive results.

(6) The rigorously ex ante *character of the Scientific discourse.*

These requirements are to be met within the framework of an account of the intelligibility of the Scientific discourse. If Hegel is right about the historical achievement of Spirit such an account is not *necessary* for the practice of the Science; the intelligibility of the discourse is an 'already acquired property' (albeit in the form of *Vorstellung*). But is one, indeed, possible?

Such accounts are the proper business of prefaces and introductions. Yet Hegel insists time and again that they are unable to capture the Science, as in the *Phenomenology*:

What is said here indeed expresses the notion, but can count as no more than an anticipated assertion.

(*P. d. G.*, p. 47)

and in the *Science of Logic*:

So what is given advance notice in this introduction does not have the purpose of founding the notion of the *Logic* or giving in advance a Scientific justification of its content and method. By a number of explanations and reflections in a common-reasoning [*räsonnierend*] and historical sense, rather, it aims to bring the point of view from which this Science is to be contemplated nearer to common consciousness [*Vorstellung*].

(*W. d. L.* I, p. 23)

This last passage suggests that Hegel thinks that the reason why the considerations given in the Introduction cannot justify the Science is that they attempt to justify in advance what can only be justified retrospectively. But, as I have shown, Hegel claims that the Science is rigorous *ex ante*. What other reason can there be?

My suggestion can be expressed in terms of Bertrand Russell's distinction between *knowledge by acquaintance* and *knowledge by description*. The essence of knowledge by acquaintance is that it is something *experienced*, something which the subject undergoes and acquires *at first hand*. Knowledge by description, by contrast, is discursive. Although, for Russell, knowledge by acquaintance is primarily knowledge of the external world gained through the senses, this is a less fundamental feature. As I argued, the ability to understand the Scientific discourse is, essentially, a practical ability. But the account given of that practical ability in introductions would be like knowledge by description: it might tell us what the understanding of the discourse consisted in but it could not give us (in the sense of substituting for) the experience of understanding itself. In this respect the status of an account of the intelligibility of the Scientific discourse is like that of art criticism. Art criticism does not capture the art experience, not because it gives an *inaccurate* representation of what that experience is like but because *acquaintance* with art is fundamental to the art experience and ineliminable from it. This contrasts with what is involved in giving an account of an argument or a theory in the normal sense. Here the aim is to give an equivalent − to give a set of more comprehensible propositions which re-express the content of the ones to be interpreted in such a way that their validity or invalidity (the structure of the argument) emerges.

This suggestion, if correct, explains why, for Hegel, an introduction does not amount to a *deduction* and *derivation* of the Science: telling us what an experience consists in does not amount to giving an equivalent substitute for that experience. It explains, furthermore, why Hegel makes his prohibition of 'external' criticism. The propositions of the Scientific discourse are, on this interpretation, not neutral semantic objects subsisting in a 'space of discourse', open to comprehension and challenge by any competent speaker of the language. Their comprehensibility, evidence and mutual relations are located within a 'movement of consciousness'. 'Ordinary' propositions, put forward as reasons for or against particular transitions, do not fall within that movement and therefore can play no rigorous part in either the *proof* or the *refutation* of Science.

Hegel makes his notion of understanding in relation to philosophy explicit in the Introduction to the *Lectures on the History of Philosophy*. It involves absorbing the intellectual content of what is written, beyond its literal perception:

For in the case of Thoughts, of speculative ones especially, understanding means something quite different than merely to grasp the grammatical sense of the words and to take them into oneself only so far as the region of figurative representation [*Vorstellung*]. One can thus possess a knowledge of the assertions, propositions or, one might say, of the *views* of philosophers, to have concerned oneself a great deal with the grounds and expositions of these opinions and still, despite all these exertions, have missed the main point, the *understanding* of the propositions.

(*Gesch. der Phil.* I, p. 17)

Hegel here emphasises that the *experience* of understanding is essential to rationality. Thus in the Preface to the *Phenomenology* he sees mathematics characterized by the *perspicuity* for the mathematician − not just the formal structure − of the proofs it gives:

As far as mathematical truths are concerned he who knew the theorems of Euclid by rote [*auswendig wüsste*] would hardly be counted a geometer without their *proofs*, without — as one might express oneself in contrast — knowing them inwardly [*inwendig*].

(*P. d. G.*, p. 35)

But is any independent account of the experience which founds understanding possible at all? The feeling that it is not rests, it seems to me, on the presumption that only people who have an experience can know what it is like. In one sense this is trivial (only the experience itself is absolutely like the experience) but in another it is false. We *can* tell a blind person what seeing colour is like and although this may never amount to — it certainly cannot substitute for — the experience itself this is not to say that it is something useless or inaccurate. The question 'what does the intelligibility of the Scientific discourse consist in?' can be reformulated, I suggest, as 'what is the experience *like* which gives the discourse its comprehensibility?'

Associated with this is the question 'what sort of a consciousness is it that undergoes the experience?' As we saw in the discussion of Habermas, it is not the common empirical consciousness. Hegel himself actually rejects the use of the name 'consciousness' to describe the process:

If other Kantians [i.e. Fichte] have expressed themselves regarding the determination of the object by the Ego in such a way that the objectification of the Ego is to be regarded as an *original and necessary act of consciousness...* then this objectifying activity, freed from the opposition characteristic of consciousness [*Gegensatz des Bewusstseins*], is nearer to that which can be taken simply as Thought as such [*Denken als solches*]. But this activity should no longer be called *consciousness*. Consciousness has within itself the opposition between the Ego and its object, which is not present in that original activity. Calling it 'consciousness' casts on it even more the illusory appearance of subjectivity than does the expression 'Thought', which, however, is here to be taken in the absolute sense as infinite Thought, not affected with the finitude of consciousness, in short as *Thought as such*.

(*W. d. L.* I, p. 45)

It is this infinite Thought as such which will be the object of investigation; the ineliminable experiental component in Hegel's conception of Science is pure Thought as represented in the *Logic*. This is the pure form of the rationality underlying all other intellectual processes. If we were able to characterize the higher consciousness of Thought we would know the nature of the animating Spirit of speculative discourse.

3
The Dialectical Movement

The safest general characterization of the European philosophical tradition is that it consists in a series of footnotes to Plato.

A.N. Whitehead

I argued in the previous chapter that the distinctive feature of determinate negation — that it should produce a positive result — received no independent justification sufficient to persuade the resolute sceptic in his own terms. The consequence is that, rather than taking determinate negation as a presuppositionless feature of rationality in general, it should be seen as a feature which only displays itself in pure form in the context of the 'movement of the pure essentialities', i.e. as part of the *Logic*.

Acquaintance and Description

The ability to understand the Scientific discourse is, I claimed, something like tacit knowledge. Its presupposition is the possession, by the person who understands, of a form of consciousness with which he is acquainted as a matter of lived experience. In giving an account of what this experience is like we are not thereby providing an initiation into it.

Yet it might be thought that Hegel's own text contradicts my suggested separation for the purposes of commentary between the Scientific discourse and an external ('narrative') characterization of it. We read, for example:

That with which one is acquainted [*das Bekannte*] is not, because a matter of acquaintance, thereby something known cognitively [*erkannt*].
(*P. d. G.*, p. 28)

The contrast between the '*Bekannte*' and the '*Erkannte*', as Hegel understands it, is the contrast between natural thought, which has attained Science in the form of *Vorstellung*, and true Science. But this suggests that the task of knowing what we are acquainted with is a task which cannot be carried out except as part of the transition from Science in the form of *Vorstellung* to pure Science. In order to deal with this objection it is necessary to distinguish two distinct connotations of what is *bekannt*.

In the first place the contrast between what is *bekannt* and what is *erkannt* expresses the contrast between what we know at first hand and what we only have descriptive knowledge of — like the contrast between our knowledge of the 'look' of anger in someone's face and the information *that* they are angry. But, in the second place, there is a quite separate distinction between something which is known 'only' implicitly (and hence not with full clarity) and what is fully explicit. There is a tendency to elide the two distinctions into a single contrast — encouraged, no doubt, by the everyday use of contrasts like 'conscious'/'unconscious'. But the difference between the two is very important. For there are evidently some sorts of knowledge which have the first characteristic of being inherently 'first-hand' — our knowledge of the redness of red, our ability to steer a car — but which are not implicit in the second sense, for they could not be improved or clarified by being made explicit. Philosophers who *are* aware of the distinction may be tempted, however, to assume that knowledge which is inherently first-hand ('knowing how' as it is often, misleadingly, called) cannot be fully cognitive because it is only such knowledge as can be expressed in descriptive, propositional form which it makes sense to call more (or less) *adequate*. On this view *all* our inherently first-hand knowledge is like our knowledge of the redness of red; not being something that could be re-expressed in descriptive form, it is, for that reason, not something which we might aspire to have *better* knowledge of.

But whatever one thinks in general of the reasoning that the possibility of a better or worse for knowledge presupposes some kind of propositional structure, it is important to see that Hegel would not endorse it. For Hegel all Science, both the *bekannt* and the *erkannt*, has this feature of necessary first-handness — acquaintance — which prevents the simple re-expression of its propositions into the neutral discourse of '*Räsonnieren*'. Both the *bekannt* and the *erkannt* are forms animated in virtue of the Scientific consciousness. But, while one of these forms of consciousness is in the form of *Vorstellung* (and therefore, in some way, only imperfectly self-aware) the other — Thought — as Absolute Knowledge is completely self-transparent.

For this reason a descriptive account of the experience by which the Scientific discourse acquires rationality should concentrate on Thought (the subject-matter of the two *Logics*) rather than the Science in the form of *Vorstellung* of the *Phenomenology*. The Logic presents explicitly that structure which forms the rational foundation for the *Phenomenology*'s progress (and hence for the achievement of its own starting point):

> But the progressive movement of [consciousness] rests solely − as does the development of all natural and spiritual life − on the nature of the pure essentialities [*reinen Wesenheiten*] which constitute the content of the *Logic*. Consciousness, being Spirit as it appears, which has freed itself from its immediacy and external concretion, becomes pure knowledge [*reines Wissen*] which gives itself as its object those pure essentialities as they are in and for themselves... This expresses the relationship between that Science which I call *Phenomenology of Spirit* and the *Logic*.
>
> (*W. d. L.* i, p. 7)

In this chapter I intend to carry out two main tasks:

(a) To give an account of the relationship between the pure Science of Thought, expressed in the *Logic*, and the everyday consciousness of *Vorstellung*.

(b) To give an account of the role of Thought in the system which meets the requirements set out in the last chapter, and deals with both those features which supported the understanding of dialectic as immanent critique (notably the unity of method and system) and also with those which were the stumbling-block for that interpretation (the positive result of determinate negation and the rigorously *ex ante* character of the Science).

It is to the first of those tasks that I now turn.

From Vorstellung *to Thought*

Although I have argued that we cannot find a justification of determinate negation as a presuppositionless feature of rationality in general and that, therefore, it must be understood in terms of the speculative discourse of the *Logic*, this does not mean that (if Hegel is right) determinate negation is not a characteristic of rationality in general. The significance of determinate negation would be restricted to the immediate domain of the *Logic*, only if it were the case that the Science of Logic was a science whose discourse was in principle separate from that of 'common sense' and ordinary theoretical knowledge. But the Scientific discourse, although not part of a common framework of '*Räsonnieren*', is not simply an alternative to the discourse of common sense. If Hegel is right, Spirit's achievement is to have brought that common consciousness itself to the point of Science. The science of Logic is not just one type of science among others, and thus as dispensable to its fellow-sciences as the science of botany is to that of astronomy.

Determinate negation will have a role in ordinary discourse and empirical science to the extent that the *Logic* does. The point is, however, that the *Logic* is not an instance of dialectical reasoning so much as the other way around: dialectical reasoning incorporates the 'movement of the essentialities' presented in the *Logic*. It is clear that Hegel makes very ambitious claims for the extent of this operation:

> Thus Logic is the all-animating spirit of all the sciences, and the Thought-determinations of the *Logic* are the pure Spirits. They are the heart and centre of things, and yet at the same time they are always on our lips − apparently at least − perfectly familiar objects. But things thus familiar are usually the greatest strangers... It is commonly supposed that the Absolute lies far away in a world beyond [*jenseits*]. Rather the Absolute is directly before us, so present that, so long as we think, we must, though without express consciousness of it, always carry it with us and always use it. These Thought-determinations are deposited primarily in language.
>
> (*Enz.*, para. 24, *Zusatz* 2)

So Hegel claims universal applicability for the categories of the *Logic* − including, as we have seen, applicability to the Science by which its own starting-point is attained. But if philosophy makes us conscious of the activity of this 'all-animating Spirit', what consequences does this consciousness have? To put the question in terms of an anachronism familiar to analytical philosophers: is the *Science of Logic* an exercise in *descriptive* or *revisionary* metaphysics? For there is a dilemma here; if the Science of Logic is revisionary then in what sense has ordinary consciousness already 'attained possession' of Science? Yet if the *Logic* is descriptive are we to conclude that dialectic has no *critical* role and that the interest of the discipline is − in the disparaging phrase − 'merely academic'? Given what we know of Hegel's view of the importance of philosophy, it would be surprising were he to endorse this second position, and, indeed, he goes out of his way to deny it:

> As of thought, so also of the Science of Thought, a very high or a very low opinion may be formed. Any man, it is supposed, can think without logic, as he can digest without studying physiology. If he has studied logic he

thinks afterwards as he did before, perhaps more methodically, but with little alteration. If this were all, and if logic did no more than make men acquainted [bekanntmachen] with the action of merely formal thought, it would produce nothing which one could not have done equally as well before. And in point of fact logic hitherto had just this attitude.

(Enz., para. 19, Zusatz 2)

But, as we have seen, Thought is not something with which we are 'unacquainted'. The role of philosophy is to work a transformation from this acquaintance of Vorstellung to Thought:

The difference between common conception [Vorstellung] and Thought [Gedanke] is of special importance because philosophy may be said to do nothing but transform conceptions into Thoughts — though it works the further transformation of the mere Thought into the notion [Begriff], of course.

(Enz., para. 20)

Our acquaintance with thoughts is such, however, that they are known only as embedded in 'sensuous and intellectual material':

Thoughts, in our common consciousness, are affected and united with common sensible and intellectual [geistigem] material.

(Enz., para. 3)

Hegel compares the relationship between the Thought and the Vorstellung in whose material it is embedded to that of a metaphor:

Ordinary conceptions [Vorstellungen] such as these may be regarded as the metaphors of Thoughts and notions. But to have these conceptions does not imply that we appreciate their significance for Thought, the Thoughts and notions which belong to them.

(Enz., para. 3)

The transformation of Vorstellungen into Thoughts has the purpose of bringing something that is unconscious and whose significance is not appreciated to consciousness. As such the Logic is — to use a phrase of Carnap's recently revived by Jürgen Habermas — a procedure of rational reconstruction:

Thus the Logical Science, insofar as it deals with the thought-determinations which unconsciously, in the manner of instincts, pervade our mind [Geist] and remain non-objective and unnoticed even as they emerge into speech, will also be the reconstruction of these thought-determinations extracted by reflection and which are treated by it as forms external to the matter and content.

(W. d. L. I, p. 19)

So the Science, one might say, is both descriptive and revisionary in that its aim is to bring to full consciousness something already present as a matter of acquaintance. But in doing this it is contributing something more to our self-understanding than just 'telling us what we are doing', in the sense of giving theoretical expression to a practical capacity which operates quite adequately in the absence of such an account. Our immediate acquaintance (by contrast with Hegel's example above of the digestive processes) is actually *inadequate*:

With this *Thinking* way of looking at things it soon becomes apparent that Thought carries the requirement of showing the necessity of its content, of proving both the existence [*Sein*] and the characteristics of its objects. Our original acquaintance with them is thus discovered to be inadequate.

(*Enz.*, para. 1)

The mere fact that our ordinary empirical consciousness lacks a theoretical account of a practical ability is not necessarily a *deficiency* in our awareness of that ability. So Hegel needs to give us some reason to think that *Vorstellung* is inadequate in terms of its own aspirations, and not just with respect to an external ideal of philosophical cognition.

He does indeed indicate such an immanent deficiency; the consciousness of *Vorstellung* lacks *necessity*:

In point of *form* the subjective reason desires a further satisfaction than empirical knowledge gives; and this form is, in the widest sense of the term, *necessity* [*Notwendigkeit überhaupt*].

(*Enz.*, para. 9, Wallace trans.)

According to Hegel this lack of necessity in ordinary empirical science takes two forms; there is no intrinsic connection between universal and particular in its judgements and it depends on immediate data:

It is partly that in that [empirical] mode of science the universal or general principle contained in it, the genus or kind etc., is, on its own account, indeterminate and vague and therefore not autonomously [*für sich*] connected with the particular. Each is external and accidental to the other just as the particular facts which are brought into union are each external and accidental to the others. And it is partly that the beginnings are in every case immediate elements, data or presuppositions [*Unmittelbarkeiten, Gefundenes, Voraussetzungen*]. In both these points the form of necessity fails to get its due.

(*Enz.*, para. 9)

The contrast is, however, not an absolute one, for the empirical sciences do not operate solely according to this empirical method.

They themselves also incorporate the (as yet unconscious) activity of Thought, to which the *conscious* development of Thought in philosophy connects up:

The empirical sciences do not stop short at the mere observation of the individual features of a phenomenon. By Thought they have prepared the material for philosophy in the shape of general uniformities ... The reception into philosophy of this content, now that Thought has removed its adhering immediacy and mere givenness, forms at the same time a development of Thought out of itself. Philosophy, then, owing its own development to the empirical sciences, gives their contents in return that most essential form, the freedom of Thought: an *a priori* character. These contents are now warranted as necessary instead of depending on the evidence of facts merely as found and experienced. The fact becomes a presentation [*Darstellung*] and copy [*Nachbildung*] of the original and entirely independent activity of Thought.

(*Enz.*, para. 12)

The quoted passage seems to suggest that in developing towards philosophy the empirical sciences are aspiring to a state in which they consist of nothing but *a priori* propositions, where there is no longer any external data, but the world is 'deduced' (although not, of course, by the logical procedure which we now call *deduction*) from some first principle. To modern ears such a suggestion sounds strange, not to say outrageous, brought up, as we have been, to believe that it was the experimental method by which the empirical sciences led the West out of the night of dogmatism and priest-ridden ignorance. Does Hegel indeed propose its replacement with an utterly *a priori* metaphysics?

Certainly, one highly-regarded philosopher of science has made just the opposite claim:

Hegel and Popper represent the only fallibilist traditions in modern philosophy.[1]

Other defenders of Hegel might make a more conciliatory reply to this *a-priorist* suggestion: Hegel's criticism of the empirical sciences is not a proposal to do away with them. The claim is that the experimental method, left to itself, stands in need of justification or warrant. The role of Hegel's philosophy is exactly that of Kant's transcendental philosophy; it does not displace empirical science but, by giving a *rational reconstruction* of the categories involved, philosophy *warrants* them.

However, this is only the first step towards meeting the objection

1   Lakatos, *Proofs and Refutations*, p. 139.

of *a-priorism*, for there are significant differences between Kant's and Hegel's enterprises; in the first place Hegel's enterprise is considerably more far-reaching than Kant's (and the defenders of transcendental arguments nowadays find even that excessively ambitious). Hegel says that Thought aspires to prove 'both the existence [*Sein*] and the characteristics of its objects', in explicit contrast to Kant's assertion that 'existence cannot be constructed'. The wealth of detailed content in the *Science of Logic* demonstrates the far greater scope which Hegel's rational Science has than Kant's transcendental philosophy. Where Kant restricts the scope of philosophy by his fundamental division between form and received content (the latter being an indispensable feature of empirical propositions), Hegel demands that the sciences of nature be fully transformed into rational *a priori* ones. Their categories are more than just means of subsuming whatever content is derived from experience; the 'propositional link' between universal and particular is to be a matter of inner, living unity. Even where philosophical activity is not explicitly present this is the goal of the unconscious drive of intellectual progress:

It is possible that the form of the scientific exposition [*wissenschaftlichen Darstellung*] merely is empirical, but that the meaning-grasping intuition [*sinnvolle Anschauung*] orders phenomena according to the internal sequence of the notion.

(*Enz.*, para. 16)

But, in addition to the greater scope of Hegel's enterprise, the parallel with Kant leaves open another question, namely, *how* Hegel intends his process of 'rational reconstruction' to take place. For, even if we concede that Hegel's enterprise has the same goal of *warranting* the thought-determinations as Kant's 'transcendental logic' does the categories, it does not seem that we can look for Hegel's achievement of this goal by similar means, for the following reason. Kant's enterprise starts out from the attempt to bring about a 'Copernican revolution' in philosophy (*K. r. V.*, Bxvi). This revolution enables the transcendental philosopher to arrive at truths about the way reality *must* be, by relating it to 'our knowledge', i.e. to the constitution of the subject who knows it:

We then assert that the conditions of the *possibility of experience* in general are likewise conditions of the *possibility of the objects of experience*, and that for this reason they have objective validity in a synthetic *a priori* judgment.

(*K. r. V.*, B197)

There is, however, a price to be paid for the possibility of such transcendental arguments, which is that the reality they tell us about is always the *ontologically dependent* reality experienced by finite human beings, and not the absolute and independent reality of things-in-themselves. Yet, when we come to look at Hegel's attitude towards Kant's transcendental philosophy, it is just this necessary consequence of the Copernican revolution which he finds objectionable:

> [Kant's] primary thought is to vindicate the categories to self-consciousness, the subjective ego. Because of this concern the approach remains in the sphere of consciousness and its opposition; beyond the empirical of feeling and intuition there still remains something not posited [*nicht gesetzt*] and determined by the thinking self-consciousness, namely, a thing-in-itself, alien and external to thought... Because the interest of Kantian philosophy was directed towards their so-called 'transcendental' character its treatment of the thought-determinations came to an empty conclusion.
>
> (*W. d. L.* I, pp. 45, 46)

So, even if we admit that it makes sense to call Hegel's warranting of the thought-determinations a *transcendental* enterprise, the means by which this is achieved cannot be by Kantian transcendental arguments — ones which relate knowable reality to the constitution of a self-conscious, receptive, experiencing subject. (This is not to say that all transcendental arguments must be of this sort. The analytic philosopher, for example, may well try to construct arguments which make the conditions of the possibility of *intelligible discourse* substitute for the conditions of the possibility of *experience* as being the conditions of the possibility of objects in general. Nonetheless my point remains: reference to the Kantian *function* of the thought-determinations does not establish that the derivation they require can be given on a Kantian basis.)

Transformative and Generative

There are two quite different lines of approach to the way one sees Hegel's philosophy going about the task of *warranting* the contents of everyday consciousness. The first approach sees the process in the following terms:

(a) We have a *Vorstellung* of X. That is to say we perceive an object X only imperfectly rationally, or we have only an abstract or reflective judgement of X.

(b) Dialectical philosophy treats the *Vorstellung* of X in such a way that it is transformed into a Thought, and, hence, our imperfect vision of X becomes a fully cognitive one.

I shall call this the *transformative* approach.[2] Naturally the crucial question for this approach is just *how* step (b) is to be thought of as taking place. As we have seen, Hegel's own text uses figurative language to talk of the 'purity' of Thoughts compared with the common material with which, as *Vorstellungen*, they are incorporated, and which occludes their fundamental nature. What this first approach needs, then, is a philosophical account of how this process of 'purification' is to be understood.

The second line of approach, however, introduces an extra step:

(a') We have a *Vorstellung* of X.
(b') An autonomous cognition of X is developed out of the notion. This occurs either unconsciously (as in the course of the development of the sciences) or, when Spirit has reached the possibility of 'pure knowledge', as the free evolution of Thought in the *Science of Logic*.
(c') In virtue of the knowledge developed in step (b') our conception of X is transformed.

This I shall call the *generative* approach. The generative approach frankly adopts the option that Hegel's *Logic* involves a 'deduction of the world' (insofar as it is rational). The problem which it must solve is how, if not by taking as its starting point experience or received theories, genuine content can be derived.

Both approaches agree that the aim of philosophy is to give our knowledge the form of necessity. The transformative approach sees this as being achieved by submitting the contents of everyday consciousness to a procedure of transcendental purification – a 'reflection of reflection' – in the course of which its adventitious character as received will be eliminated or *aufgehoben*. The generative approach, by contrast, sees the transition from *Vorstellung* to Thought as merely the step *into* full-scale philosophical discourse. Within the medium of Thought, however, the reference to *Vorstellungen* – as indeed to all received material – is absent. The relationship to ordinary consciousness is only reintroduced at the end, once the philosophical procedure

2   Examples of those adopting this approach in one way or another are: Klaus Hartmann, 'Hegel: A Non-Metaphysical View'; Arend Kulenkampff, *Antinomie und Dialektik*; Raymond Plant, *Hegel*; Michael Theunissen, *Sein und Schein* (for whom the material to be transformed is the categories of traditional metaphysics); and, as will be argued in Chapter 7, Theodor Adorno.

is completed. Although the development of ordinary consciousness may be necessary to Thought proper, in that Thought proper is only possible at the end of ordinary consciousness's formative process, this need not be taken to mean that the *Vorstellungen* are in any way the material, content or subject-matter of the dialectical process.

Hegel's text provides us with passages which *prima facie* support both approaches. Thus in paragraph 12 of the *Encyclopedia*, where Hegel discusses the relationship between the rise of philosophy and the empirical sciences, he tells us that the stimulus — the need for necessity — which leads to the independent development of Thought is, on the one hand 'but a taking up [*Aufnehmen*] of the content and its received details' but one which, on the other hand 'lets them take the form of a free emergence, after the manner of original Thought [*im Sinne des ursprünglichen Denkens*] following solely the necessity of the subject-matter itself [*der Sache selbst*]' (*Enz.* para. 12). Indeed there are passages, such as the following, in which Hegel writes as if the two approaches (although they are clearly mutually exclusive) amount to the same thing:

[The Thought] becomes the unconscious power to take up the previous multiplicity of sciences and elements of knowledge into the rational form, grasping them in their essential character, eliminating the external and thus extracting out the Logical in them — or, *which comes to the same thing*, of filling the abstract fundament of the Logical, which was arrived at previously by Logical study, with the content of all that is true.

(*W. d. L.* I, p. 41, my emphasis)

I think, however, that Hegel's text gives us sufficient evidence to prove that we should interpret it on the basis of the generative approach, without having to examine in detail how the 'reflection of reflection' or 'mediation of mediation' suggested for step (b) should be understood, and the difficulties it might face.[3] Someone who does not find this evidence convincing will, of course, have to give such an account. I myself am quite unable to see how one could be constructed which did not face objections as serious as those put up against the understanding of determinate negation as a general procedure of rationality in the last chapter.

Raymond Plant, for example, who understands Hegel to believe that:

the task of philosophy, properly conceived, is to see in detail how structuring principles can be discerned in experience; the philosopher should be con-

---

3   See A. Kulenkampff, *Antinomie und Dialektik* (especially Chapter 1) and R. Bubner 'Die "Sache Selbst" in Hegels System' for interpretations along this line.

cerned with 'the emergence of the general out of the multiplicity of existence'[4]

sees that this leads to difficulty for the claim that such a structure is *necessary*. However, he takes this as an equivocation in Hegel's text rather than an argument against his adoption of the 'transformative' approach.

The evidence in favour of the generative approach emerges when we look at precisely what Hegel sees as the deficiencies of the sciences derived from experience compared with philosophy. One of the ways in which he describes the *Logic* is as the search for definitions of God:

> All the Logical determinations – can be regarded as definitions of the Absolute, as the metaphysical definitions of God.
>
> (*Enz.*, para. 85)

Definition, then, is an essential part of philosophical procedure. But this is not to say that we are dealing with *definition* in the ordinary sense of that word. Definition must, according to Hegel, meet certain standards of rigour which are specific to philosophy:

> Philosophy does not involve just *correct* definitions (still less merely *plausible* ones) whose correctness is to be immediately apparent to the consciousness of everyday conception [*dem Vorstellenden Bewusstsein*] but rather with *warranted* ones; such definitions, that is, whose content is not simply taken up as a datum [*als ein vorgefundener Inhalt*] but as known to be warranted in free Thought and thus self-grounded.
>
> (*Enz.*, para. 99)

The key to the contrast between this philosophical definition procedure and the empirical method is that, according to Hegel, the development of philosophical definitions does not involve a procedure of *comparison*:

> A higher standpoint of intellectual development [*Bildung*] is required for interest to be directed towards such pure determinations [*the logical Thoughts*]. Contemplating them as they are in and for themselves means, further, that we derive [*ableiten*] their forms from Thought itself and see from themselves whether they are *true*. We do not accept them from outside [*sie äusserlich aufnehmen*] and subsequently define them or show their value and validity by a comparison with their appearance in consciousness... Thus in this case a notion is not determined in and for itself but with respect to a presupposition, which then functions as the criterion and standard of cor-

4   Plant, *Hegel*, pp. 140, 131.

rectness. Yet we must not use such a standard, but rather leave the determinations to their own independent life.

(*Enz.*, para. 24, *Zusatz* 2)

So Hegel is explicitly setting *his* procedure for arriving at warranted
definitions against any procedure which seeks to measure definitions
with a standard drawn from experience. But such a procedure is
just what one would normally take the procedure of *transcendental
argument* to be, namely, an attempt to show that claims about the
nature of reality, which, at first sight, appear to be arbitrary or
dogmatic assertions (e.g. 'every event has a cause'), turn out to be
necessary when related to the way that reality is given to us. In the
passage above Hegel is rejecting the whole picture which takes
'warranting' to involve a comparison between the given reality of
consciousness and a cognitive standard or ideal. Thoughts, rather,
come to be defined by being developed out of themselves. The
deficiency of what is given as experience, then, is not (as the defender
of the transformative approach has to maintain) that it is *not yet*
warranted, but that utilizing experience *at all* involves a comparison
between itself and Thought which is out of place in philosophy.

Hegel makes a similar point in his discussion of Reinhold's philosophy. Reinhold had given a criticism of Kant's transcendental
philosophy — which Hegel endorsed — for assuming the compe-
tence of Reason to investigate our cognitive capacities as an unjus-
tified presupposition of its Critical enterprise. Hegel, however, has
his own criticism to make of Reinhold's alternative:

Reinhold, who saw the confusion of this sort of commencement, suggested
as a remedy starting provisionally with a hypothetical and problematic philosophical procedure and continuing in it (however that should be possible)
until it should become apparent that one had arrived at basic truth
[*Urwahren*]. This method, when examined closely, amounted to a commonplace, namely, the analysis of an empirical fundament [*Grundlage*] or of a
provisional assumption in the form of a definition.

(*Enz.*, para. 10)

But what is here rejected as 'commonplace' in Reinhold's procedure — the provisional adoption of received material in advance of its
subsequent analysis — would seem to be precisely the structure of
any philosophy whose scientific character rested on the transformation of *Vorstellungen* into Thoughts: a *Vorstellung* is given, then
analysed and purified into the true form of Thought.

The most conclusive evidence against the transformative

approach, however, comes in the course of Hegel's discussion of the notion [*Begriff*] in the *Encyclopedia Logic*. Hegel gives an account of the independence of the philosophical procedure of conceptual development which surely excludes any interpretation which treats it as the process of transforming received consciousness into the purity of Thought:

It is an inversion of things to assume that first there are objects, forming the content of our representations [*Vorstellungen*] and that subsequently our subjective activity comes into play, forming notions by the aforementioned operation of abstracting and colligating what is common to objects. The notion, rather, is that which truly comes first and things are what they are because of the activity of their intrinsic notion, revealing itself in them. This is apparent in our religious consciousness with the effect that we say that God created the world out of nothing or, to put it another way, the world emerged from the plenitude of the divine Thoughts and decrees. We acknowledge thereby that the Thought, and specifically the notion, is the infinite form — that free creative activity which can realize itself without the need for a material present outside itself.

(Enz., para. 163)

The creative autonomy of the notion, parallel to the divine *creatio ex nihilo*, requires no material and shows that dialectical reasoning cannot be a process of transformation of received experience.

One reason why, despite these considerations, it nevertheless may be assumed automatically that Hegel adopts the transformative approach to everyday consciousness is the belief that only in this way can we do justice to the commonplace of dialectical philosophy; that *dialectical* contrasts with *formal* logic. It is important, however, to distinguish two senses in which logic might be said to be formal. In the first sense logic is formal if it lacks content and provides only a structure (a schema or set of rules) to be applied to a content derived by other means. In this sense Hegel's *Logic* is demonstrably not meant to be formal:

This objective Thought, then, is the content of the pure Science. By no means is it a *formal* science, lacking the matter for a real and true knowledge. Its content, rather, is the absolutely true, or (if one wishes to retain the word '*matter*') the *true material*. But it is a matter whose *form* is not something external, for this matter is the pure Thought and thus the Absolute Form itself.

(W. d. L. I, p. 31)

Yet this first, rejected, sense of 'formal' must not be confused with a second, distinct sense whereby 'formal' means 'rigorously *a priori*'.

The two senses are only equivalent on the assumption that whatever is rigorously *a priori* cannot generate content. But this assumes the conclusion to the issue in dispute. The text, to the contrary, shows both that Hegel distinguishes between the two senses and supports the view that the *Logic* is intended to be rigorously *a priori* and, hence, formal in the second sense.

Thus Hegel continues the passage above in which he rejects the understanding of the Logic as formal as follows:

Accordingly *Logic* is to be taken as the system of pure reason, as the realm of the pure Thought. This realm is the truth, as it is in and for itself, without any shell. One may thus say that this content is the presentation of God, as He is in His eternal being [*Wesen*] before the creation of nature and of a finite Spirit.

(*W. d. L.* I, p. 31)

Nor is this echo of Plato's *Timaios* an isolated rhetorical flourish. There are other passages in which Hegel gives us a positively *gnostic* picture of the philosopher's relation to material reality:

If the Science of Logic examines Thought in its activity and its production (and Thought is no contentless activity, for it produces Thoughts and the Thought itself) its content is the super-sensible world and to deal with the subject means to dwell for a while in that world. Mathematics deals with the abstractions of *number* and *space*, but these remain something sensible, although the sensible which is abstract and without concrete existence [*das Daseinslose*]. The Thought bids farewell to even this last sensible feature and is independent [*frei bei sich selbst*]. It renounces both internal and external sensibility and removes all particular interests and inclinations.

(*Enz.*, para. 19, *Zusatz* 2)

This double demand for a discipline which is both *formal* (in being developed in complete independence of inner or outer sense) and *not formal* (because it has a content) is further strong evidence for the generative approach. For only an account which countenances the development of content by exclusively Logical means will be able to reconcile the two.

In the course of the discussion of 'Content and Form' in the *Encyclopedia* Hegel makes it clear that he is aware of the misunderstanding to which the ambiguity of the word 'formal' can lead. In this instance he endorses the formal status of philosophy. But there is no contradiction with the passage at *W. d. L.* I, p. 31 (quoted above) for in that case it was clearly the sense of formal as 'lacking content' whereas in this case it is the sense of 'rigorously *a priori*' which is being used:

Equally, philosophical Thought is very frequently regarded as an activity which is merely concerned with form [*blosse Formtätigkeit*] and it is treated as a matter of course that Logic (which, one must concede, deals only with Thoughts as such) is without content. If content is taken to be only what is palpable and what can be sensibly perceived it will be freely conceded that philosophy in general and the *Logic* in particular have no such sensibly perceptible content ... [However], it will emerge that in the last analysis what is called content, for a cultured consciousness [*gebildetes Bewusstsein*], means nothing but conformity to Thought [*Gedankenmässigkeit*]. But we concede thereby that the Thoughts are not to be regarded as indifferent to content, intrinsically empty forms.

(*Enz.* para. 133, *Zusatz* 2)

The dual requirement of a discipline which both has content and is rigorously *a priori* seems to me to substantiate the case for the generative approach. In adopting this interpretation of the relationship between Thought and everyday consciousness a further requirement is added to the list of requirements which an account of the role of Thought in the system must meet: how Thought can generate content.

The Movement of Thought

The requirement that an account be given of how the thought-contents of the Logic can be developed in absolute independence brings the features of the Scientific discourse to be accounted for to seven:

(1) The thesis that the true is the whole
(2) The unity of method and system
(3) The prohibition of 'external' criticism
(4) The claim that immanent critique is the method of philosophical refutation
(5) The positive result of determinate negation
(6) The rigorously *ex ante* character of the Scientific progress
(7) The ability of the *Logic* to generate content independently

Of these, requirements (3) and (4) need not now detain us for long. The prohibition on external criticism (requirement (3)) has already been dealt with; it was argued that the necessary first-handness of the understanding of the Scientific discourse and its incommensurability with the 'ordinary' propositions of *Räsonnieren* imply that the Science itself and discussion of it do not take place in a common argumentative framework, a neutral 'space of discourse', and that, for this reason, such 'ordinary' propositions cannot amount to a challenge to the Science. But this does not prevent us as critics and commentators from attempting to *characterize* the understanding involved in the Science.

Nor, if the approach I am arguing is correct, should requirement (4) present difficulties. In the last chapter it was claimed that, despite his commitment to conducting refutation on the basis of immanent critique, Hegel's treatment of Kant took place on the assumption that criticism produces positive results — an assumption not shared by Kant and, hence, a violation of this very commitment. The consequence is that we cannot understand immanent critique as a universal rational procedure, for it operates on the presupposition that we have already reached (implicitly at least) the 'standpoint of Science'. As such the immanent critique of competing philosophies will be an example of the reconstructive process which is characteristic of Science's relations to all non-Scientific intellectual phenomena. It gives a reconstruction of what the philosophy is question truly is, *as the Scientific consciousness knows it to be.* But only the Scientific consciousness is in a position to grasp the inner essence of the philosophy in question, and, if it is a philosophy which rests on an unscientific consciousness, then there may well be a discontinuity between its overt presuppositions and those of the Scientific consciousness which it is being criticized by.

This is why the refutation of Spinoza takes place at a particular stage of the exposition of the *Logic* itself. It is important for Hegel that previous, partial philosophies should be integrated into the movement of his true philosophy.

Non-Scientific philosophy, like art and religion, is a sphere of culture which incorporates the self-development of the idea:

> In the history of philosophy we find the different stages of the Logical Idea in the form of successively emerging philosophical systems.
>
> (*Enz.*, para. 86)

The Idea is the intrinsic source of previous philosophies' rationality; but it is necessary to participate in Science in order to discern it.

Immanent critique, then, is immanent critique *within the system* and it stands or falls with the validity of the system's movement.

My strategy for dealing with the five remaining requirements for an account of the role of Thought in the system is as follows:

(a) Requirement (2) — the requirement of the unity of method and system — prohibits an understanding of dialectical philosophy as a philosophy whose progress is justified by reference to a set of rules of procedure, given in advance.

(b) However, requirement (6) — that philosophical procedure have a rigorously *ex ante* character — prohibits an understanding by which the moves are given a retrospective justification.

This requirement is not fully realized for both aspects of the process of development at work in the *Phenomenology*; the Science of the development of consciousness treats its object, it is true, with *ex ante* rigour, following the Scientific path which the observing consciousness has the practical ability to follow. But the *Phenomenology* has the further task of bringing this observing consciousness to full awareness of its own Scientific character, and *this* it only achieves at the end of the process, in Absolute Knowledge.

(c) Hence there is no dialectical procedure. By this I mean that the movement of the *Logic* is non-inferential, and in this sense, intuitionistic. It consists solely in holding in Thought the Thought-content; although the movement has the status of a *proof* it is not, nor does it depend on, an argument, operation or calculus.

For these reasons the aim of an account of the *Logic* cannot be to reconstruct the progress of Thought in the sense of identifying the underlying argument, reasoning process or whatever. What has to be shown is what Hegel thinks that the progress of Thought can achieve and why he thinks that it can achieve it. Since the dialectical movement cannot be justified with reference to principles, the only conclusive vindication of the movement's possibility is its actual carrying out — no 'external' discourse can adequately capture it. What *can*, however, be shown is why the objections according to which the self-developing progress of Thought is held to be impossible rest on assumptions about the nature and limits of mental life which are drawn from the limited sphere of '*Vorstellung*' and 'understanding'.

Requirements (3) and (4) have been dealt with. The conception of a *dialectical movement* meets both the requirement of the unity of method and system (requirement (2)) and of the Science's *ex ante* rigour (requirement (6)). It remains to be shown that it has the capacity to generate content independently (requirement (7)) and in doing so both show a positive result for determinate negation (requirement (5)) and give an interpretation for 'the true is the whole' (requirement (1)).

There is necessarily some overlap between the task of this chapter

— giving an account of the role of Thought in the system — and of the next one — characterizing Thought as a model of rational experience. For the movement which displays itself to the properly enlightened reader of the *Logic* is impossible if the character of Thought has been misunderstood.

Hyperintuitionism

It may be objected that to describe what Hegel is doing as intuitionistic goes against his own text. Certainly Hegel is scathing about the pretensions of intuition to displace Science. In the Preface to the *Phenomenology* he contrasts the Scientific status of philosophy with what is 'dished up with the assurance that it comes from the shrine of inward "divine intuition" ' (*P. d. G.*, p. 47).

But once we understand the nature of Hegel's objection to intuition it will become clear that this is not an objection to my claim that the movement of the *Logic* is non-inferential. Hegel's objections emerge most clearly in the sections of the *Encyclopedia Logic* which deal with 'immediate knowledge'.

What is wrong, according to Hegel, with intuition-based philosophy such as Jacobi's is its *immediacy*:

The characteristic claim of his doctrine is that immediate knowledge, treated in isolation and with mediation excluded has the truth as its content.

(*Enz.*, para. 65)

Hegel objects that there is no such thing as the purely immediate knowledge of truth which this intuition-based philosophy claims:

It is only common, abstract understanding which takes the determinations of immediacy and mediation, each independently, as absolute, and thinks that with them it has a hard and fast division, thus creating the insuperable difficulty for itself of uniting them. But this difficulty is one which, as has been shown, is not present in the *fact* and disappears in the *speculative notion*.

(*Enz.*, para. 70)

Hegel identifies three main deficiencies which are the consequence of this belief in immediate knowledge.

(1) Merely subjective certainty (as in the *consensus gentium*) is taken to be the standard of truth.

Subjective knowledge and the assurance that I find a certain content in *my* consciousness becomes the basis for what is held to be true. What *I* find in *my* consciousness is thus elevated to something found in all consciousnesses and proclaimed as being the nature of consciousness itself.

(*Enz.*, para. 71)

(2)   Immediate consciousness provides no criterion by which to discriminate among claims to truth and therefore 'all superstition and idolatry is pronounced truth' (*Enz.*, para. 72).

(3)   It fails to give a specific content to its knowledge:

> God as object of religion is restricted to God in general [*überhaupt*], the indeterminate supersensible, and religion reduced to its minimum.
>
> (*Enz.*, para. 73)

The criticisms of intuition-based philosophy attack the particularity of the consciousness which claims intuitive knowledge and the one-sided immediacy of its content. But it should not be assumed from this criticism of immediate knowledge that Hegel is an advocate of *mediate*, in the sense of *inferential, knowledge*. To the contrary, in the discussion of intuition-based philosophy, Hegel cites Descartes's understanding of the *Cogito* with approval:

> Descartes's statements regarding the indissoluble unity of myself as thinking and [my] being — that this relationship is contained and shown in a *simple intuition* of consciousness, that this relationship is the absolutely primary, the principle, the most certain and evident thing of all, so that no scepticism could be conceived so gross as not to concede it — are so eloquent and precise that the modern propositions of Jacobi and others on this immediate connection can only be needless repetitions.
>
> (*Enz.*, para. 64)

Moreover he is emphatic that the *Cogito* is no inference:

> If one takes this as an inference [*Schluss*] then it must be because one knows little more of the nature of inference than that in inferences the word 'ergo' is present.
>
> (*Enz.*, para. 64)

Hegel stresses the *observing* character of the Scientific activity as part of its unity with its content, and contrasts this with the common conception of argument, as *Räsonnieren*.

> Argumentation [*Räsonnieren*] is freedom from its content and vanity towards it. What is required of it is the effort of giving up this freedom and, instead of being the arbitrary moving principle of the content, to sink its freedom into the content and to allow the content to move itself spontaneously according to its own nature — viz. the self as its own self — and to observe this movement. To refrain from intruding into the immanent rhythm of the notion and not to intervene arbitrarily or with wisdom obtained from elsewhere is itself an essential moment of attention to the notion.
>
> (*P. d. G.*, p. 48)

The activity of the Science thus has in common with Descartes's *Cogito* that it is not the outcome of an inference, or of an operation performed by rational reflection on a mental content which is different from its own self. In fact, as Hegel puts it, it is not obviously *activity* at all but:

pure self-equivalence in otherness [*reine Sichselbstgleichheit im Anderssein*]; thus it is the cunning which, seeming to abstain from activity, *observes*.

(*P. d. G.*, p. 46)

The movement of the *Logic* consists in participating in the autonomous movement of its content, and this is what guarantees its rigour:

To ensure that the commencement of the Science remains immanent in proceeding from the determination of *pure knowledge* nothing needs to be done but to observe; or, rather, putting aside all reflections, all opinions that one otherwise has, to take up what is present at hand.

(*W. d. L.* I, p. 53)

This idea of philosophical cognition as the participation of consciousness in the self-development of the subject-matter does not contradict the requirement that dialectic furnish *proof* — unless, that is, we make the characteristically modern assumption that proof is a matter of establishing something by means of grounds or reasons. But, in fact, Hegel explicitly rejects this common understanding of the nature of proof for leading to a regress, and puts in its place the idea of a dialectical movement.

This form of grounding and conditioning belongs to that form of proof which differs from the dialectical movement and is thus part of external cognition. Regarding dialectical movement; its element is the unique notion and herewith it has a content which is a thoroughly independent subject [*Subjekt an ihm selbst*].

(*P. d. G.*, p. 53)

The objection that inferences lead to a regress (which goes back to Aristotle) applies to all forms of inferential proof. (This is why all attempts to understand dialectic as a non-standard or non-Aristotelian logic seem to me quite misguided: substituting a non-standard for a standard logic only puts one set of rules of inference in place of another. But Hegel's objection is to the whole inferential procedure itself.) Science, on the other hand, has its character of rigorous proof just because of the self-movement of its content:

This spiritual movement, giving itself its determinacy in its simplicity, and thereby its own self-equality, is thus the immanent development of the notion. It is the absolute method of cognition and at one and the same time the immanent soul of the content itself. Only upon this self-constructing path, I maintain, is philosophy capable of being objective and demonstrated Science.

(*W. d. L.* I, p. 7)

The vital point that my description of the movement of the *Logic* as 'intuitionist' was meant to emphasize was that the progress of the dialectic is *non-inferential*. Nevertheless it is true to say that the word 'intuition' is misleading to the extent that it suggests that what is taking place is a sort of 'inner picturing', a holding before the 'mind's eye' by the empirical subject. Such inner picturing only gives a one-sided, immediate, quasi-sensible content, and the consciousness it gives it to is limited, particular and everyday. As Hegel puts the point in the *Encyclopedia*:

Complete cognition belongs solely to the pure Thought of comprehending [*begreifenden*] Reason and only the person who has raised himself to this Thought possesses a fully determinate, true intuition. Intuition is, for him, merely the genuine form into which his fully developed cognition recompresses itself. It is true that in immediate intuition I have the whole subject-matter before me. But only when the cognition of the object, developed in all its aspects, has returned into the form of simple intuition does the subject-matter stand in front of my mind as an internally articulated, systematic totality.

(*Enz.*, para. 449)

Philosophical Thought has a universal content and is carried out by a self-consciousness which is beyond the empirical self. Only then is the unity of the consciousness which thinks with the content that is thought complete:

The pure Science thus presupposes the liberation from the opposition of consciousness. It contains the Thought insofar as it is equally the subject-matter itself [*Sache an sich selbst*] or the subject-matter itself as it is equally the pure Thought. As Science the truth is the pure self-developing self-consciousness and takes the form of the self, which is the notion known in and for itself, the notion as such but which is in and for itself [*an und für sich Seiende*].

(*W. d. L.* I, p. 30)

Only what emerges on this higher plane is philosophically acceptable. Because of this, Thought cannot be accused, as was the immediate consciousness, of being indiscriminate and accepting whatever comes along. To emphasize the difference between the progress of Thought and 'inner picturing' one might call the dialectical process of the *Logic* a process of *hyperintuition*, to indicate that it is a non-inferential form of development whose specific character consists in being *beyond* the 'inner picturing' which intuition is normally taken to be; it is accomplished by the *purified* consciousness of Thought, rather than the everyday one of *Vorstellung*.

Knowledge of the Infinite

We saw above that the *Logic* claims to give empirical science that 'form of necessity' which, in the form of *Vorstellung*, it lacked. But this does not exclude the theological dimension. The *Logic* claims to give us both 'knowledge of God' and a 'rational science of nature'. This implies that the *Logic* has a greater scope than empirical science of nature and includes, in fact, the traditional objects of metaphysics:

> However satisfying this [empirical] knowledge may be in its own field, there shows itself in the first place another sphere of objects which it does not include, namely Freedom, Spirit, God. The reason why they are not found there is not that they do not belong to experience. Perhaps they are not *sensibly* experienced, but whatever is in consciousness at all is experienced (this is, indeed, a tautology). The reason is that these objects by their very content show at once that they are infinite.
>
> (*Enz.*, para. 28, *Zusatz*)

This dual task draws attention to one of the most important features of Hegel's enterprise, namely, its reworking of the relationship between immanence and transcendence. We should not see the *Logic* as divided between two domains of objects — the empirical and the metaphysical — with only the common method of dialectic running between them. On the one hand it is the distinctive feature of Hegel's understanding of the infinite objects that they are not static entities subsisting in a separate transcendental realm. On the other, once they are given the 'form of Thought', even the empirical categories of natural science are given an infinite character as part of the speculative movement:

> In speaking of Thought, the finite, merely understanding, thought must be distinguished from that which is infinite and rational. The thought-determinations as they are met with immediately and in isolation are *finite* determinations. But the true is the intrinsically infinite, which does not allow of being expressed and brought to consciousness by means of what is finite. The expression *infinite Thought* may seem striking if one adheres to the conception of recent times that thought is always limited... Thought is only finite insofar as it keeps to limited determinations which it treats as

ultimate. Infinite or speculative Thought, on the other hand, likewise *deter-mines*, but in determining, limiting it sets aside this deficiency in turn [*hebt diesen Mangel wieder auf*]. Infinity is not, as in the common conception, to be taken as an abstract 'onwards-ever-onwards' but in the simple manner which has been indicated previously.

(Enz., para. 28, *Zusatz)*

When the infinite is conceived as a mathematical infinity or as a special transcendental realm violence is done to the nature of the infinite and it is actually reduced to a sort of finitude. Thus, in answer to the old metaphysical question 'is the world finite or infinite?', Hegel objects:

Infinity and finitude are rigidly opposed to one another here. But it may easily be seen that, when the two are opposed to one another, the infinite — which is supposed to be the whole — appears as only one side and is thus limited by the finite. But a *limited* infinity is itself only finite.

(Enz., para. 28, *Zusatz)*

This special feature of Hegel's conception of the infinite has frequently brought him the accusation from orthodox Christians of *pantheism*, of dissolving God into His creation. But Hegel's attack on traditional oppositions between 'transcendence' and 'immanence' does not amount to such a dissolution. This can be made clear from the discussion in the previous section. The ordinary determinations of consciousness are given the 'form of necessity' by being developed in the course of the independent self-articulation of pure Thought. But it is the self-development of Thought which is the truly pure and infinite (hence the description of it as 'God's essence') and empirical reality is only infinite insofar as it embodies the structure of Thought.

The function of the *Logic*, then, is to develop in the medium of Thought the structure of reality insofar as it is rational. This is what gives point to the claim that philosophy is *theodicy*:

Philosophy is the true theodicy — in contrast to art and religion with their sensibility [*Empfindungen*].

(Gesch. der Phil. III, p. 455)

For if we have a means of generating those contents which are found in reality, but which itself does not depend on any content *derived from* reality, then, in a clear sense, we have demonstrated the rationality of the contents of reality. Philosophical activity produces, to borrow the name from M.H. Abrams, who adopts it from the eighteenth-century writer, Baumgarten, a *heterocosm*. Abrams, considering the development of romantic poetics, writes:

We also find in eighteenth-century criticism the beginnings of a more radical solution to the problem of poetic fictions, one which would sever supernatural poetry entirely from the principle of imitation, and from any responsibility to the empirical world. The key event in this development was the replacement of the metaphor of the poem as imitation, a 'mirror of nature', by that of the poem as heterocosm, 'a second nature' created by the poet in an act analogous to God's creation of the world.[5]

Perhaps it is somewhat misleading of Abrams to say that this development 'severs poetry from imitation'. What happened was in one way not an *abandonment* of the concern with imitation, so much as a transformation of the way in which it was to be carried out. Imitation no longer lies in the correspondence between the work and reality so much as in the correspondence between the two creators, God and the artist. Thus the representational element in the *Logic* lies in reality being 'a presentation and copy [*Darstellung und Nachbildung*] of the original and entirely independent activity of Thought' (*Enz.*, para. 12), rather than in Thought functioning as a 'mirror of nature':

What is real nature is the image [*Bild*] of divine Reason. The forms of self-conscious Reason are also forms of nature. Nature and the spiritual world — history — are the two realities. We saw the emergence of the Thought which grasps its own self, which strove to make itself concrete. Its first activity is formal. Aristotle was the first to say that *nous* is the Thought of Thought. The result is the Thought which is independent [*bei sich*] and at the same time encapsulates the universe and transforms it into an intelligible [*intelligente*] world. The natural and spiritual universe permeate one another in the activity of comprehension [*Begreifen*] as a single harmonizing universe which, fleeing into its own self, develops the sides of the Absolute into totality, so as to be conscious of itself in its unity, in Thought. Thus far has the World-Spirit progressed.

(*Gesch. der Phil.* III, p. 455)

The independent development of the structure of the *Logic* means that Hegel's notorious endorsement of existing reality — 'What is rational is actual, and what is actual is rational' (*Rechtsphil.*, p. 24) — is something more than the historicist statement that thought is always limited to its own time, and so contemporary reality is the sole standard of rationality. What makes reality rational is its independent constructibility in Thought, and not the mere fact that it now exists. Were there no Logical derivation of reality Hegel would have no

5   Abrams, *The Mirror and the Lamp*, p. 272.

grounds for claiming philosophy as a *theodicy*.

The Science, then, is just as much rational theology as it is rational science of nature:

> To know God by means of Reason is the highest task of Science... [Theology becomes Scientific] only when it progresses to comprehending Thought [*begreifendes Denken*], which is the business of philosophy ... But Thought must move freely within itself — at which point one must add that the result of free Thought is an agreement with the content of the Christian religion, for the latter is the revelation of Reason.
>
> (*Enz.*, para. 36, *Zusatz*)

To be sure most modern defenders of religion find Hegel a dubious ally. They prefer Kant's 'denial of knowledge in order to make room for belief' to Hegel's unified Science of belief. However Hegel robustly takes issue with such religious non-cognitivism:

> God has revealed Himself in the Christian religion, He has given us to know what He is, so that he is no longer a concealed or secret Being. With this possibility of knowing God it becomes a *duty*. God wishes as his children no narrow-hearted souls and empty heads but rather those whose Spirit is poor in its own self but rich in its knowledge of Him, and who regard this knowledge of God as what is uniquely valuable. The development of revelation of the Divine Being must flourish to the point of grasping in Thought what was first presented to the feeling and merely conceptualizing [*Vorstellenden*] Spirit.
>
> (*Phil. der Gesch.*, p. 27)

Hegel identifies this demand for theological knowledge with the spirit of Protestantism:

> It show a great obstinacy (and one which does Man honour) to refuse to accept anything into one's convictions that is not ratified by Thought. This obstinacy is the characteristic of the modern epoch and the specific principle of Protestantism. What Luther initiated as *faith* in the sphere of feeling and of the witness of the Spirit is the same thing as the Spirit now, having further matured, endeavours to grasp in the *notion*, and thus to liberate and find itself in the present.
>
> (*Rechtsphil.*, p. 27)

The Activity of Consciousness

This further maturation is that self-consciousness, in Science, is not merely its own *authority*, but its own *source*; it produces *content* out of itself. Certainty and the production of content are now united:

> Absolute Knowledge is the truth of all modes of consciousness because (just as consciousness's progress produced it) only in Absolute Knowledge has

the separation of the object from the certainty of its own self completely dissolved and the truth become equivalent to this certainty, just as the certainty has become equivalent to the truth. The pure Science thus presupposes liberation from the opposition of consciousness... As Science the truth is the pure self-developing self-consciousness and takes the form of the self.

(*W. d. L.* I, p. 30)

This active, productive vision of the Protestant consciousness surely explains the equation — incredible to Anglo-Saxon ears — which Hegel makes in the *Lectures on the History of Philosophy* between Catholicism and empiricism:

This conception that knowledge comes from without is to be found in modern times in completely abstract, vulgar philosophers of experience, who have asserted that everything which Man knows of the Divine and holds to be true comes to him as a result of upbringing and habit and that soul and Spirit are nothing but indeterminate possibility. The extreme case is *revelation*, in which everything is given externally. This vulgar conception is not present in its abstraction in the Protestant religion. Here the witness of the Spirit is an essential component of belief. The individual subjective Spirit, in and for itself, contains within itself, posits and makes this determination which has come to it in the form of something external and merely given. Plato argues against the former conception.

(*Gesch. der Phil.* II, p. 55)

Hegel's own doctrine, by contrast, of the production of content out of the self, stands in the tradition of Plato's doctrine of *anamnesis*, which he gives his qualified approval:

In one sense recollection [*Erinnerung*] is an inappropriate expression, namely in the sense that one *reproduces* a conception [*Vorstellung*] which one has already had at some former time. But *Erinnerung* has another sense, which is given by etymology, namely that of internalization, of going into oneself. From the point of view of Thought that is the deep sense of the word. In this sense one can say that cognition of the universal is nothing but a recollection or internalization.

(*Gesch. der Phil.* II, p. 44)

What Hegel is stressing, then, is the independent *productive* role of the self, rather than the mirroring, *reproductive* one. The *Logic's* role as heterocosm, resting on philosophy's ability to generate content independently, corresponds to the theological problem of the *creatio ex nihilo*. The notion, the self-movement of which constitutes Science, is that form which produces content out of its own self. Hegel opposes this explicitly Christian cosmology to the Greek tradition:

This conception of matter as originally present and inherently formless is very ancient. It is to be found among the Greeks, at first in the mythical form of Chaos, which is conceived as the formless substratum of the existent world. It is part of the consequences of this conception that God is regarded not as the Creator of the world but as a mere world-former or demiurge. The deeper insight is that God created the world out of nothing. This expresses on the one hand that matter has no intrinsic independence and, on the other, that form does not reach matter from outside but that, as a totality, it carries the principle of matter within its own self. This free and infinite form will shortly show itself to us as the notion.

(*Enz.*, para. 128, *Zusatz*)

Hegel is actually claiming to be able to make this creation out of nothingness *intelligible*. But, traditionally, the creation from nothingness was the point at which Christian doctrine had to be acknowledged to go beyond rational intelligibility, for the impossibility of conceiving how any content could develop out of absolute nothingness marked it out as a mysterious exercise of will on the part of an omnipotent being.

The doctrine of creation from nothingness contains, however, an important dilemma for theology: if we claim that the process of creation is *intelligible* are we not, by submitting God to the standards of human reason, limiting his omnipotence and doing violence to his nature? But if the process of creation is *not* intelligible but an incomprehensible act on the part of the Creator how can God's creation be a revelation for us of his nature?

Now Hegel (perhaps unexpectedly for such a self-consciously Protestant thinker) is certainly not prepared to give up the claim that God reveals himself through his creation. Indeed it is an aspect of Christian doctrine that he is concerned to reinforce:

Those who regard the essence of nature as something that is merely inward and, hence, as inaccessible to us, take up the same position as those ancients who regarded God as *jealous* — a position which Plato and Aristotle already set themselves against. God *communicates* what he is and reveals it — in the first instance, in and through nature.

(*Enz.*, para. 140, *Zusatz*)

Hegel is faced, therefore, with the first horn of the Christian dilemma: how to make God's creation intelligible without thereby imposing human limitations on him. Naturally, Hegel will argue that the mere fact that human beings can know God does not of itself violate his nature. For, imperfect beings though we are, we *do* participate in God's nature and it is this 'divine spark' which enables us to know him. The argument that knowledge of God violates his nature must be that to *know* God is to see his nature as part of a *necessary order* and, in this way, to place him under constraint. Hegel, however, would reply that to see something as part of a necessary order is not always to *constrain* it. This is indeed the case with finite, discursive reasoning processes, for here to grasp that something is *necessary* means to derive it as something that is conditioned from antecedent conditions. But the necessity involved in the free self-development of Thought is not of this finite kind and so cannot be said to subject God to constraint. The freedom of Hegel's self-developing Thought is like that of Kant's *categorical imperative*; it does not imply the arbitrary choice between alternatives but rests, rather, on the *autonomy* of the way in which a determinate result is arrived at.

Creation and Development

The creation from nothingness is a mystery for Christian theology because it is the founding act by which rational content comes on the scene at all. This content cannot have been implicit in the previous nothingness (for precisely its character as nothingness means the absence of content) but must therefore have emerged as the result of an act of divine will which remains thoroughly mysterious from the human point of view. We shall see, however, that, for Hegel, the premise of this argument rests on a crucial misconception of the nature of 'nothingness' and of what it is to have content emerge from it.

The ancient non-Christian cosmologies did not share the doctrine of an omnipotent personal creator, and so did not have to face the objection that, in making creation intelligible, they were violating the creator's nature. Nevertheless, as Hegel points out, if one conceives what is rational on the Platonic model of a world of eternal forms, the rationality of the relationship between that transcendent world and the world of finite existence becomes problematic. The demiurge, in order to realize the world of forms, cannot himself be part of that world of forms, and so, presumably, his activity cannot have its rational nature. If, on the other hand, one tries to make the *realization* of the world of forms part of the rationality of the transcendental realm itself, one is forced to conceive it in terms of a *reflection* or *falling away* (involving the implication that creation is a 'loss' or imperfection in the form world — an implication which leads in the direction of Gnosticism) or as an *overflow*. But this metaphor suggests the addition of a *new* content beyond what is contained in the world of forms. Now, by the assumptions of the model, whatever content is rational is so by corresponding to something in the world of forms. Can this new content, then, also be understood as rational in relation to it?

My intention is not to explore the intricacies of Platonism and Neo-Platonism. My point is that Hegel himself attributed this dilemma to them. Moreover, he believes that he is in a position to solve their riddle and to give a *rational* account of creation in such a way as to accommodate it to the Christian doctrine of creation out of nothingness. To do so his philosophy, in raising itself to the purity of Thought, has had to break with those preconceptions which led to the impasses of ancient thought. The ancient conceptions all depend to some extent on a visual way of thinking for the construction of their cosmologies – a point most clearly seen in the prevalence of 'light metaphysics'. Thus the Platonist conceives of the archetypes as subsisting in a 'world of forms' – a world spatially removed from the empirical world, perhaps – whose realization in the empirical world is, for that reason, deeply mysterious. Similarly, in the Christian picture, the nothingness which precedes God's creation is conceived as a sort of inert, empty space which could acquire content only as the result of an utterly unintelligible divine act.

The use of light metaphysics to express the Christian doctrine of the subordination of the human to the divine mind is given its classic statement in the writings of St Augustine: '*Lumen tibi esse non potes, non potes, non potes!*' he thunders.[6]

When we try, in like fashion, to find metaphors out of which to construct an image of Hegel's cosmology the system appears to be paradoxical and contradictory. Yet, crucially, for Hegel this is just the point. The progress of Thought is something that cannot be pictured, and so long as we try to do so we shall find ourselves falling back into the impasses of the traditional cosmologies. The insights which philosophy can now incorporate as part of an 'objective and demonstrated Science' were once regarded, because they went beyond what everyday consciousness could conceive, as *mystical*. Science, however, means that the mystical is now no longer paradoxical. Despite the feelings of exasperation which Hegel has produced in so many of his readers he is – in intention at least – the least paradoxical of thinkers; Thought must recuperate 'paradox' for Reason:

6   'You cannot be your own light – you cannot, you cannot!' St Augustine, *Sermones*, CLXXXII, 5, quoted in Blumenberg, 'Das Licht als Metapher der Wahrheit', p. 440. See also *On the Trinity*, Book XV.

It should be mentioned here, regarding the significance of the speculative, that it means the same as what was formerly called, in connection with religious consciousness and its content, *mystical*. Nowadays when people speak of mysticism this is usually taken to be equivalent to what is mysterious and incomprehensible. This mysterious and incomprehensible matter is taken by some as the true and authentic while others, according to culture and temperament, see it as a piece of superstition and deception. But first it must be said that the mystical is only a secret for *understanding*, because the latter has *abstract identity* as its principle. The mystical, however, (as equivalent to the speculative) is the concrete unity of those determinations which the understanding only takes as true in separation and opposition. But, by the same token, if those who acknowledge the mystical as what is true are content for it to remain something utterly mysterious, they demonstrate that as far as they are concerned Thought only means abstract identification [*Identischsetzen*] and that, therefore, in order to acquire truth, one must renounce Thought or, as it is frequently put, 'place Reason in thrall'. But, as we have seen, the abstract thought of understanding is by no means something fixed and ultimate but shows itself as the constant setting aside [*Aufheben*] of its own self. Everything rational is thus equally to be called mystical — which is only to say that it extends beyond the understanding. But by no means is it to be regarded as something which is incomprehensible and inaccessible to Thought.

(*Enz.*, para. 82, *Zusatz*)

The impasses of traditional cosmologies came from trying to construct them on the basis of such abstract picturing. The language which Hegel uses to describe his own system is frankly oxymoronous and impossible to use to construct a model or a picture. Thus in the following passage the self-development of the philosophical Idea is described in terms of the association of features — extension/ intention; dispersal/comprehension; centre/periphery — which on any normal understanding are mutually exclusive:

Whilst the emergence [*Hinausgehen*] of the philosophical Idea in its development is not a change, a becoming something other, but equally an internalization [*Insichgehen*], a process of self-deepening in its own self, its progression makes the previously general, less determinate Idea more determinate in itself. [*Hegel's marginal note*: Is a difficult point. Reduction of development, of the different to simplicity, determinacy.] The further development of the Idea or its greater determinacy are one and the same thing. The most *extensive* is also the most *intensive*. The extension as a development is not a scattering and dispersal [*Zerstreuung und Auseinanderfallen*] but, equally, a comprehension [*Zusammenhalt*] which, the more powerful and the more intensive with the extension, enriches and furthers this comprehended content.

Such are the abstract propositions concerning the nature of the Idea and its development. This is how the developed [*gebildete*] philosophy is constituted its own self. It is one single Idea in the whole and all its members, just as through a living individual there beats a single pulse. All the parts that emerge in it and their systematization emerge from the one Idea. All these particularizations are but mirrors and copies [*Abbilder*] of this single vitality. They have their actuality solely in this unity and, together, their differences, their different determinations are themselves only the expression and the form contained in the Idea. Thus the Idea is the *centre* which is at one and the same time the *periphery*, the light-source which in all its expansions does not go outside itself but remains present and immanent in its own self. It is thus the system of necessity and its necessity is its own and thereby equally its freedom.

(Gesch. der Phil. III, p. 477)

Hegel's transition from *passivity* to *activity* goes beyond Abrams's opposition between *mirror* and *lamp* (see above, p. 79). It is only by breaking with the metaphors drawn from light-metaphysics, and endorsing what would be paradoxical from its point of view, that Hegel can express the self-realizing nature of the Idea. But that he has *not* abandoned the traditional Neo-Platonic enterprise, can be seen from the fact that he continues to talk of the 'particularizations' of the Idea as '*Abbilder*'—images, copies or ectypes—in keeping with Platonism. Instead of being *copies* of a 'world of forms', however, they are now seen as *particularizations* of the single, self-developing Idea. The features of this development — its ability to generate content, the positive result for negation — are impossibilities only if we hold apart as opposite features that in Thought go together.

Determinate Simplicity

In the passage quoted above Hegel indicates that one such opposition is that between *simplicity* and *complexity*. His marginal note shows that he was himself aware that common sense suggests that whatever is simple must, for that reason, lack determinacy. It is easy to see how such a presumption could be justified; if we think of something as determinate only if it possesses some attributes, namely *determinations*, and of what is simple as what lacks attributes, then evidently determinacy and simplicity must be mutually exclusive. But this would exactly misconceive the nature of 'determination', as Hegel understands it.

In calling the categories of the Science 'determinations' or 'thought-determinations' (rather than just continuing with the Kantian term 'category') Hegel is, I think, expressing two important points. The first of these is that the thought-determinations —

unlike Kantian categories – are not *forms* to be united with matter given from experience in order to constitute *judgements*. They produce content out of their own selves. The second, which is of particular relevance here, is that the word determination (*Bestimmung*) can mean either the *act* of determining or the *outcome* of such an act. Hegel is making use of this ambiguity to emphasize that the act of determining and what is determined are parts (or moments, as he calls them) of a single process. It is this process which generates 'determinate simplicity':

> The movement of what there is [*des Seienden*] is on the one hand to become another, and thus its immanent content. On the other hand it takes this unfolding, its existence [*Dasein*] back into its own self, i.e. it makes itself into a *moment* and simplifies itself into determinacy. In the former movement negativity is the differentiation and positing of *existence*; in this recuperation into itself it is the genesis of determinate simplicity.
>
> (*P. d. G.*, p. 44)

Similarly it would seem to be a matter of common sense that *mediation* and *immediacy* are mutually exclusive. It will be recalled from the discussion of intuition that Hegel objects to the claim that consciousness can have immediate knowledge. The famous arguments of the beginning of the *Phenomenology* (the chapter on 'Sensible Certainty') have made the attack on immediate knowledge familiar. We are asked there to conceive an immediately sensing consciousness. As soon as this sensing consciousness tries to *think* (that is to say, to *pick out* and *identify*) its contents, it discovers that this is only possible by relating them among themselves and, hence, *mediating* them.

It would be wrong, however, on this basis, to understand Hegel as claiming just that whatever *seems* to be immediate will turn out, in fact, to be mediated. Although there can be no such thing as *pure* immediacy, immediacy itself is no more illusory than is mediation. Hegel's point is that mediation and immediacy go together:

> There is *nothing*, nothing in Heaven or in Nature or in Spirit, which does not contain equally both immediacy and mediation, so that these two determinations show themselves inseparable and united, and the opposition above shows itself to be null.
>
> (*W. d. L.* I, p. 52)

Naturally this unity of immediacy and mediation presents difficulties of comprehension which the simpler doctrine that whatever seems to be immediate will turn out to be mediated does not. To think of something as both mediated and immediate is as hard as it is to think of something being both simple and determinate. Yet the fact that it is counterintuitive does not mean that it is not Hegel's doctrine; to the contrary, we should *expect* Thought to have such unpictureable features.

The same applies to the 'nothingness' out of which the process develops. It is natural to conceive of development as a making explicit of something that is implicit, and to think of this as something that is 'prefigured' or pre-existing in a 'logical space'. In most languages the word for development has a cognate contrary (English: *development—envelopment*; German: *Entwicklung—Einwicklung*; Latin: *evolutio—involutio*) and the spatial metaphor of folding is strongly present. If we think of development in this way and of the nothingness out of which it emerges as if it were just an emptiness (an empty space or an absence) then again the movement would seem to be impossible, or at least possible only if the method of philosophy itself has some means of generating the complexity which the initial content lacks (for example, by criticizing the initial content's deficiencies and lack of content). But to have to rely on the method in this way to generate what does not emerge spontaneously would be to claim something much weaker than what Hegel wants. It would be to reintroduce a separation between method and content for the sake of generating new content. But, for Hegel, this forward movement is in virtue of an impulse which is immanent in the initial situation, not the product of a process of reflection or analysis:

> With such consciousness, which only wished to take the beginning further for the sake of the method, this would be something formal, posited in a process of external reflection. But, because the method is the objective, immanent form, the immediate beginning must have what is lacking in its own self and be endowed with the drive [*Trieb*] to lead itself forward.
>
> (*W. d. L.* ii, p. 489)

This is the crucial point for understanding the *Logic's* generation of content; to say that further development is *implicit* in the beginning does not, in Hegel's view, contradict the *simplicity* of that beginning, for neither is what is developed 'drawn out' of some quasi-space where it pre-exists, nor is the nothingness a mere emptiness. In Thought the oppositions which are characteristic of *Vorstellung* and understanding — between 'simple' and 'complex', 'implicit' and 'explicit', 'mediated' and 'immediate' — can no longer be pictured as mutually exclusive. Thus it is by no means self-contradictory for Hegel to describe the movement of Thought as both analytic and synthetic:

The absolute method, by contrast, does not behave as an external reflection, but it takes what is determinate from its object itself, for it is itself its soul and immanent principle ... The method of absolute cognition is thus analytic. The absolute objectivity of the notion, whose certainty the method is, lies in finding the further determination of its initial universal in that universal alone. But it is equally *synthetic* to the extent that its object, determined immediately as a simple universal, shows itself as another by means of the determinacy which it has itself in its immediacy and universality. This relationship to something different, which it is in its own self, is, however, no longer what is meant by synthesis in finite cognition. The very fact of its analytical determination, that it is the relationship within the notion, distinguishes it entirely from such synthesis.

(*W. d. L.* II, p. 491)

Such a unity of the analytic and the synthetic would be quite impossible if one took the definitions of those terms from Hegel's predecessor, Kant. For Kant the analytic and the synthetic are mutually exclusive;

In all judgments in which the relation of a subject to the predicate is thought ... this relation is possible in two different ways. Either the predicate B belongs to the subject A, as something which is (covertly) contained in this concept A; or B lies outside the concept A, although it does indeed stand in connection with it. In the one case I entitle the judgment analytic, in the other synthetic.

(*K. r. V.*, B10)

But it is clear that Kant's contrast is made in terms of an analogy drawn from the visual or spatial realm — what is 'contained in' is set against what 'lies outside' a concept. Hegel must argue that the opposition hereby created between what is 'inside' and what is 'outside' the 'logical space' of a concept is ultimately false.

To understand the movement of Thought, then, we must realize that Hegel sees it as operating in a way that the finite understanding would find paradoxical or mystical — hence he is led to describe it in terms which are oxymoronous from the finite understanding's point of view. But if we understand the claims that Hegel makes for the movement of Thought we can see that they incorporate the three requirements which remain from those set out earlier in the chapter — the thesis that the true is the whole (requirement (1)), the need for determinate negation to have a positive result (requirement (5)) and the need for an independent development of content (requirement (7)).

The thesis that the true is the whole is intelligible when we realize that the movement of Thought is not a progress by Thought *along* a sequence of categories to a fixed end point (like a railway train going past a succession of stations) in which, as it were, the Thought moves on unchanged, leaving the determinations on its way behind it. Because the movement of Thought is a self-development the determinations are carried along with the progress of the *negatio negans*. But if the development is not a linear one nor should it be thought of as pyramidal, that is to say as a constant accretion of determinations. To the contrary the movement of Thought is a movement *from* simplicity *to* simplicity, but the end is a *determinate* simplicity which contains its own progress. Yet if we ask how this 'containment' could take place without violating the simplicity the only answer can be that Thought is no longer limited to the spatial form, and its plenitude is not one that *contains* anything. It is an *intensive* plenitude. To think of the process according to the spatial metaphor (like the snake Ouroboros with its tail in its own mouth) can only lead to paradox and self-contradiction.

The nature of the dialectical process shows us, furthermore, that determinate negation, so far from being a feature of rationality in general, is a feature quite specific to the sphere of Thought. It is the dynamic principle which leads the Thought's progress:

That by means of which the notion leads itself forward is the previously discussed negative which it has in its own self. This constitutes the truly dialectical.

(*W. d. L.* I, p. 37)

The thesis that 'the true is the whole' and *determinate negation* coincide as characteristics of Thought's dynamic, productive negativity. As little as the nothingness out of which development takes place can be conceived as an empty space, can the self-moving negativity in Thought be conceived as if negation were an 'erasure' or a 'wiping out' of something present, the content. Negation is *not* an operation performed upon a content, but is itself the living, self-developing substance, *negatio negans*. It is impressive evidence of the consistency of Hegel's thought that the clearest statement of the nature of this process, which receives its full presentation only in the *Logic*, should have been given in the Preface to the *Phenomenology* (which was announced as a preface to the 'System of Science' as a whole):

The living substance, further, is being which is in truth *subject*, or, what is the same, is in truth actual only in so far as it is the movement of positing itself, or is the mediation of its self-othering with itself. This substance is, as subject, pure *simple negativity*, and is for this very reason the bifurcation of the same; it is the doubling which sets up opposition, and then again the negation of this indifferent diversity and of its antithesis the immediate simplicity. Only this self-*restoring* sameness, or this reflection in otherness within itself — not an *original* or *immediate* unity as such — is the true. It is the process of its own becoming, the circle that presupposes its end as its goal, having its end also as its beginning; and only by being worked out to its end, is it actual.

(*P. d. G.*, p. 20)

Thought develops content by the simple fact of its own nature and vitality. Hegel's dialectic does not provide a *method* by which we can turn what is simple into something complex. Rather he turns the tables on his objectors. Instead of thinking of the initial content as an inert emptiness, which we are then faced with the problem of giving movement to, we should realize that only this way of thinking of things, drawn from finite cognition, sets up the problem of a 'source' of complexity. Thought is self-moving and our task as speculative philosophers is just to *follow* that non-inferential movement. The dialectical method is 'the consciousness of the form of the inner self-movement of the content' (*W. d. L.* I, p. 35) — nothing more, nothing less.

4

Imageless Truth

Alles Vergängliche ist nur ein Gleichnis.

Goethe

In the previous chapter I tried to explain how the movement of Thought has features which are, from the point of view of 'ordinary common sense', flatly self-contradictory. They are self-contradictory for a metaphysical philosophy which conceives transcendental or absolute reality by extending ways of thinking derived from empirical reality, as Neo-Platonism does with its light-imagery. In this chapter I intend to characterize the nature of Thought. I have argued that it is a specific feature of the dialectical movement that we cannot answer such questions as 'what does the dialectical movement consist in?' by giving an argumentative equivalent in ordinary discourse; the *experience* of Thought is an ineliminable feature of the dialectical progress, and, moreover, cannot be given an equivalent in the ordinary propositional form. It is only open to the critic and commentator to *characterize* the experience, not to give an equivalent which might substitute for or translate it.

But this clearly raises a problem; when we characterize an experience we try to answer the question 'what is it like?'. But the experience of Thought is an experience which is *sui generis*; the point is that it is not *like* finite experience at all, and it was the extension of such finite ways of thinking to the transcendental realm that led to the self-contradictions of traditional metaphysical philosophy. Hegel's Science, animated by the 'movement of the notion' is the *radically non-metaphorical discourse*. Its deep truth is imageless. As Hegel says, speculative philosophy is difficult *just because* we naturally demand an image to go with our thinking and this is why people complain of its 'unintelligibility'. The search for an analogy linking Thought with everyday consciousness makes understanding *more*, not less difficult:

The other aspect of its unintelligibility is the impatient wish to have as a figurative conception [*Vorstellung*] what is present in consciousness as Thought and notion. The expression is used that one 'does not know what to think' in respect of a notion which has been grasped; but there is nothing further to think with respect to a notion than the notion itself. The significance of the expression, however, is a yearning for the familiar conception drawn from common acquaintance. It is as if in losing the mode of common conception [*Weise der Vorstellung*] consciousness had the ground drawn away from under it, where it had once had a firm and familiar stance. When it finds itself transported to the pure region of the notion it has no idea *where* in the world it is.

(*Enz.*, para. 3)

So the question 'what is Thought like?' is unanswerable if we expect to be able to give an account in terms of a positive analogy. What *can* be done, however, is to explain the nature of Thought in terms of what it is *not* like — to express its distinctness from alternative conceptions of the nature of rational experience.

Only this 'weaker' sort of characterization can avoid violating Thought's infinite character. I want to argue that we should understand the nature of Thought as a rejection of two traditional models or paradigms (Wittgenstein would have called them 'pictures') of the nature of mental life and as a criticism of the misunderstanding of a third. It is the hegemony exercised by these models which prevents us from thinking pure Thought appropriately. (This is, of course, no accidental hegemony but one which corresponds to particular stages in the development of *Geist*.) Between them these three basic models cover, Hegel believes, the range of traditional answers to the question 'what is the nature of our rational experience?' The three models can be identified with his division of mental life between the faculties of *sense*, *understanding* and *reason*; either we misconceive the nature of rational experience by restricting it to sense and understanding or we misconceive the nature of reason, the true source, in fact, of rational experience.

The three basic models are, then:

(1) An understanding of the rationality of our mental life which sees it passively, as 'sensing' or 'imaging' or 'mapping' external reality.

(2) An understanding of the rationality of our mental life which acknowledges the role of judgement in experience but sees the latter essentially in terms of the subsuming, ordering activity of the understanding.

(3) An understanding of the rationality of our mental life which acknowledges that it contains experience of the infinite, the transcendent and unconditioned.

Hegel objects to those versions of this third model which misconceive the infinite as an infinite progress, as a 'world behind the world'
or as something known only indirectly.

Against this misunderstanding of the nature of Reason Hegel advances an understanding of the Idea as a self-realizing subject. This
itself does not amount, however, to a positive characterization of the
nature of Thought. The subject in question here is not the discursive
subject of ordinary consciousness, so we must also answer the question of how this self-realizing subject resembles — or differs from —
the empirical subject.

The Imaging Model

I shall consider the models in turn. Against the first, sensing model of
experience, Hegel holds a thesis of the *imagelessness* of truth. Our
inability to picture pure Thought should not just be taken negatively, as an obstacle to understanding. The imagelessness of truth is, to
the contrary, an essential positive feature of the theory. In this Hegel
is at one with the mainstream of Protestant theology. As Jürgen
Habermas has put it:

> The perception of the divine *Logos* in history, mediated by hearing and
> obedience [*durch Gehör und Gehorsam*], has alienated Protestant philosophy
> from nature, just as the intuition of the divine Logos in nature, mediated by
> the eye, has alienated Catholic thought from history.[1]

Herder, for example, a Protestant minister, makes a special connection between language and the sense of hearing in his *Essay on the
Origin of Language*.[2] He sees the special status of hearing as a consequence of its intermediary position between feeling and vision, with
neither the overwhelming immediacy of the former nor what he
regards as the excessive clarity of the latter. Hegel gives hearing a
similar priority, although his view of the matter (as will be argued in
the next chapter) is more philosophically sophisticated.

Opposition to the image has usually gone together in the Protestant tradition with an emphasis on community, history and the immediate, unconditional reality of obligation — the 'call'. Against the

1   Habermas, 'Ein marxistischer Schelling', p. 70.
2   Herder, *Abhandlung über den Ursprung der Sprache*, p. 59.

Catholic emphasis on nature as a channel of grace (a manifestation of the Creator's goodness) the Protestant tradition has emphasized the *break* which man's sin has introduced between himself and the Creator's benevolence. But, by this standard, Hegel would have to be placed firmly in the Catholic tradition. For, as was seen in the previous chapter, he wishes to insist on nature as a revelation of God's will. But what is vitally important is that this understanding of nature depends on a consciousness with the ability to participate in an essentially *imageless* truth. Hence a 'Catholic' goal is achieved by inherently 'Protestant' means (thus confirming Hegel's own self-understanding as the culmination of *both* traditions). Moreover it is the modern principle of subjectivity (the process of the *Logic* understood as the self-development in the medium of Thought of an elevated, purified self) which is the key to its achievement.

The internal structure of speculative philosophy and Hegel's philosophical approach to history support one another here. Speculative philosophy is possible only at the end of Spirit's process of development, for only then is it given to the individual to think 'pure' Thought. The history of religious ideas preceding it clearly shows the traces of *impure* Thought; on the one side, a tradition which, lacking the full understanding of the meaning of selfhood, can only conceive the relations between the creator and his creation by visual or spatial metaphors; on the other, one whose conception of the authority and independence of the individual has led it to cut itself off from external reality, instead of 'turning inwards' to find in its own self the lineaments of reality's structure.

This thesis of the imagelessness of truth is not unambiguous; its significance is a function of the conception of 'image' with which it is contrasted. Historically, this has moved between two poles: the finite conception and the infinite one. The infinite, transcendental conception of the image is historically prior. It derives both from the Greek concept of the *eikon* and the Old Testament doctrine of man as a creature created in God's image. Fundamental to this conception is that it is possible for copying or imaging presentation to take place not just within a single medium but between media; there can be an *epiphany* of the infinite within the finite realm. The later, secularized conception of imagery, on the other hand, restricts copying to within the spatial field. (It would be interesting to determine the role that the rise of a secular, geometrical theory of vision in the seventeenth century played in destroying the credit of medieval attempts to synthesize immanent and transcendent elements in knowledge.)

The criticism of images is as old as the tradition of the image as a presentation of the infinite itself. The two, in fact, go together in the ancient criticism of the *inauthenticity* of *human* images. The prophet Hosea reproaches the Israelites for having said 'ye are our gods' to the work of their own hands (Hosea 14.3). The true image is the one produced by God, the false by man. For Hegel, however, the point of criticism does not lie in the inauthentic authorship of images so much as in the character of the visual, sensible medium itself. (Like Kant he considers vision to be the paradigmatic case of sense-perception.) Space and a linearly-conceived time are, in Kant's view, the forms of sense. Our sense-perceptions therefore take on the features of multiplicity and mutual exclusion. All sensations are intrinsically particular. Such universality as our perception shows may hence be inferred to be the outcome of the synthesizing activity of the mind. Hegel describes this Kantian account of the nature of sensation approvingly in the preliminary paragraphs of the *Encyclopedia*:

The representations [*Vorstellungen*] which are given by feeling and intuition are manifold as to their content and equally in their form, by the mutual externality of sensibility in its two forms, space and time ... This manifold of sensation and intuition is brought into identity, into an original connection as the 'I' relates it to itself and unites it in a single consciousness (pure apperception).

(*Enz.*, para. 42)

Hegel agrees with the Kantian criticism of the deficiencies of the sensible realm. Lacking intrinsic universality, if the image shows a cognitive character then this must have its origin in some other source. He expresses this very succinctly in the following passage:

There is an old saying, commonly though falsely attributed to Aristotle and supposed to express the viewpoint of his philosophy: '*nihil est in intellectu, quod non fuerit in sensu*' – there is nothing in thought that was not in sense and experience. It could only be regarded as a misunderstanding if speculative philosophy refused to acknowledge this phrase. Conversely, however, it will equally assert '*nihil est in sensu, quod non fuerit in intellectu*, in the very general sense that *nous* (and, as more profoundly determined, *Spirit*) is the cause of the world.

(*Enz.*, para. 8)

Although they are agreed that there must be some source other than sensibility itself for the order and universality in our experience of the world, Hegel objects to Kant's conception of this source as a transcendental subject on the grounds that this makes the source something subjective and quasi-psychological:

It must be said at the same time that it is not the subjective activity of self-consciousness which introduces absolute unity into the manifold. This identity is, rather, the Absolute and true itself.

(*Enz.*, para. 42, *Zusatz* 1)

Hegel's conception of the 'source', then, is not as a synthesizing power located (although just how it should come to be *located* is never very clear in the Kantian picture) in the knowing subject, but an *absolute* subject, which is itself part of the *objective* (in the sense of independent of the knowing subject) world process. The contrast can be made explicit by comparing the differing views on the part of the two authors of the nature of *time*. For Kant, time, like space, is a form of sense whose structure can be determined without reference to the activity of the synthesizing subject. According to Hegel, on the other hand, the objective synthesizing agency and the nature of time itself are connected.

Because time is a form of sense we are naturally and inevitably led, according to Kant, to analogize time and space:

Time is nothing but the form of inner sense, that is, of the intuition of ourselves and of our inner state... And just because this inner intuition yields no shape, we endeavour to make up for this want by analogies. We represent the time-sequence [*stellen...die Zeitfolge...vor*] by a line progressing to infinity, in which the manifold constitutes a series of one dimension only; and we reason from the properties of this line to all the properties of time, with this one exception, that while the parts of the line are simultaneous the parts of time are always successive. From this fact also, that all the relations of time allow of being expressed in an outer intuition, it is evident that the representation [*Vorstellung*] is itself an intuition.

(*K. r. V.*, B49)

Time, for Kant, is like space in being a form of intuition. For Hegel, however, it is *vital* and *dynamic*, and these are features which distinguish it from space and the mathematical mode of cognition which, for Hegel as for Kant, is connected with spatiality:

As regards *time* of which one might think that, as a corresponding feature to space, it would constitute the material of the other part of pure mathematics, it is the existent notion itself [*der daseiende Begriff selbst*]. The principle of *magnitude*, of notionless difference, and the principle of *equality*, of abstract and lifeless unity, are incapable of dealing with that pure unrest [*reine Un-ruhe*] of life and absolute differentiation.

(*P. d. G.*, p. 38)

Time for Hegel, in contrast to Kant, cannot be represented spatially or grasped mathematically because it is the form of existence of the notion, that is to say of the source of order and universality which has a higher reality than space:

The actual [*das Wirkliche*] is not something spatial, as it is regarded in mathematics.

(*P. d. G.*, p. 37)

Time is the form of existence of the notion. It is not, however, the notion's entirely adequate medium for it also has partially the linear and self-external character of space:

Time is the same principle as the I = I of pure self-consciousness; but it is the latter (or the simple notion) still in complete externality and abstraction... Thus the finite is transitory and *temporal* for it is not, like the notion, in its own self total negativity. Although it has the latter as its universal essence, it is not adequate to it − it is *one-sided* and thus relates itself to this negativity as the power over it. But the notion in its freely existing identity with its own self as I = I is intrinsically [*an und für sich*] absolute negativity and freedom. Time, therefore, is not the power over it. Nor is it something temporal and in time but it is itself the power over time which is only this negativity as externality.

(*Enz.*, para. 258)

So the image, as sensory and spatial, intrinsically lacks the cognitive character which has the notion as its source. The notion, pure negativity, is by no means a *spatial* source, however. As *negatio negans* it is a vital 'pure unrest' which externalizes itself when it takes on existence. So, although an image may incorporate an expression of the true, the character of this truth has been violated by its translation into an intrinsically inappropriate medium. It can only show itself as beauty or *Schein* − illusory radiance.

This medium of finitude − intuition − cannot grasp the infinite. It is only an intended [*gemeinte*] infinity. This God as a statue, this world of melody which encompasses heaven and earth and the universal essences, self-consciousness and the individual essences, in a mythical and individual form, is an *intended* and not a true conception [*Vorstellung*]. Necessity, the form of Thought, is absent from it. Beauty is the veil which covers truth rather than its presentation [*Darstellung*].[3]

3   Hegel, *Jenenser Realphilosophie* II, p. 265.

This doctrine of the inability of the sensible to present the truth can be instructively contrasted with the doctrine of presentation (*Darstellung*) advanced by Kant in the *Critique of Judgement*. In Kant's view whenever a concept is capable of figuring in cognition it must be possible for it to be displayed in intuition:

> *Concepts of the understanding* must, as such, always be demonstrable (if by demonstration we understand, as in anatomy, merely presentation [*darstellen*]) i.e. the object corresponding to them must always be capable of being given in intuition (pure or empirical), for thus alone could they become cognitions. The concept of *magnitude* can be given *a priori* in the intuition of space, e.g. of a straight line, etc.; the concept of *cause* in impenetrability in the collision of bodies etc. Consequently both can be authenticated by means of an empirical intuition, i.e. the thought of them can be proved (demonstrated, verified) by an example; and this must be possible, for otherwise we should not be certain that the concept was not empty, i.e. devoid of any object.
>
> (*K. Uk.*, para. 57)

and

> Intuitions are always required to establish the reality of our concepts. If the concepts are empirical, the intuitions are called *examples*. If they are pure concepts of the understanding, the intuitions are called *schemata*.
>
> (*K. Uk.*, para. 59)

This doctrine, requiring concepts used in cognition to be presentable in such a form that they can be intuited, is itself a result of Kant's view of the finitude of human cognition. We finite beings have only finite cognition. But we are not wholly finite in the sense that (even in the cognitive sphere) we find ourselves necessarily led to the idea of an infinite mind, an *intellectus archetypus* operating 'in contrast to our discursive, image-requiring [*der Bilder bedürftigen*] understanding.' (*K. Uk.*, para. 77)

The presentability of concepts for intuition by means of images is required where the concepts involved are to figure in cognition. But not everything which plays an important role in our mental life *can* figure in cognition. Most notably the ideas of reason have an infinite character which means that they can never be employed as empirical concepts are. They are *indemonstrable*. At this point Kant attaches his own doctrine to the Judaeo-Christian tradition which prohibits images. The sublime can only be presented negatively. Yet such a presentation is more appropriate and, even, more powerful than any attempted positive, sensible presentation could ever be; it evokes the thought of the unconditioned.

We need not fear that the feeling of the sublime will lose by so abstract a mode of presentation [*Darstellungsart*] — which is quite negative in respect of what is sensible — for the imagination, although it finds nothing beyond the sensible to which it can attach itself, yet feels itself unlimited [*unbegrenzt*] by the removal of its boundaries; and thus that very abstraction is a presentation of the Infinite, which can be nothing but a mere negative presentation, but which yet expands the soul. Perhaps there is no sublimer passage in the Jewish law than the command, 'Thou shalt not make to thyself any graven image, nor the likeness of anything which is in heaven or in the earth or under the earth etc.'

(*K. Uk.*, para, 29, *Allgemeine Anmerkung*)

So, according to Kant, there is no way for the infinite vital thought to be positively presented. The effect of a positive presentation in a sensible form is to distort its infinite character. But, given Kant's wider views on the complementary functions of sense and understanding in cognition, such a presentation would be required for knowledge. Hence it must remain unknowable for us. For Hegel, on the other hand, a contrast between what can be *known* and what can (indeed, on Kant's doctrine, must) only be *thought* is completely out of the question. Thought is the true method of knowledge. Both Kant and Hegel agree that the sensible is inadequate for the presentation of the infinite, but Hegel does not draw Kant's conclusion that the infinite must be unknowable. His claim is that it can be adequately known *in another medium*, namely, the medium of *Thought*. Images have the characteristics of sensible intuition — particularity and mutual externality — and, insofar as they show intelligible characteristics, these must be the product of the activity of a higher agency.

The criticism of sensibility plays a crucial role in Hegel's critique of common consciousness. In the first place *Vorstellung* takes its content from sense, giving it the form of consciousness, but remaining infected with sensibility's deficiencies; even where the material for *Vorstellung* is not derived from sense, its presentation as *Vorstellung*, Hegel says, imparts some of sensibility's deficiency:

The distinction of the sensible from Thought lies in this; the determination of the former is individuality and, insofar as this individual (abstractly the *atom*) stands in relation, it is an *externality* whose abstract forms have it standing side by side or in succession... But common conception has, besides the sensible, material which has arisen from self-conscious Thought, as in juridical, ethical and religious conceptions — that of Thought itself, also — and it is not obvious where the difference lies between common conception and Thought regarding such content. In this case there is both Thought as the content and the presence of the form of universality, which lies in the very fact that a content is in *me*, that it is a *conception*. But the peculiarity of common conception is, in general, to be seen also in this respect, that in it such content stands isolated also.

(*Enz.*, para. 20)

The fact that a content is 'present to the mind' is sufficient to give it a certain universality. But, at the same time, even where the content is not completely particular (as where the material is purely sensible) the very fact of being a content of *Vorstellung* isolates it. *Vorstellung*, as Hegel understands it, has affinities with the classical empiricist 'ideas' — mental contents whose cognitive character rests on their mere presence before the mind of a knowing subject. So the criticism of this first model of rational experience leads naturally to discussion of the second model — the view of the mind as ordering or subsuming — for it was Kant's advocacy of this second model which, historically, provided the most effective challenge to the empiricist doctrine.

The Subsuming Model

Kant's epistemology is based on the thesis of the complementary role of intuition and understanding in cognition. Knowledge, he argues, involves more than just 'presence before the mind'. As one of the most famous apophthegms of the *Critique of Pure Reason* puts it:

Thoughts without content are empty, intuitions without concepts are blind... The understanding can intuit nothing, the senses can think nothing. Only through their union can knowledge arise.

(*K. r. V.*, B75)

Understanding is defined by Kant as the 'faculty of rules' and judgement as 'the faculty of subsuming under rules' (*K. r. V.*, B171). All our cognition involves, even though we are not aware of its operation, a judgement which acts as a 'function of unity among our representations' (*K. r. V.*, B94). It is this judging activity which introduces the order and universality which we find in our mental life, and furnishes the basis for the distinction made between the self and the mental contents of which it is conscious. Although he concedes that this account is an advance from the view of mental life as a direct 'imaging', Hegel, nonetheless, does not find it satisfactory. What he objects to is the fixed character of the universals of the understanding and to the fact that the understanding only determines the object as a matter of 'either-or' — it can only determine whether the object falls under the classifying rule or not. Hegel distinguishes his sense of *Begriff* and *begreifen* (which I have translated as 'notion' and 'comprehend' for that reason) from their common, Kantian sense, in which *Begriff* is properly translated as 'concept'. For Hegel the Kantian *Begriff*, applied by the understanding, is only an *abstract* universal:

> It is common when speaking of Thought or, more specifically, comprehension [*Begreifen*] to have only the activity of the understanding in mind. Now it is true that Thought is in the first instance *understanding* Thought, but it does not stop at this point and the notion [*Begriff*] is not a mere determination of the understanding. The activity of the understanding consists in giving its content the form of universality and the universal which is posited by the understanding is an abstract universal, held rigid as such with respect to the particular, and which, thereby, is itself in turn determined as a particular. In its separating and abstracting behaviour towards its objects the understanding is the opposite of immediate intuition and sensation, which have to do entirely with what is concrete and remain bounded thereby.
>
> (*Enz.*, para. 80)

Abstract universality is deficient because, although the particular may be subsumed under the universal, there is no intrinsic relation between the two. If we picture judgement as the process of submitting a given material to the test of a set of rules, there is no way of telling whether these rules themselves are an appropriate or an inappropriate way of classifying the material. Put in Kant's and Hegel's terms the 'movement of the judgement' goes 'only one way' – from the *universal* to the *particular*. A richer conception of rationality requires a way of moving from the *particular* to the *universal* so that we can say that the latter is adequate to the former. This, according to Kant, is the requirement of *reflective* judgement. Because experience, being the material for subsumption by the understanding, can never furnish such a principle itself it must be given by the reflective judgement 'as a law from and to itself '. This principle is that empirical laws 'must be considered in accordance with such a unity as they would have if an understanding (although not our understanding) had furnished them to our cognitive faculties' (*K. Uk.*, Intro. Section 4, Bernard trans.). So this reflective movement from particular to universal can only take place, in Kant's view, as a result of the application of a transcendental principle, and it cannot have the full, objective cognitive status of an empirical principle.

Many of Kant's readers, including Hegel, were dissatisfied with this solution. For Goethe, for example, the real point was that Kant's simply receptive, subsuming conception of experience had to be supplemented with a richer conception by which universals should actually be *developed out of* (and not just applied to) experience. The appropriateness of the universals should be established by experience itself. Goethe adopted the idea of what he called an 'intuitive power of judgement' [*anschauende Urteilskraft*], which would grasp the universal element in a phenomenon in a more direct way than subsumption. The enrichment of the concept of experience which this entails is of the greatest importance to Goethe's philosophy and aesthetics for it informs his conception of *symbolism* and of its relation to *allegory*. The former, which is the truly *poetic* form, depends on the ability of the poet to *see* the universal *in* the particular:

It is a great difference whether the poet searches for the particular to go with the universal or whether he sees [*schaut*] the universal in the particular. From the former there arises *allegory*, where the particular is only an example, an instance of the universal; the latter is actually the true nature of poetry: it utters a particular without thinking the universal or indicating it. Whoever now vitally grasps this particular acquires the universal at the same time, although not then aware of it, or only later.[4]

But Hegel's response is different, although he shares the criticism of abstract universality and the dissatisfaction with a reflective principle of unity operating only within the faculty of judgement. Hegel pays tribute to Goethe's genius and acknowledges the richness of the experience which that great man in fact had. But this is not to endorse the Goethean notion of experience. Goethe's is a mind whose experience is, in fact, animated by the (unconscious) operation of Thought. The very fact that it is *experience*, however disqualifies it, in Hegel's view, from being the adequate form for the presentation of the true:

What is important in experience is in what spirit one approaches reality. A great sensibility [*Sinn*] has great experiences and perceives the point of real significance in the motley play of appearance. The Idea is present and actual, not something away and beyond. The great sensibility, that of Goethe, for example, looking into nature or history perceives the rational there and expresses it... Reflection, too, is a method of knowing truth ... But the true as it is in and for itself is not yet present in its proper form in these two modes. The most complete mode of cognition is that in the pure form of Thought.
(*Enz.*, para. 24)

So, against Goethe's '*zarte Empirie*', a 'gentle', non-authoritarian attitude to experience which allows the universal in the object to 'emerge', rather than imposing it as part of the organizing function

4   Goethe, *Maximen und Reflexionen*, No. 279.

of the knowing subject, Hegel puts the completely *a priori* 'movement of the notion'. In this case the opposition between the universal and the particular is to be overcome by the universal's own creative power. The notion – the *Logos* of the world-process – has to 'bring forth' the particular from its own self:

> Merely *understanding* Thought is restricted to the form of the abstract universal and is not capable of progress to the particularization [*Besonderung*] of this universal.
>
> (*Enz.*, para. 37, *Zusatz*)

Hegel and Goethe would be in agreement that we cannot derive universals by abstraction, by 'leaving out' the inessential features of an object given in experience to arrive at its essential ones. But whereas for Goethe this implies that there can be a non-abstracting '*Schau*', Hegel rejects deriving universals from experience *at all*. They are acquired in the autonomous self-development of Thought, and it is this, rather than its receptiveness, which is the true source of the richness of Goethe's experience.

This feature of self-creativity is one of the most important reasons why it is misleading to translate Hegel's *Begriff* as 'concept'; the notion is self-particularizing and therefore is more than just the sum of the features held in common:

> Now the universal of the notion is not just a common feature which has its own subsistence [*Bestand für sich*] in relation to the particular, but rather it is what is self-particularizing (specifying) and what in undimmed clarity remains at home in its other.
>
> (*Enz.*, para. 163, *Zusatz* 1)

The inability to develop content out of its own self reduces the abstract universal into a 'particular' itself; the particular is what can be brought under fixed boundaries of identity. But the universal can have no such static identity if it is to meet the demand of having an *intrinsic* relation to the particular.

To sum up: Hegel and Kant agree that sense or intuition are cognitively deficient because of their intrinsic particularity. Their joint position can be expressed as a simple argument:

(1) Intrinsically what we receive through our senses is a manifold of particulars.
(2) *But* our experience shows order and universality; it is cognitive.
(3) *Therefore* our experience contains a further component which is the source of this order and universality.

The two disagree, however, about the nature of this source. Hegel rejects Kant's transcendental psychology according to which the synthesis is a subsuming, ordering activity of the knowing subject. The source of order is now a realistically construed component of reality, the Absolute Subject as *Logos*. The knowing subject comes into harmony with reality not by imposing his order on a received material but because there is present and active in himself (even if unconsciously) the freely self-developing Thought.

The *transcendental* subject is now an Absolute Subject and the problem no longer how to conceive of the understanding imposing its form on the formless material of sensation, but the creative development of that content out of the form. As Karl-Heinz Haag expresses the point, after Kant 'the place of transcendental processes of determination is taken by transcendental processes of generation'.[5]

The Model of Manifestation

The criticism of the model of rational experience as subsumption leads to a conception of the particular as produced by an active universal. We thus come to the third model, according to which our experience takes its rational character (*order* and *universality*, but also certain characteristics which empiricists would count as non-rational, such as aesthetic *harmoniousness*) in virtue of being a *manifestation* or *embodiment* of the transcendent.

Once again I turn to Goethe's doctrine of symbolism to elucidate the conception. It was pointed out above that the theory of symbolic art was the result of Goethe's hostility to the *subsuming* picture of the human intellect to be found in Kant. In contrast to this — the province of the concepts of the understanding — Goethe postulates an attitude which will make use of reason and the *Idea*:

Concept is the *sum*, Idea is the *result* of experience. To draw the former understanding is required, to grasp the latter reason.[6]

Hegel shares this belief that we can only grasp reality as rational insofar as we perceive in it the manifestation of what is infinite, the Idea (this, of course, rather than affinities with Bishop Berkeley, is the sense in which German Idealism is *Idealism*). His affirmative attitude to the infinite is expressed in explicit contrast to Kant's critical one:

5   K.-H. Haag, *Philosophischer Idealismus*, p. 31.
6   Goethe, *Maximen und Reflexionen*, No. 1135.

When one speaks of Thought it is important to distinguish the finite thought of understanding from that which is infinite and rational.

(Enz., para. 28)

and philosophy need not be restricted, as Kant had thought it must, to the finite, merely discursive, sphere. Kant's philosophy, Hegel tells us, establishes the result that the content of our cognition is only appearance. But true philosophy goes beyond this:

One must agree with this result insofar as finite thought is only concerned with appearances. However, this stage of appearance does not complete the matter, for there is a higher region, yet it is one which remains an inaccessible beyond [*Jenseits*] to the Kantian philosophy.

(Enz., para. 60, *Zusatz* 1)

The infinite *can* be grasped by Thought and it is just this that distinguishes the speculative *Begriff* from the sense of 'concept' in which it resumes the features of diverse objects:

The notion [*Begriff*] in the speculative sense is to be distinguished from what is commonly called concept [*Begriff*]. It is in this latter, one-sided sense that the assertion has been made, repeated countless times and turned into a common prejudice that the infinite cannot be grasped by concepts.

(Enz., para. 9)

From this general position of Idealism Hegel attacks three main misconceptions of the nature of the infinite. The first of these is the Platonic misconception (or perhaps, as Hegel suggests, a misconception of Platonism) according to which the realm of ideas is thought of as if it were a world of individuated entities — the archetypes — existing in separation from the finite world. This misconception is the result, he says, of the mythical way in which Plato's philosophy is presented. The criticism of mythical presentations of philosophical content reiterates the general criticism of the sensible as a mode of presentation of Thought. For the characteristic feature of myth according to Hegel is its use of sensible imagery. The mythical presentation of philosophy is thus characteristic of a less developed stage of Thought:

Many elements of philosophy are made approachable by means of mythical presentation [*Darstellung*] but this is not the true mode of presentation. The elements of philosophy are Thoughts and must, in order to be pure, be set forth as such. Myth is always a presentation which makes use of sensibility, and introduces images designed for common consciousness, not for Thought; it is the powerlessness of Thought which does not know yet how to hold itself for its own self and is not self-sufficient.

(Gesch. der Phil. II, p. 29)

The consequence is that in this heteronomous style of presentation the infinite itself comes to be modelled on the finite and its authentic, infinite character lost:

Equally, when Plato speaks of the main feature of his philosophy – the Ideas, the universal, as the permanent and independent, as the patterns of sensible objects, one can easily proceed to think of these Ideas after the fashion of the modern categories of understanding, as substances which exist in the mind of God or for themselves as independent (as angels, for example) beyond reality.

(*Gesch. der Phil.* II, p. 31)

But, as I have argued, Hegel believes that the visual model of the 'world of ideas' leads to paradoxes in understanding dialectical movement which only the non-sensible grasp of pure Thought can avoid. Hence Platonism needs to be rescued from its form of presentation. Whereas Schelling had seen the task of Idealist philosophy as involving the rehabilitation of myth, Hegel's speculative philosophy requires its elimination.

The second of Hegel's attacks is on the 'bad infinity' (*schlechte Unendlichkeit*), derived from mathematics, but taken by Kant, as the *progressus in infinitum*, to embody the impossibility of man's attaining the unconditioned, and hence as being of ethico-religious significance. This conception is unable to capture the essential features of the dialectical movement:

But this progression to infinity is not the truly infinite which consists, rather in remaining by itself [*bei sich selbst*] in its other or, taken as a process, to come to itself in its other.

(*Enz.*, para. 94, *Zusatz*)

It is the movement of the Idea, its development from and to simplicity, which is the true infinite. The mathematical infinite, by contrast, merely separates off the finite and the infinite, thereby distorting the nature of both. The former is given an unwarranted autonomy while the latter is limited and hence not truly infinite. But we should be careful to note that the fact that Hegel's infinite is not to be limited does not mean that it is absolutely unarticulated. Hegel requires that the infinite should be self-differentiating as part of the movement of Thought, but not divided by a limit or a boundary from the finite:

Such an infinite which is only a particular *alongside* the finite and which has its bound [*Schranke*] or limit [*Grenze*] therein is *not* what it ought to be, not the infinite, but only *finite*. In such a relationship, with the finite *here* and the infinite *away yonder*, the one immanent [*diesseits*] the other transcendent [*jen-*

seits], the finite is invested with the same dignity of permanence and independence as the infinite.

(Enz., para. 95)

Both the Platonic and the quasi-mathematical conception of the infinite introduce an absolute separation between finite and infinite.
Hegel, however, believes that the infinite cannot be conceived 'as a
mere realm beyond the finite [*ein blosses Jenseits des Endlichen*]'.
(*Enz.*, para. 104, *Zusatz* 2)

There is a third account of the infinite which Hegel rejects but
which does not depend on such a separation. This is the doctrine of
contemporary Idealism which rehabilitated Platonism in a way that
did not emphasize the existence of an individuated realm of entities
beyond the immanent so much as the quality which the Idea (or
Ideas) gave to experience itself as *manifestation* or expression. For the
clearest example of such views we should return to Goethe's doctrine
of the symbol and its contrast to allegory. In symbolic art the Idea is
said to show itself *indirectly*. Because only the manifestation of the
Idea is experienced it cannot be identified determinately so that we
could answer the question 'which Idea?'. The symbolic work of art
has 'meaning' but it does not mean something specific. So, for example, Goethe writes that the artist's activity is determined:

> By a deep feeling which, if it is pure and natural, will coincide with the best
> and the highest objects and in the best case will make them symbolic. The
> objects presented [*dargestellt*] in this way appear to stand independently and
> are, again, most deeply significant, and this in virtue of the ideal which ever
> brings a universality with it. If the symbolic expresses [*besagt*] anything apart
> from the presentation then it does so in indirect fashion.[7]

The suggestion, then, is that the Idea always presents itself in
occluded form to our experience, that, as Coleridge puts it:

> A symbol ... is characterized by a translucence of the Special in the Indi-
> vidual or of the General in the Especial... Above all, by the translucence of
> the Eternal through and in the Temporal.[8]

The crucial point in this doctrine is the conception of a manifestation or expression taking place in a medium which, not being wholly
infinite itself, necessarily gives it an occluded '*Schein*' character.

This change of emphasis away from the clarity and determinacy of
the Idea itself to the quality of the *experience* of manifestation is a

---

7   Goethe, 'Über die Gegenstände der bildenden Kunst', p. 461.
8   Coleridge, *The Statesman's Manual*, p. 30.

distinctive feature of the romantic and Idealist rehabilitation of Platonist styles of thinking. It also has a lot to do with their elusiveness;
it is only a short distance from the doctrine of *occluded manifestation*
and of an Absolute which is simultaneously *self-revealing* and *self-
concealing* (Schelling's doctrine) to a position in which the manifestation of transcendence is at most an *interruption* or *hiatus* in the course
of the finite (as in Hölderlin). Romanticism, therefore, often seems
to hover between affirmative and negative theology.

But Hegel himself is quite emphatic that the Idea can be known
adequately and determinately. This is possible because, whereas for
Goethe the Idea always presents itself *through* the medium of experience, for Hegel it is apprehended by the philosopher in its own element, Thought:

> The *Logic* is the Science of the *pure Idea*, that is of the Idea in the abstract
> element of Thought.
>
> (*Enz.*, para. 19)

So, unlike beauty which, being sensible, is at best, a 'veiled' or
'occluded' presentation of the truth, the *Logic*, the 'realm of pure
Thought' 'is the truth as it is without veil [*Hülle*] in and for itself '
(*W. d. L.* I, p. 31).

The element of Thought cannot be conceived as another medium
analogous to the medium of sensible experience (looked at,
perhaps, with 'the mind's eye'); the very idea of a medium is itself a
prime piece of visual thinking. It is just because it is *not* a medium
for a content which comes to expression *in* it that the philosopher
who attains pure Thought can have adequate knowledge where
even a genius such as Goethe, restricted to intuition and experience,
has only intimations.

The Synthesizing Subject

The Idea, then, for Hegel, is not part of a 'world beyond the world'.
It is the true source of the order and rationality found in reality, even
when this is experienced through the senses.

Like the synthesizing activity of Kant's transcendental subject it is
buried beneath the surface of consciousness, but, unlike Kant's
synthesis, it is not an ordering or subsuming operation performed
upon an externally given material. The contrast was illustrated by
the comparison of the two authors' views of time. In its free form
the notion is, in the strongest sense, *creative*, that is it acts as a productive source of new content.

Reason, then, properly understood as the Idea, displaces *sense* and *understanding* as a model of the nature of rational experience. It does so not just because there are aspects of reality which go beyond what sensible imaging or subsuming judgement could account for – the contents of art and religion or the moral imperative, for example – and, which only the Idea can make intelligible; the Idea is itself the source of the rationality of even the 'subordinate' spheres of sense and understanding:

If one attributes the determinations of *individuality* and *mutual externality* to what is sensible it may be added that these are themselves Thoughts and universals. It will be shown in the *Logic* that Thought and the universal consist in precisely this, that it is itself and its other, that it takes the latter over [*über dieses übergreift*] and that nothing escapes it.

(*Enz.*, para. 20)

Unlike the world of forms, standing behind reality, the Idea produces out of its own self, and the world is its self-realization. In this way the Idea fulfils the famous programme of the Preface to the *Phenomenology* that the true should be grasped 'not as *substance*, but equally as *subject*' (*P. d. G.*, p. 19). Yet, in order to characterize the nature of Thought, we need to understand in what sense 'subject' is intended here. This understanding may not be assumed, for, notoriously, no philosophical concept has shifted its significance in the modern epoch more radically. Yet it is easier to establish senses in which Hegel is clearly *not* using the concept than how he does. It must be evident, for example, that Hegel cannot be using it in the traditional grammatical/logical/ontological sense in which the subject, as *hypokeimenon*, underlies and supports the predicates and/or accidents which are attached to it. For then it would be no novelty to say that the substance should become subject – in this sense *substance* is precisely what *subject* means. In fact, Hegel explicitly contrasts the nature of the *Begriff* with this static conception of the subject:

Since the notion is the object's own self, which presents itself as the *coming-to-be of the object*, it is not a passive subject, inertly supporting the accidents; it is, on the contrary, the self-moving notion which draws its determinations back into itself. In this movement this inert [*ruhende*] subject itself perishes.

(*P. d. G.*, p. 49)

Yet, on the other hand, no more can we take Hegel as adopting the modern, Cartesian view of subjectivity, for which the subject is a personal region of cognitive presence, whose contents can be contemplated without existential commitment; the consciousness of Thought is *supra-individual*.

The attempt to clarify Hegel's concept of *subject* should start from the thesis that the self-movement of the notion is the act of a purified self. The first point I wish to clarify concerns the sense in which we think of the movement as an *act*. It is important that this is not misconceived. One common conception of the nature of action would be to see it as involving the transition to reality (the 'putting into practice') of something that had previously only existed as an intention. But, if I am right to maintain that the crucial sense in which the notion develops itself is as a movement within the 'ether' of pure Thought, then this understanding of the realization of Thought, as if it involved the transfer of a content between media, is out of place. Although the structure of Thought and the structure of external reality, taken as a whole, *correspond*, the relations between the two cannot be used to try and explain a development *within* Thought. Thought's activity cannot be a matter of realizing the same content in a different medium, as if the intention which precedes the action were a 'shadowy anticipation' of the realized action.

The self-realization of the Idea should not be thought of as such a *transfer*, as if something which previously subsisted implicitly in Thought becomes explicit in reality. The Idea does not externalize itself as part of a temporal process (it is – a different matter – the power *over* temporal process) and its embodiment in reality is not a loss or transfer. Once again Hegel's attempt to articulate philosophical truth in common language leads to what is (interpreted according to criteria drawn from the understanding) a self-contradiction:

> The task of philosophy had also been so expressed that it has to answer the question how it is that the infinite decides to emerge from its own self. To this question, which is founded on the presupposition of a fixed opposition between the infinite and the finite, one can only reply that this opposition is an untrue one and that the infinite is in fact eternally outside its own self and eternally not outside itself.
>
> (*Enz.*, para. 94, *Zusatz*)

This can be acceptable only if we concede that it is inappropriate to think of the dialectical process in terms of 'inside' and 'outside'. Development within the medium of Thought involves a generation of content, and this means that we cannot think of the relationship between what is implicit and what is explicit as if the former were a prefiguring of the latter. The critique of spatialized ways of thinking explains why we should not conceive the working out of purposes in this way. The alternative conception of development is tied to the sense of *subject* which Hegel is using:

> Further, the living substance is being which is in truth *subject*, or, what is the same, is in truth actual only in so far as it is the self-positing movement, or is the mediation of its becoming-other with itself.
>
> (*P. d. G.*, p. 20)

The conception of the self-realizing subject *is* to be related, however, to the grammatical-epistemological conception of a subject whose role is to be the *subject of judgement*. For Hegel explicitly describes the relation between the Idea and its particular realizations as one of *judgement*:

> The Absolute is the universal and *one* Idea which, in an act of *judgement* [*urteilend*] particularizes itself into the *system* of determinate Ideas. Their nature as Ideas is only to return into the one Idea, into their truth. Emerging from this judgement the Idea is, in the first place, the single universal substance. But its true developed actuality consists in being as a *subject* and thus as Spirit.
>
> (*Enz.*, para. 213)

Hegel plays on the etymology of *Urteil* to suggest this self-particularizing role of judgement and to balance the conception, suggested by the word *synthesis*, of judgement as a 'holding together' in thought of disparate materials:

> The etymological significance of *Urteil* in our language is deeper and expresses the unity of the notion as what is first and as the *original* division, which is what the *judgement* is in truth.
>
> (*Enz.*, para. 166)

But to say that the Idea is a subject which realizes itself by an act of judgement is only to expand the circle of concepts for interpretation. To say that the self-developing subject *judges* seems to lead to another paradox; for how can there be an act of judgement if the subject is an infinite one, operating in a domain where the subject–object division of a knowing subject from its received material is no longer present? To answer this we must return once again to Kant.

Kant's doctrine of judgement had established a connection between the traditional logical and ontological conception of the subject (as subject governing predicate, as substance bearing accidents) and the modern cognitive conception of a knowing subject which, by an act of judgement, comes to be aware of an objective reality. They are brought together in such a way that what one might call the 'discursive difference', the 'break' between subject and predicate, is related to a cognitive break between the merely formal self of judging consciousness and the content *of which* it is conscious, but which it receives from outside its own self, by sensibility.

But, in contrast to this formal, Kantian self, Hegel's purified self, whose activity constitutes the self-development of Thought, is an infinite and non-discursive subject. It might seem therefore that its operation would be such as to leave the distinction between subject and predicate behind. Yet, as I shall argue, the connection between subject and predicate is vitally important to the speculative enterprise. What Hegel is concerned to do is to *free* this connection from its finite, discursive element, which, as he sees it, limits its applicability and significance. How he envisages this becomes apparent from his critique of Kant.

To understand Kant let us start by considering the nature of the relationship between consciousness and what it is consciousness of. It is surely evident that this is no ordinary relationship. Specifically we cannot understand it as a *connection* of some sort made between two independent items – the mind and its contents. On the interpretation of Kant adopted by the German Idealists (and, in my view, this was an accurate interpretation) Kant was not out to deny the reality of self-consciousness, to dissolve it into something that is no more than a *construction* from the fact that our experience takes an orderly and coherent path through a world of objects. Kant was, however, concerned to deny that this self-consciousness amounted to the consciousness of an independent item, the self. Hence self-consciousness is called *apperception*, rather than perception. For this reason we cannot think of the relationship between consciousness and its content as if it were a connection made between two items, the self on the one hand, and its experience on the other.

Although Kant *identifies* this self which figures in formal self-consciousness with the synthesizing subject it is crucial to the argument that we should distinguish, on the one hand, the relationship obtaining between consciousness and the content of experience from, on the other, the relationship introduced by the activity of synthesis among the contents of the manifold of experience. The synthesizing activity connects up the received manifold in such a way that it constitutes experience. But its constituting activity is not itself an element of, or in, experience. Consciousness is always conscious of constituted, synthesized experience. We are not directly aware of our active role in constituting experience; once it has become experience the duality between active synthesizing subject and received material of experience has been resolved.

The point is expressed by Kant (with customary obscurity) in the following passage of the *Transcendental Deduction*:

I am conscious to myself *a priori* of a necessary synthesis of representations — to be entitled the original synthetic unity of apperception — under which all representations that are given to me must stand, but under which they have also first to be brought by means of a synthesis.

(*K. r. V.*, B135)

That is to say the synthesis precedes self-consciousness. Thus I am aware of the unity of my self-consciousness, which is what makes all my experiences *mine*, but it is the *prior* fact of their synthesis in the manifold which brings them under that single self-consciousness (and that, in its turn, is not a matter for awareness).

The distinction is important for, in my view, it is just the *dislocation* between the relationship of consciousness to its content (of which we are aware) on the one hand, and the synthesizing relationship operating upon the manifold of perception (of which we are not) which acts as a fulcrum for Kant's argument. Were the self a 'thinking substance', as Descartes suggested, then the distinction which is made in all judgements between subject and predicate could simply be referred directly to the distinction between consciousness and its contents. Consciousness would function as the permanent substratum. Yet, just because in Kant's view consciousness is only a *formal* unity, such a distinction can only be made if the experience itself provides the necessary articulated structure for it to be drawn. *Objective* judgements involve a distinction between subject and predicate and can only be made if the received content is referred to a *concept* and so given the general form of object-hood.

From the fact that, as finite, discursive beings, our transcendental self-consciousness is purely formal, the necessity of a synthesizing act can be inferred. Yet, for a non-discursive subject with a consciousness which were actually *productive* of content, no such synthesis would be necessary. As Kant puts it:

This principle of the original synthetic unity of apperception is not, however, to be taken as applying to every possible understanding, but only to that understanding through whose pure apperception in the representation 'I am', nothing manifold is given. An understanding which through its self-consciousness could supply to itself the manifold of intuition − an understanding, that is to say, through whose representation the objects of representation should at the same time exist − would not require, for the unity of consciousness, a special act of synthesis of the manifold.

(*K. r. V.*, B138)

Hegel's Misreading of Kant

Turning now to Hegel we find that the most extensive discussion of the Kantian *Transcendental Deduction* is given in the chapter of the *Science of Logic* dealing with the *notion*. This is appropriate in the light of my claim that the *notion* takes over for Hegel the role played by the doctrine of *synthesis* in Kant as the source of order and universality in experience.

The nature of the notion and the nature of the self are, Hegel makes clear, intimately connected with one another. Indeed the self is a form of existence of the notion:

The notion, to the extent that it has developed into such an existence as is itself free, is nothing other than *I* or pure self-consciousness. I certainly *have* notions, particular [*bestimmte*] notions, that is; but 'I' is the pure notion itself which has come to existence as a notion.

(*W. d. L.* II, p. 220)

This identification of the notion with the self was, according to Hegel, one of the chief doctrines of Kant's philosophy. But the self which is involved here is not the self as we are used to conceiving it in everyday consciousness as a simple Cartesian 'thinking substance':

[It is] a fundamental proposition of the Kantian philosophy that in order to know what the notion [*Begriff*] is, one recalls the nature of the 'I'. But for this, correspondingly, it is necessary to have grasped the notion of the 'I' as previously put forward. If one remains fixed at the mere common conception of the 'I' as it comes to mind for our ordinary consciousness the 'I' is merely the simple thing, also called *soul*, in which the notion inheres as a possession or property.

(*W. d. L.* II, p. 222)

But nor does it appear to be the self of conventional readings of Kant. In fact Hegel takes a conception of the self as content-producing from his reading of the *Transcendental Deduction*. In view of my argument above this must be astonishing. For it appeared from that that Kant's argument for the necessary operation of a synthesis of the manifold turned on precisely the fact that the self of self-consciousness was not content-producing but purely formal, and therefore unable to give its perceptions the articulation necessary for them to figure in strictly *objective* judgements. For a non-discursive, truly *creative*, self, however, this synthesis would be unnecessary. Yet this creative self is just the sort proposed as the nature of the notion in the *Logic*.

The reasoning behind Hegel's reading emerges when we look at his account of the doctrine of synthesis. It will be recalled that I distinguished the relationship introduced by synthesis between the contents of the manifold and the relationship between consciousness and its contents. Hegel, too, understands Kant as making a distinction; but it is a significantly different one:

This unity of consciousness is that which alone constitutes the relationship of the representations [*Vorstellungen*] to an object and thus their objective validity, and the very possibility of the understanding itself rests on it. Kant distinguishes from this the subjective unity of consciousness, whether I am conscious of a manifold as simultaneous or successive, which depends on empirical conditions.

(*W. d. L.* II, p. 221)

So, for Hegel, the principle of the relationship introduced into the manifold by synthesis is the (objective) transcendental unity of consciousness, the principle of the self, whereas self-consciousness is only a subjective unity. The implication is that the concepts which unite the manifold of perception must themselves have the form of self-hood, and are, in this way, unlike subsuming concepts as commonly conceived:

According to this common conception *I* have notions [*Begriffe*] and *the* notion, just as I have a robe, a colour and other such external properties. Kant went beyond this external relationship of the understanding as the faculty of concepts and of the notion itself to the 'I'. Amongst the most profound and correct insights to be found in the *Critique of Reason* is that the unity which constitutes the essence of the notion is recognized as the original synthetic unity of apperception, as the unity of the 'I think' or of self-consciousness.

(*W. d. L.* II, p. 221)

Therefore the synthesis of the manifold is connected with self-consciousness in a more intimate way than that the latter's purely formal nature makes synthesis necessary. Hegel makes self-consciousness the *principle* of synthesis itself. Synthesis is not to be conceived as an 'external relation' — as if it were the connecting up or classifying of a disparate material — but on the model of the self's relationship to its contents. Thus *comprehending* is not restricted to the understanding's function of picking out and classifying, but involves the *permeation* of an object by consciousness:

Comprehending [*Begreifen*] an object consists, in fact, in nothing other than that 'I' makes it its own, permeates it [*ihn durchdringt*] and brings it into its own form, i.e. the universality which is immediate determinacy or the determinacy which is immediate universality.

(*W. d. L.* II, p. 222)

In this way, the characteristic feature of the relationship between consciousness and its content, identified above — that it cannot be treated as if it were a connection made between two independent items — is made into the characteristic feature of the relationship between the contents of the manifold.

But this conception of synthesis as a non-subsuming, permeating, *intrinsic* relationship is demonstrably a misreading of Kant; indeed it is an inversion of Kant's own conception. Kant writes, for example, that:

Plato very well realized that our faculty of knowledge feels a much higher need than to spell out appearances according to a synthetic unity [*nach synthetischer Einheit buchstabieren*] in order to be able to read them as experience.

(*K. r. V.*, B370)

Although this need can be satisfied in the moral sphere, our *knowledge* is restricted to just a synthetic 'spelling out', the sort of external ordering process that Hegel thinks that Kant has 'gone beyond'. In the Transcendental Deduction itself Kant actually calls the 'synthesis of apprehension' a *holding together* of the manifold of empirical intuition [*Zusammennehmung*] (*K. r. V.*, A99): an external relating *par excellence*.

What really interests Hegel in the *Transcendental Deduction* is not that the purely formal nature of self-consciousness makes the ordering operation of a synthesis of the manifold necessary but that the intrinsic relationship which self-consciousness has to its contents should give synthesis its principle. This opens up the possibility of a synthesis which is truly *creative* — not just the act of an abstract universal classifying a manifold of content received from outside. Hegel cannot, of course, attribute such a synthesis to Kant. But he claims that Kant fails to follow up the breakthrough which his initial discovery of the intrinsic relationship of synthesis represents and regresses to a 'psychological' picture of the relationship between the concept and received materials of experience:

> This *original synthesis of apperception* is one of the most profound principles for speculative development; it contains the starting point for a true grasp of the nature of the notion and is completely opposed to that empty identity or abstract universality which is no synthesis in itself... The very expression: *synthesis* easily leads to the conception of an external unity and mere connection of things which intrinsically are separate. Thereupon the Kantian philosophy came to a halt at the psychological image of the notion and regressed once more to the assertion of the permanent conditionedness of the notion by a manifold of intuition.
>
> (*W. d. L.* II, p. 227)

The contemporary pressure towards Hegel's misreading of Kant's doctrine of synthesis should be noted: Kant had rejected the ruling empiricist-associationist doctrine of the passivity of the human mind. It appeared only natural to challenge at the same time empiricism-associationism's other key doctrine – the doctrine of the atomic character of experience, and the external character of the relations introduced by the mind. But Kant, as we saw, does not take this further step; although he was aware of the current of thought which was trying to rehabilitate conceptions of intrinsic unity, such conceptions feature in his own thought only as subjective propensities of our power of judgement, not as objective features of cognition.

We can turn, once again, to Goethe, for an example of 'synthesis' being used in a sense antithetical to that of 'combining'. He writes that:

> The analyst must examine... whether he is really dealing with a mysterious synthesis, or whether that which he is concerned with is merely an aggregation, a coexistence [*Nebeneinander*].[9]

No doctrine is more characteristic of Idealism's desire to extend Kant's critique of empiricism-associationism into a doctrine of 'intrinsic unity', than Coleridge's opposition between *imagination* and *fancy*. *Imagination* unifies experience in the emphatic, intrinsic sense – Coleridge calls it *esemplastic* – whereas *fancy* 'must receive all its materials ready made from the laws of association'. The pre-eminence of imagination over fancy is such that Coleridge goes so far as to call it:

> the living power and prime agent of all human perception, and ... a repetition in the finite mind of the eternal act of creation in the infinite I AM.[10]

9   Goethe, 'Analyse und Synthese', p. 299.
10   Coleridge, *Biographia Literaria*, p. 167.

Hegel himself, in the *Systemprogramm* (a fragment from the year 1796 which is now generally agreed to be of Hegel's authorship) uses the motif of the 'spelling out' of letters (which goes back to Plato's *Thaetetus*) to characterize what was to be rejected in contemporary philosophy:

men without aesthetic sense are our literal philosophers [*Buchstaben-philosophen*].[11]

A final contemporary influence on Hegel's reading of Kant must be mentioned — Fichte. The influence of Fichte is apparent in the language which Hegel uses for describing the relationship between the notion and its object; the 'being in and for itself' of the object is transformed, he says, into — a key Fichtean term — 'positedness' [*Gesetztsein*]. (*W. d. L.* II, p. 222) The distinctive element which Fichte contributes is his emphasis on the *active* nature of consciousness, an activity which emerges most clearly in the *moral* sphere. In the moral sphere consciousness relates to its content as a will does to its realization, without the restriction of a received manifold. The relation between consciousness and content has thus become, in the highest degree, intrinsic.

We can now summarize the contrast between the two views of the self. For Kant it was the formal quality of the self, its inability to produce content, which allowed the inference of the necessary operation of a synthesis, which would be superfluous for an intuitive understanding. For Hegel, the principle of selfhood itself gives the principle of synthesis, namely, that the relationship between synthesizing agency and what it synthesizes is intrinsic and rational.

But Hegel is dissatisfied even with this conception of synthesis, for, even though the relationship between the two poles is now claimed to be intrinsic, there still remains a bifurcation between synthesizing activity, on the one hand, and received content, on the other. This bifurcation is itself to be overcome in the *Logic* which shows 'the elevation of the Idea to that level from which it becomes the creator of nature'. (*W. d. L.* II, p.231) In the context of the Science of Absolute Form, which the *Logic* embodies, the notion develops content from its own self:

This Absolute Form has its content or reality in its self [*an ihr selbst*]; the notion, insofar as it is not trivial, empty identity, has the different determinations in the moments of its negativity or of its absolute activity of determi-

11   Hegel, *Frühe Schriften*, p. 235

nation [*Bestimmen*]; the content is nothing at all other than such determinations of the Absolute Form — posited by it itself and therefore its appropriate content.

(W. d. L. II, p. 231)

So, whereas Kant sees the idea of an intuitive understanding as implying a being for whom synthesis would be *unnecessary*, Hegel, inspired by the Fichtean conception of the free, moral self, takes it as an anticipation of the truly *creative* synthesis, carried out in the *Logic*. This synthesis, the Absolute Form, is, as we saw, both analytic (it does not depend on externally received content) and synthetic (it actually *generates* content). Had he accepted such a conception of synthesis, Hegel says, Kant would not have been forced to reject the definition of truth as correspondence: 'a definition of great, yes, of the highest, value' *(W. d. L.* II, p. 231):

If Kant had held the idea [*Idee*] of an intuitive understanding up against that definition of truth he would not have treated this idea, which expresses the required correspondence, as a mere thing of thought, but as the truth.

(W. d. L. II, p. 232)

It is certainly surprising to find the arch-Idealist endorsing the correspondence definition of truth, but when we examine what he means we find that it has little to do with the simple, traditional picture of the truth relation as a reflection between the mental life of a knowing subject and mind-independent reality. Where that picture envisages a relationship between judgements and reality Hegel sees the correspondence as obtaining *within* the judgement itself. We can understand this if we recall Hegel's claim that the movement of the notion is a *judgement*. The correspondence that Hegel sees is between *source* and *product* in the self-particularizing movement of Thought's development. It is achieved by *productive* Thought.

I have described Hegel in this chapter as seeking to achieve a Catholic goal (the understanding of creation as a revelation of God) by Protestant means (an imageless conception of truth). Yet one might, with equal justification, describe him, as Gadamer does, as seeking to achieve an ancient goal (the rehabilitation of the understanding of reality as *Logos*) by means of a modern conception of subjectivity:

Absolute Knowledge, then, is the result of a purification, in the sense that the truth of Fichte's transcendental concept of the Ego [*Ich-Begriff*] has emerged not merely as being subject, but reason and Spirit and thus, everything actual. That is Hegel's characteristic foundation by which he re-establishes Absolute Knowledge as the truth of metaphysics, as Aristotle had considered it *Nous* or St Thomas *intellectus agens*, and thus renders possible a universal Logic (which unfolds the thoughts of God before the Creation). His concept of Spirit, which goes beyond the subjective forms of self-consciousness, has its origins in the *Logos—Nous* metaphysics of the Platonic—Aristotelian tradition, located prior to any problem of self-consciousness. Thus Hegel solved his problem of establishing anew the *Greek Logos*, on the basis of the modern, self-knowing Spirit.[12]

Our two characterizations do not conflict with one another. In Hegel's estimation, at least, speculative Thought is the resolution of *all* the deep-rooted antitheses of intellectual history.

12   Gadamer, *Hegels Dialektik*, p. 51

5
The Prose of Thought

Perhaps there is no greater defect in Hegel's system than the want of a
sound theory of language.

Jowett

At this point the main features of my interpretation have been developed. In the next two chapters I will illustrate this interpretation
by a discussion of two topics which have been prominent in recent
discussion of Hegel's theoretical philosophy — the role of language
for the system[1] and the beginning of the *Science of Logic*. I intend to
support the line which my interpretation has followed by showing
that it provides a more convincing account of these questions than its
main rivals.

Although it is true to say that Hegel gives comparatively little
explicit attention to the problem of language, this does not mean that
the question is unimportant for him. Two points should be emphasized; the first is that, if language is given little treatment *within* the
system, this does not preclude it from playing a vital role *for the system itself*. We should not mistake the place accorded to a topic within
the encyclopedic system of Science for the role which it plays for that
system. The second point is that we should realize that what counts
as a philosophical treatment of *language* is not fixed. Certainly, Hegel
is not particularly interested in the diversity of grammars and voca-
bularies, the topics dealt with at length by Wilhelm von Humboldt.
But this is not simply an omission; there is positive significance behind their neglect. Hegel does not consider these formal aspects of
language to be of particular philosophical interest. Their richness and
diversity belong to a more primitive stage of the development of
Spirit. This formal element is subordinate:

But the *formal* element of language is the work of the understanding which

---

1   The outstanding treatment is D. J. Cook's, *Language in the Philosophy of Hegel*.

THE PROSE OF THOUGHT

informs language with its categories [*in sie einbildet*]; this logical instinct produces its grammatical character.

(Enz., para. 459)

There actually seems to be, Hegel says, referring to the empirical
work of von Humboldt, an *inverse* relationship between the development of a people's culture and the development of grammar. Philosophy, being concerned with Spirit, is primarily concerned with
culture at its highest stage of development.

The *philosophical* problem of language is its role as a vehicle of
Thought:

Language here comes under discussion only in the special aspect of a product
of intelligence for manifesting its conceptions [*Vorstellungen*] in an external
medium.

(Enz., para. 459)

Where we are dealing with Thought in its developed form those
topics dealt with by comparative linguistics recede in importance for
here *Reason* rather than *understanding* gives the underlying principle.

Hegel has a good deal to say about such topics as *judgement* (and its
articulation into subject and predicate), the *proposition* [*Satz*] and the
sign, for it is these universal features of all developed languages which
he considers to be of true philosophical interest. In this we already see
an implicit contrast between Hegel's views and those of von Humboldt. Von Humboldt, too, is interested in language as a vehicle of
thought. He describes it as a product of the 'labour of mind' [*Arbeit
des Geistes*]:

[Language] itself is no work (*Ergon*) but an activity (*Energeia*)... It is, in fact,
the labour of mind, eternally repeating itself, to make the articulated sound
capable of the expression of thought. [2]

It follows from this doctrine that the diversity of languages is itself
of philosophical significance; given the unity of thought and language it means that each language embodies a unique way of thinking. Charles Taylor has described a position fundamentally of this
sort as *expressivism*.

On this theory words have meaning not simply because they come to be
used to point or refer to certain things in the world or in the mind, but more
fundamentally, because they express or embody a certain kind of consciousness of ourselves and things, peculiar to man as a language-user, for which
Herder used the word '*Besonnenheit*'. Language is seen not just as a set of

2   Humboldt, *Über die Verschiedenheit des menschlichen Sprachbaus*, p. 46.

signs, but as the medium of expression of seeing and experiencing; as such it is continuous with art. Hence there can be no thought without language; and, indeed, the languages of different people reflect their different vision of things.

... There is no thought without language, art, gesture or some external medium, not just in the sense that the former could not be without the latter, but also in that thought is shaped by its medium. That is, what from one point of view might be described as the same thoughts are altered, given a new twist, in being expressed in a new medium, for instance, translated from one language to another. [3]

Expressivism

I want to argue in this chapter that Taylor's attribution of this expressivist doctrine to Hegel is mistaken and misleading. Indeed it would be more accurate to call Hegel's views on language *anti-expressivist*. Taylor characterizes expressivism in terms of a dual thesis about language. The expressivist believes, he says, that (a) 'there is no thought without language' and (b) that 'thought is shaped by its medium'. Now, since Hegel says explicitly (*Enz.*, para. 462) that thought without language is impossible, part (a) of the expressivist thesis must be accepted. However it does not entail the second part, and I shall argue that, so far from holding it, Hegel in fact sees the progress of consciousness as the process of *emancipation* of Thought from such an expressive dependence on its medium. It is in this sense that he is an anti-expressivist.

The existence of an opposition between Hegel's views and those of expressivism becomes clear from a comparison between their respective attitudes to the nature of poetry. For truly expressivist views of language, poetry (or, rather, *Dichtung* – the sense of the German word escapes the English restriction to *verse*) has a special dignity. [4] Poetry, it is held, combines the highest degree of meaning with untranslatability. So poetry can be seen as a vindication of the expressivist view of meaning, for the expressivist thesis of the dependence of meaning on its embodiment in a medium implies just this possibility of untranslatable (or only imperfectly translatable) meanings. A view of meaning, on the other hand, which saw meanings as detachable from their embodiments would correlate with the view that whatever is meaningful is translatable.

In the light of this, Hegel's position is clearly opposed to express-

3   Taylor, *Hegel*, p. 82.
4   For example: Gadamer, *Truth and Method*; Heidegger, 'The Origin of the Work of Art'.

ivism, for, according to him, true poetry is *indifferent* to the external form in which it is expressed, to the extent that it can be translated without loss between different languages:

Thus it is a matter of indifference in the case of what is authentically poetic whether a work of poetry be read or listened to, and it can be translated into other languages without significant detriment to its value, transposed from verse into prose and thus brought into quite different tone-relationships.

(*Ästh.* III, p. 229)

It is true that Hegel, too, gives particular importance to poetry. He calls it the highest form of art. But this dignity lies in the fact that its content is *Spirit*. The function of poetic language is the instrumental one of *communicating* this content, rather than the expressivist one of acting as a medium which shapes or constitutes content:

In this way Spirit becomes objective to itself on its own territory and has the element of language only as a *means*, partly as communication [*Mitteilung*] and partly as the immediate externality from which, as a pure sign, it has withdrawn into its own self.

(*Ästh.* III, p. 229)

The fact that Hegel is not an expressivist does not imply that the problem of *expression* is irrelevant to Hegel's philosophy. To the contrary, the problem of the expressibility of truth is crucial to it. But it is wrong to see that problem in the framework of the doctrine of expressivism. For expressivism the problem is to find a truly expressive medium (one capable of *symbolizing*, in Goethe's sense) in which the form–content relationship will be as intrinsic as possible. For Hegel, however, the suitability of language for the expression of Thought does not lie in language's expressive or symbolic character but in its character as a system of *signs*. In contrast with expressivism for which, according to Taylor, language is 'not just a set of signs', it is *precisely this* which makes language, in Hegel's view, the sole adequate vehicle of philosophical expression.

The Problem of Expression

In order to explain this let us consider the problem of expression with which Hegel is faced. I have argued that the subject-matter of philosophy is the process of the self-development of Thought. This Thought is *sui generis*, an imageless Truth. But, if so, must it not, for that reason, always be inexpressible? For whatever medium we try to express Thought in will always have a sensible character, and this will surely occlude the purity of the content to be presented in it. We would then be returned to something like a Kantian division between what is *thinkable* (pure Thought) and what is objectively *presentable* (the Thought as occluded by its medium of expression). *Prima facie*, at any rate, this undermines the claim of philosophy to be a presentation of the Absolute, the 'unveiled truth' of the *Logos*.

We can see how Hegel intends this problem to be solved by considering his account of the development of art. The role of art is, Hegel thinks, to provide a sensible presentation of Spirit, at whatever stage its development has reached. Thus, he says, its value is a function of 'the degree of internality and unity [*Innigkeit und Einigkeit*] in which Idea and form [*Gestalt*] appear as worked into one another [*ineinandergearbeitet*]'. (*Ästh.* I, p. 103)

From this we can see that art operates in the context of just that tension between content and medium of expression which, for expressivism, is characteristic of all thought.

As consciousness develops over time so, too, according to Hegel, the focus of art changes. Different epochs aim at different contents and different arts are pre-eminent. Finally, the function of art itself is superseded by philosophy: 'Thought [*der Gedanke*] and reflection [*Reflexion*] have overflown fine art'. (*Ästh.* I, p. 24)

With the development of consciousness the nature of the Idea which art is to represent is grasped in increasingly sophisticated ways. But this more developed conception is, for that very reason, less capable of artistic representation. The most significant of the stages in the development comes when art is superseded as the highest form of awareness of the Absolute with the transition from the Greek to the Christian world-view:

For, by its form, art is restricted to a certain content. Only a certain sphere and level of truth is capable of being presented [*dargestellt*] in the element of the work of art; it must still be part of its determination to externalize itself in what is sensible, and to be adequate to its own self therein, for it to be an authentic content for art – as was the case, for example, with the Greek gods. But there is a more profound conception of truth, on the other hand, according to which it no longer has such an intimate relationship and affinity to the sensible as to be absorbed and appropriately expressed by this material: such is the Christian conception of truth and the Spirit of our modern world – in particular our religion and the development of reason – appears as past that stage at which art represents the supreme mode of awareness of the Absolute.

(*Ästh.* I, p. 23)

Externalization and Realization

This specifically Christian principle is the principle of *subjectivity*. As was argued in the previous chapter there are particular reasons why this should not be sensibly representable. The principle of the Idea as *subject* means understanding it as a source which is in a strong sense productive or creative, that is to say as one which does not just externalize a content conceived of as pre-existing in some mental or logical space. Corresponding to this development the characteristically Christian art form is *romantic* art, whose content is 'inwardness' and 'subjectivity':

The true content of the romantic is absolute inwardness, and its corresponding form spiritual subjectivity as the grasp of its independence and freedom.
(*Ästh.* II, p. 129)

It would be easy — but wrong — to interpret this turn to inwardness and subjectivity as a transition from the world-view of an active, realized *Logos*, embodied in the world (the Greek ideal) to an isolated Cartesian (or Protestant) subjectivity. This would be a decisive mistake. In fact Hegel's understanding of the transition is more complicated.

The modern conception of subjectivity does not involve the substitution of a static, withdrawn, for an active, realized, subject. The transition, as Hegel sees it, involves two elements. In the first place Spirit makes its *withdrawal* from externality. As Hegel puts it, in romantic art:

[Spirit] only becomes sure of its own truth in that it withdraws out of the external into its inwardness with itself, and posits external reality as an existence which is inadequate to it.
(*Ästh.* II, p. 129)

But this withdrawal itself enables consciousness to become aware of its truly *active* character, for only in inwardness can its free self-development take place. Significantly, in view of the contrast which I have suggested between Hegel's views and those of traditional Platonism and Neo-Platonism, Hegel explains the modern turn to subjectivity by means of a contrast between the nature of *natural* and *spiritual* light:

For infinite negativity, the self-withdrawal of the Spiritual into its own self, sets aside its pouring forth [*Ergossenheit*] into the corporeal; subjectivity is the Spiritual light, which shines into itself, into its own place which was previously dark, and — in contrast to natural light, which can only illuminate an object [*nur an einem Gegenstande leuchten kann*] — is ground [*Boden*] and object for itself, which it shines on and which it knows as its own self.

(*Ästh.* II, p. 132)

The analogy between consciousness and natural light suggests that the subject—object structure of a separation between the knowing subject and the object which it knows is a permanent feature of all cognition. Self-consciousness on this model comes to be conceived as a 'looking inward', as consciousness of an inner item, the self. Against this, Hegel's view is that, once consciousness has developed to the stage where it is truly *productive*, light imagery is inadequate to represent its activity and must, like the opposition between subject and object in consciousness, be superseded.

In the course of an ideal form of such inward self-activity a purified self generates the contents of philosophy which give the rational structure of *all* reality. This theoretical intelligence is more freely active, Hegel says, than practical will, for will always faces opposition in its realization. It aims to realize itself against a medium which resists it. But the medium in which true theoretical intelligence realizes itself is unresisting. Hegel calls it (we shall see why below) the *Word*. The freedom of Spirit and the ideal character of the Word (the fact that it lacks determinate, external material characteristics) go together:

The will can be said to be the more limited for it engages itself in struggle with external, resistant matter, with the exclusive singularity of what is real [*des Wirklichen*] and has other human wills set against it also. Intelligence, however, proceeds only as far as the *Word* in its externalization [*Äusserung*] — this fleeting, disappearing quite *ideal* realization, which takes place in an element without resistance — and thus remains completely at home with itself [*bei sich*] in its externalization.

(*Enz.*, para. 444, *Zusatz*)

Against expressivism it is vital to emphasize that Hegel distinguishes between *externalization* (the putting forth of content into an external medium) and *realization* (the development of the content). Not all such developments involve externalization into a sensible medium. The full realization of Spirit is only possible because of the *internalization* of the modern turn to subjectivity. The Word is its vehicle of expression.

Self-consciousness itself comes to presence in language, whose vital characteristic is to function as if it were a resistanceless medium. For example, in the chapter on 'Mechanism' in the *Science of Logic*

Hegel compares material with Spiritual processes of communication. Spiritual communication, he says,

takes place in that element which is the universal in the form of universality [i.e. in the element of Spirit] and is autonomously [*für sich selbst*] an ideal relationship in which a determination continues from one person into another and universalizes itself without alteration – as a scent diffuses itself in the unresisting atmosphere.

(*W. d. L.* II, p. 365)

Sound and Sign

The vehicle of Thought (contrary to what expressivism suggests) *does not* shape or limit it.

The turn to subjectivity of romantic art leads to the dominance of an art form which aspires to represent this inwardness. This art is, according to Hegel, poetry. Here there is no inner connection between the content and the means of its expression. The words are not symbols or manifestations of the content but only signs. In poetic expression, Hegel writes:

The word and the sounds of words are neither a symbol of Spiritual representations [*geistiger Vorstellungen*], nor an adequate spatial externality of what is inward, as in the embodied forms of sculpture and painting, nor a musical resonance [*Tönen*] of the whole soul, but a mere sign.

(*Ästh.* III, p. 274)

Because the material embodiment of poetry is the sign the work of art's material character is reduced to the minimum. Thus there is no longer the constraint on organization of earlier art-forms that the work of art has to be adapted to the sensible characteristics of the medium. But this does not mean that poetry *lacks* a principle of organization. Now, no longer having to organize itself by the characteristics of the medium, it can arrange its content by *Phantasie*, using the 'Spiritual forms' as the guiding principle. (*Ästh.* III, pp. 229, 230)

We should understand statements on the priority of hearing over vision in this context. Where Herder had justified the special affinity between sound and language on the somewhat feeble grounds that the sense of hearing occupied a middle role between sight and pure feeling, Hegel's justification continues his criticism of the 'externality' of space. Sound is, he says, *temporal* rather than *spatial* in character. As such, sounds have less of an independent, material identity than visual objects. Moreover, vision places a distance *between* the perceiver and the object of perception which sound does not. Thus the basic element of music − the musical tone − is described as 'an externality which destroys itself again as it arises by its own existence and disappears intrinsically [*an sich selbst*]'. (*Ästh.* iii, p. 134) The character of the musical tone as a 'disappearing-appearance' and its lack of substantial independence makes it an appropriate medium for the direct expression of our inner life (a view of music which Hegel shared with Rousseau). This is why, Hegel says, the sounds of music have a *soulful* quality. Musical sound is the sensible domain which is immediately at one with inwardness.

The next stage, poetry, however, transforms the sound from a *tone* into a *sign*. The 'negative point' of sound becomes the 'concrete point', the Word, which: 'unites the infinite space of representation [*Vorstellung*] with the time of sound'. (*Ästh.* i, p. 122)

So the Word, the concrete point, is the proper embodiment of that *intensive* plenitude, the *determinate simplicity*, of developed Thought. The sign can represent precisely intellectual content in a way that an 'expressive object' (where content and expression are a unity-intension) can never do. In the *Science of Logic* Hegel makes this absolutely explicit:

In symbols the truth is still dimmed and veiled [*verhüllt*] by the sensible element; it is only entirely revealed [*ganz offenbar*] to the consciousness in the form of Thought; the meaning is only the Thought itself.

(*W. d. L.* i, p. 211)

The development of art is the development of Spirit away from dependence on media which occlude or veil the truth to *language* which represents it adequately. But this itself leads us beyond art:

Poetry is the universal art of the Spirit which has become free in itself and which is not tied down for its realization to external sensuous material; instead it launches out exclusively in the inner space and the inner time of conscious representations [*Vorstellungen*] and feelings. Yet, precisely at this highest stage, art now transcends itself in that it forsakes the element of a reconciled embodiment [*Versinnlichung*] of the Spirit in sensuous form and passes over from the poetry of representation [*Vorstellung*] to the prose of Thought.

(*Ästh.* i, p. 123)

Hegel is here opposing a long German (and romantic) tradition according to which the 'mere sign' represents a subordinate form of mental life. It is important, then, to be clear about what the understanding of language as a system of signs might involve − the more so because the German tradition has often defined itself in opposition to a crude empiricist view, as if this were the only possible form the understanding of language as a system of signs could take.

Language as a System of Signs

I think that it is possible to identify four interwoven strands in this crude empiricist picture of language as a system of signs which, in fact, do not mutually entail one another. These four strands of belief are:

(1) That there is no resemblance between words and their meanings (referents).
(2) That signs are motivated (their systematic use is underpinned) by psychological causality operating either directly and naturally (by habit and association) or indirectly (by convention).
(3) That what is designated by a sign can *be* (exist in the mind, at least) independently of the sign associated with it.
(4) That the primary function of language is to designate, to represent in the form of relationships between signs, the relations obtaining in reality.

The German tradition, including 'expressivism', of which Heidegger and Gadamer are representative examples, concentrates its opposition on (3). In this sense Heidegger describes words as *showing* or *revealing* significance. This leads naturally to opposition to (2). For if causality requires the independent indentifiability of cause and effect, our inability to separate the sign from what it designates (the consequence of the rejection of (3)) means that a causal relationship between sign and referent is excluded. (1), moreover, becomes meaningless, for there are no longer two separate items which we could compare for resemblance or difference.

The key question, then, is Hegel's attitude to (3); does he think that there can be designata in separation from signs? In answering, it becomes clear that Hegel's views on language cannot be assimilated to either expressivism or (classical empiricist) 'designativism'. For, unlike the classical empiricists, Hegel denies that we could hope to think without words. On the other hand, against expressivism, Thoughts are not *constituted* by the signs which represent them. The sign, we might say, *evokes* the meaning and is therefore indispensable to it; but it is not *part of* the meaning. For expressivism what linguistic tokens disclose is never absolutely self-transparent. As Taylor puts it:

If we focus on disclosure we must see all clarity, all explicit articulated thought, as surrounded by a horizon of the unclear, implicit, inarticulate.[5]

On Hegel's view, however, the claim that there can be no thought without language does not conflict with the claim that the content of the *Logic* is the adequate, transparent awareness of the rational structure of reality.

Consequences of Expressivism

Seeing Hegel as an expressivist distorts our understanding of his philosophy in three main ways. In the first place, by identifying the conception of *self-realization* with *externalization* (calling both 'expression') it over-simplifies Hegel's position on the relationship between thought and reality. For the expressivist, mind can only be conceived as one pole of a basic continuity. So, according to Taylor, expressivism:

takes just those functions, of pure thought, reflection, deliberation, which one would be most tempted to attribute to a disembodied mind, and reclaims them to embodied existence as necessarily couched in an external medium.[6]

But this is to ignore the way in which, as we have seen, Spirit is said to have its *own element*, Thought, which is indeed logically independent of its embodiment (to the extent that *anything* is independent in Hegel's system), although of course it is not to be conceived as a kind of separable mental space. Only by *withdrawing* into this 'realm of truth' can Spirit attain free self-realization.

A second way in which expressivism distorts our understanding of Hegel is in *appearing* to offer a solution to what Hegel means by *subjectivity*. As we saw, for expressivism 'the languages of different peoples reflect their different visions of things'.[7] The suggestion is that, because *what* comes to expression is not a content which is determinate and independent, the role of the representing medium is not just to transmit. The medium *in which* the content is represented can also express the particular nature of the representing subject. Now, in actual fact, Hegel *does* think of the contents of the *Logic* as determinate and independent of their embodiment, so there is no room for expressivism's (characteristically romantic) reconciliation

5   Taylor, *Hegel*, p. 475.
6   Taylor, *Hegel*, p. 82.
7   Taylor, *Hegel*, p. 82.

of subjectivity and objectivity in the unity of the expressive object. We need, then, another account of what Hegel means by subjectivity (an account which I tried to give in the last chapter). This point is of special importance for the assessment of Hegel's political philosophy. For if one wishes to defend Hegel — as Taylor does in some measure — from the charge of political authoritarianism, by the claim that the realized state is one which acknowledges the 'principle of subjectivity', then it is important whether this principle amounts to a recognition of the value of what is personal or not. Expressivism suggests that it does, whereas, on my account, subjectivity is first and foremost a general metaphysical principle of activity, not a private possession.

'Linguistic-tension' Theories

The third consequence which I want to draw attention to is more general and applies not just to expressivism but to the family of interpretations of Hegel (of which Taylor's is one of the most distinguished) which locate the operation of the dialectic in terms of a tension between *what* is said in a language and the language *in which* it is said. Such interpretations (let me call them 'linguistic-tension' interpretations) are part of an attempt to find a 'motor' for Hegel's categorial development. The approach has consequences, in turn, for the way in which one gives sense to the claim that the subject-matter of the *Logic* is Absolute Knowledge.

Linguistic tension theories appear to offer an answer to the problem of how an increasingly complex sequence of determinations can be generated starting from a point which is genuinely one of contentless simplicity, if this is not to be a process with only a retrospective justification. The 'inner articulation necessary for contradiction'[8] does not lie in the determination itself — for this, it is held, would conflict with its character as 'indeterminate immediacy' — but in the attempt to give thought articulation. According to Rüdiger Bubner, for example, 'movement only takes place insofar as the assertion of the utterance of the Absolute and the utterance which is possible in each case do not coincide'.[9] If by thought we can only mean 'thought as expressed in a medium' then the fact that a pure Thought is internally self-contradictory does not violate the requirement that the *Logic* be presuppositionless. For the tension which leads to

8   Taylor, *Hegel*, p. 130.
9   R. Bubner, 'Strukturprobleme dialektischer Logik', p. 49.

contradiction is no *presupposition* but an incliminable feature of thought itself. One may still raise the objection that, in rooting complexity in the distinction between the determination itself and the attempt to articulate it, the linguistic-tension approach makes progress the result of a *reflection on* the content, rather than part of the content itself. To defend itself the linguistic-tension approach has to understand Hegel's claim that the subject-matter of philosophy is self-moving as referring not to the determination treated in isolation, but to the *unity* of the determination with the attempt to articulate it. The claim is that it is part of the nature of the thought-determinations to strive to articulate themselves so that, properly conceived, there could never be such a thing as a set of disembodied categories. All determinations strive to articulate themselves against the limitations set for them by the medium in which they are expressed.

Yet here is a dilemma. The *Logic* is the 'realm of pure Thought', 'the truth as it is without veil in and for itself', its content is what is 'absolutely true'. (*W. d. L.* I, p. 31) Does this, then, mean that the nature of the Absolute — 'Spirit thinking its essence' — itself incorporates such a tension between content and its expression?

To see God as engaged in a struggle to articulate himself against the 'principle of resistance' of externality is to make him into something quite different than the Christian omnipotent creator. But, as we saw, it is the emphatic Christian sense of *creation* that Hegel himself appeals to for the understanding of the self-development of the notion. The failure to distinguish between *realization* and *externalization* encourages this picture of the Absolute as engaged in a gnostic struggle for self-realization. Although it is true that God's nature is externalized in the world, the active self-realization process of the *Logic* reproduces, in the famous phrase, 'God... *before* the creation'. We cannot understand its progress by referring to the externality which it takes on at the point of its completion.

But the only alternative to ascribing such a thoroughly un-Christian conception of God to Hegel for someone who takes up the linguistic tension interpretation is to revise the sense in which the *Logic* deals with Absolute Knowledge. Wolfgang Wieland, for example, tells us that:

Hegel's *Logic* has, to be sure, the Absolute as its object, but it is no speculation, which could lay claim to standing on the standpoint of the Absolute. What is being dealt with, rather, is the endeavour of finite Spirit, attempting to develop and grasp the categories which are necessary for an appropriate exposition [*Auslegung*] of the Absolute.[10]

This revision is made because of Wieland's awareness that the limitation that content can only be thought within a finite medium of expression is inappropriate to the nature of God himself.

If the linguistic-tension conflicts with Hegel's Christian conception of the Absolute, Josef Simon's interpretation takes things to what is, in a sense, their logical conclusion. He complements the Heideggerian twist which the approach gives to the understanding of language with an interpretation of the Absolute which brings it into line with Heidegger's *Sein*. Thus, in his view, the Absolute never entirely discloses itself in experience (it would not seem to be the truth 'without veil') and language, which is the medium of its revelation, is the ' "ground" of the dissimulation of the Absolute [*"Grund" der Verstellung des Absoluten*]'.[11] I can see no textual evidence for the thesis that Hegel's Absolute 'dissimulates' itself in the *Logic*. Indeed, the point of the contrast between Hegel's Idealism and that of such predecessors as Goethe and Schelling lies in the claim that the *Logic* provides a transparent knowledge of the Absolute, by contrast with their occluded visions. But the linguistic-tension approach necessarily leads its adherents to downgrade the importance of this self-transparency, to make it a final outcome rather than a permanent feature of the process.

The Inadequacy of the Proposition

I have argued that the sign character of language is decisive for Hegel's problem of the expressibility of philosophical truth because by its means alone is Thought enabled to go beyond the expressivist problem of the tension between a transcendental content and its presentation in a finite medium. Only in this way can we accommodate the thesis that the *Logic* expounds the nature of the Absolute. However, there is one feature of Hegel's writing on language, with which I have not yet dealt, which might be thought to count strongly in favour of the linguistic-tension approach. In four passages at important stages of major works Hegel tells us explicitly and in some detail that, in his view, language is *inadequate* for the expression of speculative truth.[12] Surely if, on the one hand, philosophy takes place in the 'prose of Thought' and yet, on the other, 'the proposition

10   W. Wieland, 'Bemerkungen zum Anfang von Hegels Logik', p. 405.
11   J. Simon, *Das Problem der Sprache bei Hegel*, p. 14.
12   *P. d. G.*, pp. 51–4 (the *Preface*); *W. d. L.* I, pp. 75–7 (the chapter on being);

[*Satz*] in the form of a judgement is not appropriate to express speculative truths' (*W. d. L.* I, p. 76), this must support the view that
speculative philosophy operates in the tension between the necessity
of language for the realization of expressive intentions and the limitations it imposes as a medium.

In order to counter this argument it is necessary to distinguish two
ways in which language might be expressively deficient: (1) as unable to (fully) disclose correct contents, and (2) as falsifying the relationship between those contents it represents. (There is also a third
way in which language may be inadequate, and that is when we
associate it with *Vorstellungen* rather than true Thoughts. Against
this the speculative philosopher is obliged to express himself in
apparently self-contradictory terms — to say that the world both is
and is not finite, for example. But this is only necessary for a consciousness which fails to grasp the true, Hegelian sense of infinity.
These antinomies, which arise from trying to characterize speculative contents in terms of the predicates of the understanding, are
different from the problem of philosophical representation proper,
the form in which the true, speculative movement is to be
presented.)[13]

I have dealt with the first form of inadequacy under the title of
expressivism. The issue there was posed at the level of the individual
linguistic tokens. But language is certainly more than a collection of
such tokens, be they empiricist *signs* or revelatory, Heideggerian
words. As analytical philosophy has consistently emphasized, it is the
basic semantic unit — the sentence, proposition, or judgement —
which forms the starting point of philosophical interest in language.[14] I shall argue that it is in just this respect (the proposition *in
the form of a judgement*, as he says) that Hegel sees language as inadequate. The problem is not the representability of the content by signs so
much as the representability of the movement between the content's
'moments'.

The movement of the Absolute Form was described as an *ur-teilen*,
an original division, and the judgement itself must incorporate
this self-articulation. In the comprehending Thought [*begreifendes*

W. d. L. II pp. 495, 496 (the *Absolute Idea*); *Enz.*, paras. 28–32 (Hegel's discussion of traditional metaphysics under the title 'First Attitude of Thought to Objectivity').

13 *Pace* Arend Kulenkampff (see *Antinomie und Dialektik*).
14 *Traditional and Analytical Philosophy: Lectures on the Philosophy of Language*, pp.
35-50

Denken] of speculative Science 'the notion is the self of the object which presents itself [*sich darstellt*] as its becoming'. (*P. d. G.*, p. 49) But this becoming, as was argued above, is not to be thought of as a *transition* in the normal sense, as if the dialectical process transferred itself from one separate object to another. It is this, seemingly paradoxical, feature of the dialectical movement 'this course that generates itself, going forth from, and returning to itself', (*P. d. G.*, p. 53, Miller trans.) as Hegel calls it, that language has to represent.

To understand Hegel's approach to the problem we must appreciate that his discussions — obscure even by his own standards — are actually concerned with the interaction of *two* conflicts in the judgement, which, in the interests of interpretation, should be distinguished. In the first place there is the broad conflict between the nature of the dialectical movement and the external relationship of the parts of the judgement, as the judgement is conceived according to *Vorstellung*. But, within this broad conflict, there is the tension between the common conception of the judgement, according to *Vorstellung*, as if it were simply a matter of 'connecting up', and the judgement's intrinsic nature. The great importance of the second tension consists in the fact that this intrinsic nature of the judgement both makes it amenable (if not perfectly so) for the representation of dialectical movement on the one side and also acts as the drive which, operating within *Vorstellung*, gives common consciousness an innate aspiration towards speculative Science, to the point where it can only satisfy itself in Thought.

The normal understanding of the proposition, which Hegel objects to, sees it as the unification of two separate items — subject and predicate. The subject term is identified as a fixed point (the *hypokeimenon* of traditional logic) to which predicates come to be attached like lights on a Christmas tree. This picture of the judgement, which takes it to be informative because bringing together innately separate contents, creates, Hegel thinks, the need for a connecting agency, the knowing subject. But the movement of the notion, as he conceives it, is both analytic and synthetic, which is to say that the source of the content of informative propositions (and not just the tautologies which Kant calls 'analytic') lies in the nature of the subject-term, the notion.

Hegel puts these considerations against the traditional account of the proposition as follows:

The subject is assumed as a fixed point to which, as their support, the predicates are affixed by a movement belonging to its knower, and which is not
regarded as belonging to the fixed point itself; yet it is only through this
movement that the content could be represented [*dargestellt*] as subject. The
way in which this movement has been brought about is such that it cannot
belong to the fixed point. Yet, after this point has been presupposed, the
nature of the movement cannot be any other than this; it can only be external. Hence, the mere anticipation that the Absolute is subject is not only *not*
the actuality of the notion, but it makes the actuality impossible; for the
anticipation posits the subject as an inert point, whereas the notion is self-
movement.

(*P. d. G.*, p. 23)

The picture of the judgement as a process of assigning or attributing predicates to subject-terms is cognitively deficient. Hegel says of
this procedure that:

This is, however, an external reflection on the objects, for the determinations (the predicates) are ready at hand in my immediate consciousness [*Vorstellung*] and are attributed to the object merely externally. Whereas the true
cognition of an object must be in such a fashion that it determines itself out of
its own self and does not receive its predicates externally.

(*Enz.*, para. 28, *Zusatz*)

It is important (if one wishes to defend Hegel from some of his
more absurd opponents) to see that he does not mean by this charge
of cognitive deficiency that all propositions which we call 'true' in
the normal acceptance of the word are true cognitions in his sense —
in effect that all our empirical knowledge is purely *a priori*. Not all
propositions which correspond to a state of affairs in reality are
judgements:

'Caesar was born at Rome in such and such a year, waged war in Gaul, for
ten years, crossed the Rubicon etc.' are propositions [*Sätze*], not judgements.

(*Enz.*, para. 167)

But the nature of the propositions and our ordinary consciousness
contain within themselves the aspiration towards what Hegel sees as
the judgement proper:

But as the copula 'is' utters the predicate of the subject, this external, subjective subsuming is set aside again [*aufgehoben*] and the judgement taken as a
determination of the *object* itself... Of course the determinations of individuality and the universality, subject and predicate, are also distinct, but
there remains no less the quite universal *fact* that every judgement expresses
[*aussagt*] them as identical. The copula 'is' comes from the nature of the

notion which is to be identical with itself in its externalization.

(*Enz*., para. 166)

In the light of Hegel's criticism of the view of judgement as a *connection* it is quite extraordinary to read Tugendhat's claim that:

Hegel remained bounded by the prejudice of his time that judgements are a composition [*Zusammensetzung*] out of concepts and the speculative logic which he developed remains a logic of concepts and determinations. It contravenes at every turn Frege's insight that the logically primary — and, one might add, the ontologically primary — unity, behind which no-one can proceed unscathed is the sentence [*Satz*].[15]

In its quest for cognitive adequacy the mind is led away from external empirical judgement to the region of Thought. In the first place the very form of the proposition contains the demand, Hegel says, that the predicate should be an *intrinsic* characteristic of the object:

When we say 'this rose is red' or 'this picture is beautiful' there is thereby expressed that it is not *we* who attach externally to the rose that it is red, or the picture that it is beautiful, but that these are the proper determinations [*die eigenen Bestimmungen*] of these objects.

(*Enz*., para. 166, *Zusatz*)

The importance of this feature of *objectivity*, that there be a distinction between the way things are and the way that they appear to the subject, for Kant's Transcendental Deduction, has been stressed, rightly in my view, by P. F. Strawson.[16] He points out that Kant cannot found this distinction by referring to the nature of the object as it is in itself, independently of experience. Kant shares the empiricists' thesis that objects for us are always objects as given in experience. Yet, unlike them, Kant will not abandon the requirement that room for the distinction be made.

To this requirement that the attribution of the predicate be *objective* Hegel adds the stronger requirement that true judgements should not be contingent at all:

A further deficiency in the conception of the judgement common in formal logic is that, according to it, the judgement appears merely as something contingent and the transition from the notion to judgement is not demonstrated. But the notion is not, as understanding thinks, standing in immobility. It is rather, as the infinite form, purely active [*schlechthin tätig*], therein the *punctum saliens* of all vitality and thus self-differentiating.

(*Enz*., para. 166, *Zusatz*)

15 Tugendhat, 'Das Sein und das Nichts', p. 152.
16 See *The Bounds of Sense*, especially pp. 89–112.

So the movement of the notion generates a system of synthetic *a priori* propositions which satisfies Hegel's version of the correspondence definition of truth, namely, a correspondence between the two sides of the judgement. Thus the speculative judgement represents the resolution of the second tension — between the common conception of the judgement as a connection and the intrinsic nature of the copula. The transformation which it produces in the proposition is more complex, however, than the move from an extrinsic to an intrinsic connection between subject and predicate. For, in the process, the nature of the predicate is itself altered. In the normal understanding the predicate is a universal term that can be used to characterize a variety of objects. Conversely, the logical subject is taken to be capable of supporting a variety of predicates. But the speculative movement changes this:

The subject that fulfils its content ceases to reach beyond it, and cannot have any further predicates or accidental properties. Conversely, the dispersion of the content is thereby bound together under the self; it is not the universal which, free from the subject, could belong to several others. Thus the content is, in fact, no longer a predicate of the subject, but is the substance, the essence and the notion of what is being spoken of.

(*P. d. G.*, p. 50)

So we see that the proposition which is to express the speculative movement requires a sort of 'essential predication', one in which the relationship between the two parts of the judgement has an affinity both to the *is* of identity and to the *is* of predication. The speculative proposition comes *between* identical propositions (such as 'Hermes is Mercury') and predicative ones (such as 'the rose is red'). As Hegel puts it:

Formally, what has been said can be expressed thus: the general nature of the judgement or proposition, which involves the distinction of subject and predicate, is destroyed by the speculative proposition, and the proposition of identity which the former becomes contains the counter-thrust against that subject—predicate relationship.

(*P. d. G.*, p. 51, Miller trans.)

The speculative proposition, embodying the movement of the notion, is neither predicative nor merely identifying. If we construe the propositions of speculative philosophy as predicative we shall continue to regard the two sides as separable, united from outside by a knowing subject. On the other hand, identical propositions neglect the most important feature of the judgement, the fact that it is a *movement* from one side to the other, in which the predicate expresses the nature of the subject, makes explicit what is implicit in it, and, in this sense, *develops* it. Hegel compares the way in which the speculative proposition exploits the tension between these two forms to a musical rhythm:

> This conflict between the general form of a proposition [i.e. the subject −predicate form] and the unity of the notion which destroys it is similar to the conflict that occurs in rhythm between metre and accent. Rhythm results from the floating centre and the unification of the two. So, too, in the philosophical proposition, the identification of subject and predicate is not meant to destroy the difference between them, which the form of the proposition expresses; their unity, rather, is meant to emerge as a harmony.
>
> (*P. d. G.*, p. 51, Miller trans.)

If we approach the speculative proposition, however, as if the 'is' which it makes use of is the 'is' of identity, both the proposition *and* its negation will appear to be true, for it is necessary to express the fact that the predicate term is not (i.e. *is not identical with*) the subject:

> If the content is speculative then the non-identical aspect of the subject and predicate is an essential moment, but this is not expressed in the judgement taken as a judgement of identity ... This deficiency is made up for, for the purposes of expressing speculative truth, in that, in the first place, the contrary proposition is added: the proposition 'being and nothing is not the same' which was likewise expressed above.
>
> (*W. d. L.* I, p. 76)

So it lies in the nature of the proposition itself to aspire to a higher cognitive status than empirical judgement, in which a knowing subject connects up given subject and predicate. But when the stage of Thought is reached, and the predicate is the intrinsic articulation of the subject-term itself (the notion), the nature of predication has been transformed into essential or substantial predication and the proposition brought nearer to the judgement of identity. The inadequacy of language for the expression of Thought results from the fact that the speculative proposition relates its parts *neither* by means of the copula nor by an 'is' of identity.

The implication is quite different from the linguistic tension thesis. The proposition as commonly conceived fails to express the *movement between* the contents (not, as the linguistic tension approach would have it, the content itself). Furthermore, crucially, the conflict between the normal and the speculative relationship, although permanently recurring, is a problem for the expression of a movement which Thought allows us to conceive independently — it is *not* constitutive of the movement itself.

6
From Being to Nothingness (and Back Again)

Das Nichts hungert nach dem Etwas.

J. Böhme

Although I think that Dieter Henrich exaggerates when he claims that the critical discussion of the last century developed interpretation of the beginning of the *Logic* to a point beyond which no significant progress has been made, his observation that this text has been singled out, above all others, for scrutiny, is pertinent.[1] This body of discussion exerts its own force and means that the beginning of the *Logic* claims the attention even of those, like Henrich, who believe that it is a relatively trivial matter.

In this chapter I am concerned to show the consequences of three of the principles whose importance for Hegel's philosophy I have argued in the preceding ones.

(1) The forward movement of the *Logic*, if it is to be in keeping with Hegel's own understanding of his philosophy, must be rigorous and perspicuous *ex ante*. Any account which needs to supplement the forward movement with a retrospective justification must violate Hegel's self-understanding. This rules out Henrich's own attempt to contrast the progressive development of the thought-determinations in the exposition of the *Logic* with what he calls a 'metalogic' of their justification:

The *Science* of Logic must be distinguished from the process of the Logical determinations of Thought. This process takes place as a univocal development. Its Science, however, is a mode of the actuality of Spirit. To a great extent it only allows of being unfolded with retrospective justification and with regard to the whole. We need a doctrine of method of these justifications which would have the character of a 'metalogic'.[2]

1   Henrich, 'Anfang und Methode der Logik', pp. 73, 75.
2   Henrich, 'Anfang und Methode der Logik', p. 92

The argument of Chapters 2 and 3 shows that this is completely wrong. Such a 'doctrine of method' is just what Hegel *does not, cannot*, and (in his own opinion) *need not* give.

This rules out interpretations such as Klaus Hartmann's:

> The sequential forward reading cannot be the whole story. How could a presuppositionless beginning lead to anything; how could the absence of determination lead to richness? Thus there must be operative a contrary consideration pointing from the ordered richness of granted content back to its antecedents. The linear progression cannot be deduction; what it is heading for is granted.[3]

Hartmann's reasoning is consistent but its premise is drawn from common sense rather than from Hegel. He is arguing from the impossibility of content being generated from simplicity to the need for the movement of Thought to be, in some sense, retrospective. In contrast, Hegel does not think such a generation from simplicity impossible; it is the only way he can satisfy his own clearly stated demand that the forward movement be rigorous *ex ante*.

(2) The forward movement must proceed *immanently*; it must be implicit in the starting point, not something that results from an operation performed on the starting point – a 'reflection' on it. If this is not to rule out the linguistic-tension account of the progress of Thought it must be shown that the tension between the thought-determination as it immediately presents itself and the attempt to articulate it is immanent in the required sense.

(3) The *Logic* takes place in the purified self-transparency of the element of Thought, from which it follows that we cannot analogize the nature of Thought from the nature of everyday consciousness. It may turn out that Thought has characteristics which, by common consciousness's standards, are impossible and self-contradictory.

Being as Intuition

I shall start with the criticism of the beginning of the *Logic* made by Ernst Tugendhat in his article 'Das Sein und das Nichts'. Tugendhat's criticism is of particular interest for being made in the context of an ambitious reading of the history of Western philosophy. In 'Das Sein und das Nichts' and in his book *Traditional and Analytical Philosophy*, Tugendhat attempts to vindicate a picture like Heideg-

---

3   Hartmann, 'Hegel: a Non-Metaphysical View', p. 105

ger's of the history of philosophy as a process in which the 'question of Being' [*Seinsfrage*] is displaced by the 'question of what is' [*Frage nach dem Seienden*]. Against Heidegger, however, Tugendhat argues that the appropriate response is made, not by Heidegger's own 'hermeneutics of *Dasein*', but by the development of analytical philosophy of language.

Following Heidegger, Tugendhat claims that the tradition of Western philosophy has misunderstood the nature of *being*, ontology's most general term, in treating it in exclusively *positive* terms, as *what there is*, for instance, or as *substance*. By this assumption traditional ontology pre-forms the answer to its own basic question 'what is there?' by construing it as if it were asking 'what *sorts of things* are there?'. Traditional ontology of this sort Tugendhat calls 'object theory' [*Gegenstandstheorie*]. Although, in the modern epoch, new conceptions of the philosophical enterprise — epistemology and transcendental philosophy — have challenged ontology's central role, what they had *not* done until the advent of Heidegger and analytical philosophy, according to Tugendhat, was to dislodge ontology's distorting orientation towards objects.

In 'Das Sein und das Nichts' Tugendhat traces the origin of the presupposition that whatever is is object-like, an entity, to a confusion about the nature of *thinking*, which was made originally in Greek philosophy. It seems reasonable to assume that whatever *is* must (at least) be *thinkable*, even if not capable of being *known* or *encountered*. But if thinking itself is understood as a quasi-picturing, the 'holding before the mind' of a thought-object by a thinking subject, then whatever *is* will automatically be taken to be object-like. Understanding thought as quasi-perception, however, leads to the Parmenidean paradox whose form, Tugendhat says, is:

(1)   A thinks that X is not
therefore (2)   A thinks nothing
therefore (3)   A does not think

The fallacy, according to Tugendhat, lies in the move from (1) to (2). It rests, he says, on a failure to distinguish *legein* (*thinking* in the sense that what is thought is not a perceptual object but a propositional content) from *noein* (*thought* as the quasi-perceptual consciousness of an object). Although it is the former sense of 'thought' which we employ when we think something negative, as in (1), the transition from (1) to (2) only holds under the assumption that thinking is

quasi-perception; a non-existent state of affairs is construed as one
that presents itself to the mind as *nothingness*. But, in Tugendhat's
view, the whole tradition of Western philosophy falls victim to just
this assimilation of *legein* to *noein*. Only analytical philosophy once
again distinguishes *propositonal attitude* verbs and their objects from
ordinary verbs of action.

The basis of Tugendhat's objection to the equation of *being* and
nothing at the beginning of Hegel's *Logic* lies in the claim that Hegel,
too, is a representative of the *noein* tradition:

Hegel... stands at the end of a tradition which had long since accustomed
itself to speak of the *noein* of an *ousia* (*essentia*). He lies open, therefore, for a
term which is exclusively oriented towards intuition, one which is adequate
to the Parmenidean conception, and, at the same time, to his own systematic
intentions. This term is *pure being*.[4]

The argument which Tugendhat attributes to Hegel is that *being*
and *nothing* can be equated only because there is an implicit appeal to
the nature of *being* as a contentless intuition. Tugendhat claims that
Hegel wants us to imagine *being* by leaving out all determinate content from intuition. What we are left with will be *being* but, equally,
(for the two quasi-intuitions turn out to be exactly the same) *nothing*.

Every... intuited content, whether sensible or intellectual, is a determinate
one, distinguished from other contents. One 'sets aside' [*hebe...auf*] this distinction and abstracts from this and every determinacy. What one retains (if
one retains anything at all) is *pure being*.[5]

Tugendhat (like many less distinguished commentators) completely ignores the attack on the restriction of thought to *Vorstellung*
which, as I have argued, plays such a crucial role in Hegel's philosophy. The result is that he provides an interpretation which indicates
precisely what Hegel's conception of *pure being* is *not*. Tugendhat
claims that 'Hegel expressly describes the thought of *being* as
"intuition".'[6] But here is Hegel's actual text:

There is nothing to intuit in [*being*], *if one can talk of intuition here*, or it is only
this pure, empty intuition itself. There is as little to Think in it, or it is
equally only this empty Thought.

(*W. d. L.* I, p. 66, my emphasis)

The sense in which we *can* talk of intuition in the speculative Sci-

4   Tugendhat, 'Das Sein und das Nichts', p. 146.
5   Tugendhat, 'Das Sein und das Nichts', p. 147.
6   Tugendhat, 'Das Sein und das Nichts', p. 146.

ence was explained in Chapters 3 and 4. What emerged there was that this could only be in the sense that *intuition* is something non-discursive, which the subject undergoes at first hand. It could not be in the sense in which intuition is taken to be a form of mental *imaging*. For, as Hegel describes the beginning of the *Logic*:

> The beginning is *Logical* in that it should be made in the element of free and autonomous [*für sich seienden*] Thought, in pure knowledge [*im reinen Wissen*]. It is mediated herein that pure knowledge is the last, absolute truth of consciousness.
>
> (*W. d. L.* I, p. 53)

This 'absolute truth of consciousness' consists precisely in its opposition to the *Vorstellung* of immediate consciousness with which the *Phenomenology* begins:

> In [the *Phenomenology*] immediate consciousness is also what is first and immediate in Science, thus the *presupposition*; but in the *Logic* the presupposition is that which had shown itself to be the result of that study — the Idea as pure knowledge.
>
> (*W. d. L.* I, p. 53)

Only the 'Idea as pure knowledge' can give us the *Thought* of pure being. This is the point of *determinate simplicity* to which the *Phenomenology* takes consciousness, the point, as Hegel puts it, at which 'externalization is itself externalized'. (*P. d. G.*, p. 564) At this point we have left *Vorstellung* behind; this explains why the beginning of the *Logic* is not an argument drawing on the quasi-perceptual nature of Thought — a point which, in fact, Hegel spells out in the first *Zusatz* to the paragraph on *being* in the *Encyclopedia Logic*:

> [*Being*] is not to be sensed [*empfinden*], not to be intuited [*anschauen*], and not to be represented [*vorstellen*], but, rather, it is the pure Thought and, as such, it constitutes the beginning.
>
> (*Enz.* para. 86)

The beginning of the *Logic* depends on the contrast between Thought and intuition. The correspondence between Tugendhat's reading of the history of philosophy, to which he assimilates Hegel, and the understanding of mental life which, as I argued in Chapter 4, Hegel sets himself *against*, cannot be entirely coincidental. Heidegger's reading, on which Tugendhat's is based, owes more to the tradition of German Idealism than his own terminological idiosyncrasy makes apparent; certain of Idealism's crucial themes — the imagelessness of truth, the opposition between spatial externality and temporality, for example — had become part of the common stock of German intellectual life, and were treated as commonplace by later authors, including Heidegger.[7]

The Linguistic-tension Approach

If it is accepted that Thought is opposed to *Vorstellung* then Hegel could not be arguing the equivalence of *being* and *nothing* by a detour through the idea of a 'contentless intuition', as Tugendhat suggests. A second line of interpretation recommends itself to those who understand the movement of the Logic in terms of the *linguistic-tension* approach. What unites *being* with *nothing* on this approach is the expressive inadequacy of the category of pure *being* . Because when we utter pure *being* we fail to *say* anything with it — we fail to characterize reality on its basis — pure *being* is the same as *nothing*.

Thus Josef Simon:

They are the same for this reason — that *being* is the 'unutterable' [*Unsagbare*], because with the utterance of *being* nothing is said [*mit dem Sagen des Seins nichts gesagt ist*] or it can only be uttered in so far as nothing determinate is said.[8]

If this is not to fall into a horrific example of the Parmenidean fallacy the approach is forced to deny that *being* and *nothing* are legitimate thought-determinations, or to count them as thought-determinations only in a weak sense. The necessity for this can be made clear if we contrast the *linguistic-tension* view of language with a *designativist* view (which I shall call the *direct* approach). The direct approach suggests that if *being* is a thought-determination then, quite simply, 'being' means (*refers to*, or *evokes*) being. Clearly, if Hegel adopts this direct approach to language, an argument such as Simon's will commit precisely the fallacy identified by Tugendhat, namely, to think that in *failing* to thing *anything* (and thus 'thinking nothing') I am actually thinking *nothing* in the sense of referring to a thought-object: nothing. The failure to think anything and the successful thought of *nothing*, would be thereby conflated.

So, for an approach such as Simon's, the beginning of the *Logic* cannot consistently be an employment of language to *refer* to the Thought of indeterminate immediacy, pure *being*, or whatever. It is rather, the failure of language to succeed in *evoking, uttering* or *refer-*

7   A treatment of Heidegger's philosophy which acknowledges these affinities is given by Werner Marx in *Heidegger and the Tradition*.
8   Simon, *Das Problem der Sprache bei Hegel*, p. 183.

ring to anything at all. As Taylor puts it:

> The notion of pure being frustrates its own purpose. We cannot characterize reality with it alone, and we are forced to a notion of being as determinate, as having some quality and not another. Being can only be thought as determinate.[9]

An approach such as Taylor's makes *being unthinkable*. It is the thought of *nothing* only in the sense that it is no thought. But, for Hegel, it is vital that *being* should indeed be thinkable, in order to preserve the *realism* of the enterprise of the *Logic* (the sense in which the thought-determinations developed in it correspond to reality's most basic structure). If the thought-determinations are to be understood as more or less unsuccessful attempts at self-articulation then the correspondence between Thought and reality can only be saved by having the author of the universe himself engage in such unsuccessful attempts at self-realization. But, as I argued in Chapter 5, this picture of the Absolute is quite at odds with Hegel's Christian self-understanding.

Furthermore, if *being* is unthinkable, what becomes of the connection between the end of the *Phenomenology* and the beginning of the *Logic*? The description of *being* as 'indeterminate immediacy' characterizes it from the viewpoint of the beginning of the *Logic*. But there is an equally legitimate viewpoint according to which pure *being* is itself a result — the result of the *Phenomenology*, whose development leads to the return of consciousness into the determinate simplicity of Absolute Knowledge:

> Pure knowledge compacted [*zusammengegangen*] into this unity has set aside [*aufgehoben*] all relation to another and to mediation... Here in the Introduction to the *Logic being* is the beginning, presented as having come about through mediation — mediation, to be precise, which sets itself aside thereby; with the presupposition of pure knowledge as the result of the finite knowledge of consciousness. But, if no presupposition is to be made and the beginning itself taken immediately, it only determines itself thereby that it must be the beginning of the *Logic*, of Thought for itself.
>
> (*W. d. L.* i, p. 54)

The result of the *Phenomenology* is a *mediated immediacy*, whose mediation is cancelled when we come to consider it as the beginning of the *Logic*; it amounts to the transition from *consciousness* which stands 'over-against' its objects to Thought itself. Yet, if we understand what is indeterminate and immediate not just as *featureless* (this,

9   Taylor, *Hegel*, p. 232.

after all, it is) but actually as *unthinkable*, as the linguistic-tension approach makes it, then the result of the *Phenomenology* itself, effectively, becomes unthinkable.

The Direct Approach

The inadequacies of Tugendhat's detour through intuition and of the linguistic-tension approach give support, if negatively, to the direct approach: the view which says that, for Hegel, 'being' means *being* and 'nothing' means *nothing*. Following the direct approach the natural interpretation of the equivalence between *being* and *nothing* is that 'being' and 'nothing' are *coreferential*.

Henrich develops this thesis in the form of an objection to Hegel:

> The objection against the equivalence of *being* and *nothing* says that their difference is only one between *words*, whose reference [*Bedeutung*] is one and the same, namely, indeterminate immediacy. *Being* and *nothing* are distinguished from one another in what they intend [*meinen*]. The beginning of the *Logic* performs nothing more than this identification and yields no progress in Thought.[10]

Yet, for Henrich, this really is not an objection at all; to the contrary, it expresses precisely the *Logic*'s point. In contemporary terms *being* and *nothing* have different senses, but the same *reference*. There are, however, objections to this.

First, one might object that the sense–reference distinction is out of place here. *Senses* (at least in the construction put on them by Dummett) are essentially *means to the establishment of the reference* of words. Senses then involve criteria (such as those contained in definite descriptions) for the establishment of reference. But without such criteria how can one talk of *different* senses? The only determination we have for both *being* and *nothing* is 'indeterminate immediacy'; how, the objection goes, can the idea of different means to a single reference find a purchase?

Moreover the text itself appears to contradict the suggestion. The point of the distinction between sense and reference is to enable semantic theorists to explain how statements of identity such as 'Hermes is Mercury' are informative, not tautological. But, quite explicitly, Hegel objects to the construction of the relationship between *being* and *nothing* as if it could be expressed in a statement of identity:

10   Henrich, 'Anfang und Methode der Logik', p. 78.

The expression of the result that emerges from the examination of *being* and *nothing* by the proposition '*being* and *nothing* is one and the same' is incomplete.

(W. d. L. I, p. 75)

It is one-sided and so, for the purposes of the expression of speculative truth, Hegel requires that:

The opposing proposition is added: '*being* and *nothing* is not the same' which is equally expressed above.

(W. d. L. I, p. 76)

So, despite the fact that *being* and *nothing* are to be 'one and the same', their distinctness must also be preserved. How, in that case, is this distinctness to be accommodated? What is its status? It is, Hegel says, a difference which is a matter of intention [*Meinung*]:

The difference between the two is thus only an intended one — the quite abstract difference which is at the same time no difference.

(Enz., para. 87)

Yet, as Gadamer points out, contrasts of intention of this sort are only intelligible *below* the level of the *Logic*, which claims to be beyond such subjective considerations:

It is striking that 'intention' should be spoken of here. For the difference between intention and that which is actually present in the saying [*im Sagen*] really no longer belongs to the theme of the Logic of 'pure thought'.[11]

Hegel himself excludes intention from the *Logic*:

Intention is a form of the subjective which does not belong in this sequence of presentation.

(W. d. L. I, p. 78) [12]

To accommodate the difference which requires that we describe *being* and *nothing* as *not* the same we can appeal, then, neither to subjective differences in intention between the two terms (for these lie outside the domain of the *Logic*) nor to discernible differences in their properties (for both have 'indeterminate immediacy' as their sole characteristic).

The only path that appears to be open for the direct approach is to abandon the thesis of coreferentiality and turn it on its head: 'being' and 'nothing' might be 'one and the same' in sharing the same sense

11   Gadamer, *Hegels Dialektik*, p. 60.

12   The point is denied by Michael Theunissen in pursuit of his thesis that the *Logic* is 'itself Phenomenology'; he claims that *meinen* plays a constant role in moving the (objective) *Logic* forward. *Sein und Schein*, p. 83.

(or, more precisely, the same *lack* of identifying characteristics) but have *different* referents, *being* and *nothing*, respectively. Of course the objection to this is that not only does it involve standing the coreferentiality thesis on its head but that it also stands on its head the picture of the functioning of language which gave the sense –reference distinction its point. If we admit that two words have the same descriptive content yet still claim that they refer to different things then we cannot hold to the basic Fregean idea that *reference* depends on *sense*.

However, one should beware of attributing to past authors what now seems reasonable; the account of Hegel's view of language, given in Chapter 6, suggests that this may indeed be what he believed. Words, it will be recalled, were essentially *signs* which evoked the Thoughts they represented; there was no suggestion of an *intermediary* feature acting like a sense, as a means to the establishment of a reference. From this, then, it is at least consistent to suggest that for Hegel 'being' evokes the Thought of *being* and 'nothing' the Thought of *nothing*. *Being* and *nothing* are, then, *non-identical indiscernibles*.

The 'sameness' of *being* and *nothing* is not, on this interpretation, something to be established by external argument or abstract semantic theory. It is to *show* itself to the purified consciousness at work in the *Logic*. Only the *experience* of Thought can justify Hegel's claim; neither the detour through intuition nor the linguistic-tension thesis allow this self-evidence to be dispensed with.

7

A Negative Dialectic?

The worst thing about the system is the system.

Roy Harper

In this chapter I move outside Hegel's own text to discuss Theodor Adorno's attempt to produce a 'materialist' conception of dialectic in his final major work of philosophy, the *Negative Dialektik*. But considerations from Chapter 1 explain why such an examination may itself contribute to the understanding of Hegel's text. I suggested there that it is possible for concepts to turn out to have an identity which in fact goes beyond the way that they function to organize those texts in which they are originally used. That does not make the tracing of their functioning in those original texts superfluous, but it suggests that we may need to add a dimension to interpretation beyond the original text, in order to approach the concept's final identity. So, just as Marx claims that the concept of surplus value developed in *Das Kapital* represents the truth of that concept of value which the classical economists, Smith and Ricardo, had used but misunderstood, it might be that the ultimate identity of the concepts in Hegel's theoretical writings are only established after a materialist transformation of his system.

Adorno himself is committed to the possibility of such a materialist transformation by an immanent critique of Hegel's dialectic; indeed he goes so far as to make the possibility of a critique of Hegel into a condition for the continuation of philosophy:

If the concept of dialectic achieved by Idealism encompasses no experiences which are — against Hegel's own emphasis — independent of the Idealistic apparatus, then a renunciation is inevitable for philosophy. It must prohibit itself substantive [*inhaltliche*] insight, restricting itself to the methodology of the sciences and, declaring this to be philosophy, effectively cancel itself.

(*N. D.*, p. 19)

This passage also shows Adorno's answer to a question which I left open in Chapter 1. I argued there only that we should concede that it is possible for the true identity of a concept (its semantic power) to extend beyond the immediate awareness of the author using it, without, however, committing myself to an epistemological account of how this is possible. But Adorno himself does offer an explanation of how concepts extend, namely, that the *experience* which underlies a discourse leads us beyond its surface structure. When he quotes his own provocative aphorism from the *Minima Moralia* 'only those thoughts are true which do not understand themselves' (*N. D.*, p. 57) he should be understood as saying 'only those thoughts are true which contain an experience that extends beyond the immediate awareness based on them'.

The focus on the experience underlying discourse explains, furthermore, Adorno's answer to the dilemmas of immanent critique discussed in Chapter 2. It is a brilliant stratagem to avoid the, apparently exclusive, alternatives of participating in the cognitive activity of philosophy (and remaining bound by its limitation to the realm of thought) or adopting an extra-philosophical standpoint, treating philosophy as a social phenomenon, at the cost of being unable to engage with its cognitive claims. Like Hegel himself, Adorno rejects the assumption on which the first part of the alternative rests, that philosophical discourse participates in a world of neutral, independent semantic entities. Believing, as he does, that language draws its cognitive value from experience and that this experience can be shown to have a social character, Adorno holds that an an analysis of the nature of philosophical experience – the 'criticism of content' – will contribute to the argumentative practice of philosophy and also reach beyond it to social reality; yet it will do this in a way quite different from 'positivist' sociology of knowledge:

Dialectical theory must be immanent – as Marx's largely is – even if, finally, it negates the entire sphere in which it moves. This contrasts it with a sociology of knowledge, introduced from outside philosophy, and, as philosophy smartly discovered, impotent against it. Sociology of knowledge fails in the face of philosophy, substituting its social function and conditionedness by interest for its truth content, not entering into that content's criticism but acting indifferently towards it.

(*N. D.*, p. 197)

Adorno's stress on experience gives his reading of Hegel an advantage, from the point of view of the interpretation argued in this book, over many more specialist commentators, for it leads him to appreciate what I have called the 'necessary first-handness' of Thought. He is committed to the claim that Hegel misidentifies the nature of the experience on which the system's functioning is based, in taking it to derive from the subject's participation in a purified realm of Absolute Knowledge. Apparently, then, Adorno is in a position to mount an immanent criticism of the system, without losing himself in piecemeal disputes, by challenging, not the structure of the system, but the conception of experience on which it rests.

But, as we shall see, it is not possible to account for Adorno's reading of Hegel in this simple way as an *acceptance* of the structure of the dialectical movement and a *rejection* of the conception of experience which operates it. There are two reasons why not. First, Adorno thinks that Hegel's misidentification of the experience underlying the speculative movement actually leads to inconsistencies in his perception of the movement's structure, the most significant of which is that Hegel complements the intrinsically critical movement of the dialectic with a 'negation of the negation' − an unjustifiable affirmation. Thus Adorno only intends to endorse a part of the dialectical movement. Second, it can be shown, with the help of the account developed in the preceding chapters, that Adorno seriously misunderstands the enterprise being carried out in Hegel's system. The result is that the conception of dialectic which he does endorse differs significantly from that which is at work in Hegel's text.

Before arguing these points in more detail I shall examine the two fundamental criticisms which Adorno makes of Hegel's conception of experience. These criticisms are, as we shall see, logically connected to one another. The first I shall call the *transition to materialism*, and is the result of the claim that Hegel misidentifies the real nature of the synthesizing source, the origin of order and universality, which underlies the movement of the system, *Geist*.[1] Putting the claim in its most succinct form, Adorno writes: 'The World-Spirit is, but it is no such thing.' (*N. D.*, p. 298)

The Transition to Materialism

Adorno is not making the banal Marxist criticism that Hegel mistakes for *mind* what is really *matter*; a line of criticism which, it is easy

1   In this chapter it would be misleading to continue the practice of rendering *Geist* as 'Spirit'. The ambiguity of *Geist* between 'mind' in the everyday English usage and 'Spirit' in the Hegelian sense is often important to Adorno's thought. Where he does not clearly opt for one sense (as in references to Hegel, for example) I shall leave the word untranslated.

to see, leads into impasses. Interpreted epistemologically, it amounts to the claim that Hegel imputes processes to the knowing subject which are in fact features of mind-independent reality. Such criticism is beside the point, however; the dialectical development of Thought furnishes the structure of reality, and, because it encompasses both *thought* and *reality*, there is no way to play one off against the other. But how else, if not epistemologically, could the contrast between materialism and Hegel's Idealism be given purchase? If we take Hegel's own understanding of the contrast, then the issue between materialism and Idealism is one of two opposed metaphysics. The difference does not lie in competing epistemological conceptions of the *origin* of knowledge but in the different *structures* which each attribute to mind-independent reality. Materialism, in Hegel's view, is a fundamentally reductionist metaphysics, whose aim is to account for reality without having to admit developmental or teleological qualities. 'Dialectical materialism', in aiming to restore such dynamic features to materialism, would, on Hegel's understanding of the difference, undermine the basis of its own distinct identity.

For Adorno, however, the Idealist misidentification consists in the failure to identify *Geist* as *society*:

Beyond the philosophy of identity's magic circle the transcendental subject may be deciphered as *society*, unconscious of its own self.

(*N. D.*, p. 179)

At first sight this criticism, too, risks triviality. What does it matter whether Hegel calls society '*Geist*' and Adorno calls *Geist* 'society'? But, apart from the terminological difference, there is also an important change in substance. For Adorno, society is not to be understood in the affirmative way in which Hegel understands *Geist*. The Idealist conception of *Geist* is the theoretical embodiment of a false society, one whose structure subjects its members to domination. Thus the passage from which the aphorism on the World-Spirit quoted above was taken reads in full:

The World-Spirit is, but it is no such thing. It is not Spirit but, rather, the negative which Hegel shifted off it and on to those who have to bow to it. Their defeat is redoubled by the verdict that their difference from objectivity is untrue and bad.

(*N. D.*, p. 298)

Society is constituted by alienated social labour, organized as a system of exchange relationships, which represent a mechanism of compulsion — a false subject — in relation to the individual subjects who participate in them. Idealism conceals this subject's true, negative identity:

The mediation [of subject and object] is itself substantive [*inhaltlich*] — it is mediation by the social totality. But it is also formal in virtue of the abstract law-governedness of the totality itself, that of *exchange*. Idealism, which distilled its Absolute Spirit from it, also enciphers the truth that the phenomena meet this mediation as a mechanism of compulsion. That is what is concealed behind the so-called problem of constitution.

(*N. D.*, p. 57)

Philosophically, the most significant feature of the social division of labour is the separation introduced between *mental* and *manual* labour, for this is what gives rise to the illusion of autonomous *Geist*:

Geist is no isolated principle but one *moment* in social labour — that which is separated from the corporeal.[2]

The repressive character of the division of labour helps to explain why Idealism should fail to decipher *Geist's* true origin. In creating the illusion that *Geist* is autonomous, Idealism functions as part of the dominant ideology, concealing, and hence ratifying, the structure of an unequally divided society:

Since mental labour parted company with manual, under the sign of the domination of *Geist*, and of the justification of privilege, *Geist*, separated, had to vindicate the claim to domination (which it takes from the idea of itself as what is *primary* and *original*) with the exaggeration of a guilty conscience. For the claim not to collapse it had to forget entirely where that claim originated.

(*N. D.*, p. 179)

Idealism's refusal to acknowledge *Geist's* origin in labour leads directly to a distortion in the conception of *Geist* itself, the claim that *Geist* amounts to an Absolute Subject, capable of generating content without the need for a material complement or substratum. But such an Absolute Subject is out of the question, for, according to Adorno, the activity of *labour*, in which the concept of *Geist* originates, has an ineradicably bi-polar structure. He describes Marx as engaging in a polemic against the hypostasis of labour in any way:

Such a hypostasis only continues the illusion of the primacy of the generating principle. It arrives at its truth solely in relation to that non-identical element for which Marx — who despised epistemology — chose at first the

2   Adorno, *Drei Studien zu Hegel*, p. 270.

crude, all too narrow name of *nature*, later that of *natural material* and other, less burdened terms.

(*N. D.*, p. 179)

Non-identity

The transition to materialism, which recalls the origin of *Geist* in social labour, ideologically suppressed by Idealism, brings us, therefore, to the second fundamental criticism which Adorno makes of Idealism: the *transition to non-identity*. If the model for mental activity is labour, and labour always requires a substratum, then the claim of the Hegelian system to operate from a point where thought is independently productive is an illusion which owes its plausibility solely to *Geist*'s concealment of its origins. In fact, according to Adorno, *Geist* is always only the subject pole in a relationship which requires an objective material:

Hegel accordingly hypostasizes *Geist* in vain. To manage this he must inflate it to the *whole*, whereas, by its concept, *Geist*'s *differentia specifica* lies in that it is *subject*, not the whole.

(*N. D.*, p. 199)

In denying the primacy of the subject, Adorno is not just adopting the general anthropological standpoint that man is to be seen as an element in the natural order, but advancing a thesis with a specific philosophical force. The necessarily dualistic structure of *Geist*, which he argues for, undermines any attempt at an Absolute-Idealist ontology; all concepts being intrinsically related to the non-conceptual, the idea of a purely conceptual discipline is an impossible self-contradiction:

In truth, all concepts, philosophical ones included, relate to what is non-conceptual, because they themselves are moments of reality, which compels their formation, primarily for the purposes of the domination of nature

(*N. D.*, p. 23)

It is important to emphasize, however, that, although concepts originate in the domination of nature, Adorno does not restrict them to this instrumental function. The innate capacity of language to extend itself beyond the function assigned to it in an exchange-dominated society is essential to Adorno's (qualified) defence of philosophy. Language can be turned against domination. The implication of the criticism of the instrumental operation of concepts cannot be the adoption by the philosopher of a standpoint *beyond* the tension between the conceptual and the non-conceptual; the origin of thought processes in the appropriation of external reality prohibits any escape from the dualism of subject and object. The philosopher whom Adorno takes to task for this is not, as one might have expected, Hegel, but Heidegger:

> Heidegger avoids the issue, which it is one of the motivations of dialectic to deal with, in usurping a position beyond that difference between subject and object in which the incongruity of reasoning with what is thought reveals itself... Thought can conquer no position where the separation between subject and object lying in every thought – in thought itself – would disappear.
>
> (N. D., p. 92)

The concepts themselves incorporate the tension between their subsuming function (the 'compulsion to identity') and their intrinsically dynamic and expressive power. Adorno describes these subsuming functions as 'archaisms', in a way that recalls Nietzsche's criticism of the classificatory intellect. For Nietzsche, classification incorporates the Platonic myth that all cognition is a form of repetition – in effect, recognition. For Adorno such functions are 'relics of static thought and of a static ideal of knowledge in the middle of dynamized consciousness' (N. D., p. 156) and dialectic has the task of reanimating them:

> In dialectic thought makes objection to the archaisms of its conceptuality. Identifying thought reifies [vergegenständlicht] by the logical identity of the concept. Dialectic, on its subjective side, amounts to thinking so that the form of thought no longer turns its objects into invariants, always self-identical.
>
> (N. D., p. 157)

But Adorno's account of conceptual thought leads to a dilemma for his reading of Hegel. On the one side, the dualistic structure of thought clearly implies the rejection of Hegel's understanding of *Begriff* as the notion which is:

> the infinite form – the free creative activity which can realize itself without the need for a material present outside itself.
>
> (Enz., para. 163)

Yet, on the other, conceding the impossibility of such a spontaneously creative notion undermines the possibility of a dialectical movement owing anything to Hegel; the tension between the concept and the non-conceptual, supposed by Adorno to provide the very motor of dialectic, must be surpassed in order to attain Hegel's 'element of Thought'. Only a reading of Hegel which failed to take this into account would make Adorno believe that his own enterprise could draw on Hegel's.

Adorno's Account of Hegel

This supposition is confirmed when we examine what Adorno has to say about the nature of the Hegelian enterprise. He describes its uniqueness as consisting in the fact that it 'represents the unattained endeavour to match up, by the means of philosophical concepts, to what is heterogeneous to them' (*N. D.*, p. 16). Recalling the discussion of *transformative* and *generative* approaches to the understanding of Hegel in Chapter 3, we can see that this is an ambiguous characterization. It is true to say that Hegel's conception of philosophy aims to 'match up to reality by conceptual means' to the extent that it tries to generate a richer content than, for example, the purely formal structures of Kant's transcendental philosophy. It is also true to say that the structure developed in the *Logic* underlies the rational aspects of our everyday experience. But Adorno's description suggests that the activity of dialectical philosophy consists in the attempt to use concepts to *appropriate* the non-conceptual — in effect that he takes the transformative approach to dialectic which I argued against in Chapter 3. Adorno provides evidence for this in this passage from *Drei Studien zu Hegel*:

Goethe's proposition that everything which is complete of its kind points beyond itself, is canonical for Hegel, just as he has much more in common with Goethe than the surface difference between the doctrine of the *Urphänomen* and that of the self-moving Absolute gives one to suspect.[3]

In fact, Adorno is wrong: the difference between Goethe and Hegel is a fundamental one; although they share the goal of overcoming the separation which the subsuming activity of the understanding places between particular and universal, we saw that, against Goethe, Hegel explicitly describes his own philosophy as *not* being a doctrine of experience. Thought underlies experience, for Hegel, but such non-philosophical experience does not provide the starting point in the sense of being the 'raw material' for philosophy. Adorno's association of Goethe and Hegel in fact tells us something significant about his own conception of dialectic.

Only when we see that Adorno understands Hegel's 'substantive

3   Adorno, *Drei Studien zu Hegel*, p. 305.

philosophizing' on the transformative model, as an activity 'which endeavours to bring experiences to their necessity and rigour'[4] can we identify the structure of his reading of Hegel. He writes, for example, that

The contradiction is not that which Hegel's Absolute Idealism inevitably transfigured it to — no Heraclitean essentiality. It is the index of the untruth of identity, of the resolution of what is conceived into the concept.
(*N. D.*, p. 17)

The first sentence represents a clear rejection — consistent with Adorno's claims about the nature of the concept — of a fundamental feature of Hegel's enterprise, the idea that 'contradictions', as *moments* within the dialectical movement, are constitutive parts of the structure of reality, which it is philosophy's task to develop in Thought. Yet, endorse this rejection of Absolute Idealism, and what place is left for the second sentence? None within Hegel's enterprise. Hegel's 'contradictions' are not products of the 'untruth' of identifying judgements but of the unfolding Absolute Form, which can generate them solely on the assumption that the tension between concepts and the content which they apply to can be transcended.

There is a defence of Adorno which would deny that this misreading seriously undermines his criticism. Using the ideas developed in Chapter 1, one might argue that the criticisms which Adorno makes of Hegel's concepts of *Geist* and *Begriff* are in themselves sufficiently fundamental implicitly to undermine Hegel's text, despite the fact that he follows them up with an explicit misreading of it. It is the initial criticism of these basic concepts which is crucial, not the subsequent misreading of the structure based on them. But, even conceding this, the misreading is important; we cannot understand Adorno's own philosophy without it, for it serves as the basis for his fundamental distinction between *affirmative* and *negative* dialectic. Adorno's argument is founded on the charge that Hegel takes what is in essence a critical procedure — the attempt to articulate the contradiction between concept [*Begriff*] and subject-matter [*Sache*] — and turns it, by a 'negation of negation', into an affirmative one. Hegel is accused by Adorno of going beyond the proper task of philosophy, the recollection to thought of the content which subsuming judgement has eliminated, by a gratuitous 'negation of negation':

4   Adorno, *Drei Studien zu Hegel*, p. 306.

The non-identical cannot be acquired immediately as something positive, nor by negation of the negative. This is not itself, as in Hegel, affirmation. The positive which, according to him, should result from negation, has more than its name in common with that positivity he fought against in his youth. The equation of the negation of negation with *positivity* is the quintessence of identification – the formal principle brought to its purest form. With it the anti-dialectical principle gains the upper hand in the heart of dialectic.

(*N. D.*, p. 161)

Hegel is further accused of betraying his own dialectic, of practising 'abstract' negation in the course of a forward progression in which, at each 'higher' stage, the legitimacy of the act of criticism performed at the lower one is cancelled:

In forgetting – against the intermittent insight of his own *Logic* – at each new dialectical stage the right of the preceding one, Hegel produces the very image of what he takes abstract negation to task for: abstract positivity, dependent on subjective arbitrariness for its confirmation.

(*N. D.*, p. 162)

But it is apparent that Adorno's conception of determinate negation is not Hegel's and his picture of the role Hegel intends it to play is at odds with that explained earlier in this book. I argued, in Chapter 2, that determinate negation, for Hegel, amounts to the double claim that (1) negation is a procedure which adapts itself to the contours of its object, and (2) such negation leads to a *positive* result. The first claim does not entail the second. However, for Hegel, the two go together because both are justified by seeing processes of determinate negation as part of the *single* movement of Thought, presented in its pure form in the *Logic*. For Adorno the dialectical development of Hegel's philosophy consists in a double movement, of legitimate criticism and illegitimate affirmation, so it is natural for him to misunderstand determinate negation as involving only claim (1), not claim (2):

Dialectic's positive element would only be determinate negation – criticism – not a final inversion, happily emerging with affirmation in its hands.

(*N. D.*, p. 161)

But, for Hegel, the negative *is* the positive in a more profound sense than that the criticism of criticism amounts to endorsement; as 'infinite negativity' it is supposed to be the vital source from which content autonomously emerges. Thought operates from behind the point at which the common opposition between positive and negative holds, and, for this reason, Adorno's suggestion that the move-

ment of dialectic be subdivided is misplaced: if the negative movement takes place so, *ipso facto*, does the positive one.

There is, however, one further, even more radical, line of defence
to be used on Adorno's behalf. I have accused him of misunderstanding the movement of Hegel's text which the experience of Thought
generates. The evidence for this has been drawn from Hegel's own
scattered comments, in which he accounts for what he believes himself to be doing. But what if Hegel has misidentified, not just the
experience underlying the movement of Thought, as has been discussed up to now, but the very *structure* of the movement which the
experience sets in motion? In that case the statements that I have
used as evidence cannot be taken as evidence at all, and my whole
interpretative strategy of separating the experience itself (which can
only be given at first hand) from the question of what it is *like* is
undermined. For that strategy must concede authority to Hegel's
self-understanding. The interpreter who adopts my strategy lacks —
or at least brackets his possession of — the experience which alone
could prove or disprove the experience of Thought; nor does he have
the standards by which he could say that Hegel is *wrong* in what he
thinks it achieves. Only the experience of Thought could give
foundation to such a claim.

In one passage Adorno appears to cover himself against criticism
of his reading of Hegel by taking up this more radical position:

If it is objected that criticism of the positive negation of negation severs the
vital nerve of Hegel's *Logic* and no longer permits any dialectical movement
at all, this is to restrict criticism, submissively, to Hegel's own self-
understanding. Although, without question, the construction of his system
would collapse in the absence of the principle, the experiential content
[*Erfahrungsgehalt*] of dialectic is contained not in that principle but in the
resistance of the *other* against identity.

(*N. D.*, p. 163)

Yet here Adorno interprets the criticism to be made against him as
less fundamental than the one which I have made. He supposes his
objector to claim that he has undermined the dialectical movement
because negation of negation is, actually, fundamental to it — an
indispensable feature which can be separately identified. My own
criticism, however, was not that 'negation of negation' is *indispensable*, but that, in one sense, *there is no such thing*. The affirmative
movement in Hegel's system cannot be seen as *supplementing* an initial negative one, and thus subverting its critical value; the two are

not distinct. If we take 'negation of negation' as a misnomer for that aspect of determinate negation by which it produces a positive result, then its rejection amounts to the rejection of precisely that feature which differentiates true dialectic for Hegel. We are left only with 'sceptical', 'sophistic' or 'Kantian' forms.

Nevertheless, Adorno maintains, we can retain the truly dialectical feature at work in Hegel's philosophy despite the loss of the system which the criticism of 'negation of negation' implies. This amounts to something like the Marxist claim to be able to isolate a 'rational kernel' of dialectic from the system in which it is incorporated. But, crucially, for Adorno, unlike Engels, this rational kernel does not consist in a *method*. He has not claimed to have isolated a set of dialectical principles or laws of dialectic and so cannot be accused of failing to appreciate that Hegel's dialectic cannot be incorporated in 'laws' in that sense. Adorno's distinction is not between *method* and *system*, but between *experience* and *system*.

However, the only possible authority for such a radical rejection of Hegel's self-understanding is Adorno's *own* philosophical experience, and so we are returned to the problem faced in developing the initial account of Hegel's philosophy: Adorno draws on a conception of the nature of philosophical experience which it is open to us to *characterize*, but not (because it is experience) to *resume*. I shall now try to give that characterization. Although the purpose is to illuminate Adorno's reading of Hegel, we shall have to refer to what he himself takes from Hegel in order to establish what is distinctive about his conception.

An Interpretative Discipline of Experience

Adorno sees philosophy as an *interpretative discipline of experience*. By discipline of experience I mean more than just that it depends upon what its practitioners undergo at first hand (this, as we have seen, is also characteristic of Hegel), but that it takes its starting point from non-philosophical, everyday experience. Adorno's concern to bring philosophy to bear on non-philosophical experience explains his continuing respect for Husserl's Transcendental Phenomenology; in this respect, phenomenology was an ally within the camp of 'bourgeois' philosophy against those positivist and formalist trends which engaged neither Adorno's sympathy nor his understanding. For Adorno, the ideal of philosophy would be that of 'full, unreduced experience in the medium of conceptual reflection'. (*N. D.*, p. 25)

In calling his philosophy interpretative I mean to identify Adorno as part of the hermeneutic tradition in German philosophy. Two elements of this wide-ranging tradition call for emphasis. Let me start from a thesis which is uncontroversial, but trivial; the object of hermeneutic activity is meaning. As it stands this thesis is too broad to permit one to draw the tradition's boundaries. No one could deny that Quine and Wittgenstein, to name two obvious examples, have made questions of meaning and interpretation central to their philosophies. But ought that to suffice to make them hermeneutic philosophers? If the label is to have any specific historical point it should not.

If concern with meaning is not a sufficient condition for hermeneutic philosophy, is there then a characteristically hermeneutic understanding of the nature of meaning? Although the history of hermeneutic philosophy is a series of disputes (admirably chronicled by Gadamer in *Truth and Method*) on just this question, nevertheless, even these disagreements may be read in terms of two underlying agreements. The first is that for hermeneutics, although meanings are not independent and objective features of reality (in the way that objects in causal relations were for Kant or 'primary qualities' for Locke), neither are they something private and subjective, like seventeenth-century 'ideas'. In this way hermeneutics challenges the division of the world between public 'objective' and private 'subjective' features made by classical empiricism.

The second agreement flows from this; it is the view that it is impossible to try to understand what meaning is by referring to the consciousness and intentions of the subject; we can only understand the nature of the subject itself from its role in appropriating and generating meaning, so meaning cannot itself be approached through it. Thus, for the hermeneutic tradition, the question of whether meaning extends beyond its 'core sense' of deliberate human communicative action — whether, for example, there is meaning in the natural world — represents a major, substantive issue.

This consideration about meaning brings me to a second, epistemological element of the tradition, which I wish to stress. The knowing subject (possibly no longer a *subject* in any traditional philosophical sense) does not carry out its role in appropriating meaning by passive 'imaging' registration or subsuming classification of experience; it is debatable whether there is a hermeneutic analogue to the Idealists' Reason but hermeneutics follows Idealism in resisting the reduction of the subject's status implicit in sense or understanding.

From this description hermeneutic philosophy's affinities with romanticism and Idealism (again admirably stressed by Gadamer) emerge. No less then Coleridge or Goethe, it aims to build on Kant's *Third Critique* in order to challenge views of the world which restrict what is intersubjectively significant to the causal order described by natural science, and, like them, it extends the notion of meaning beyond the range of what can be determinately expressed, going so far as to conclude that, in its highest form, meaning actually resists such determination. So Adorno, in my view, is perfectly justified in moving as freely as he does between Hegel's and Heidegger's problems; the context in which they write is a continuous one.

On this description Adorno himself is certainly a hermeneutic author. He says as much explicitly. Philosophy, which participates in tradition by its dependence on texts, is interpretative:

That justifies the transition of philosophy to *interpretation*, which elevates neither what is interpreted nor the symbol into the Absolute.

(*N. D.*, p. 64)

The Goal of Interpretation

In the course of the *Negative Dialektik* Adorno expands on the nature of this interpretative process in terms of a range of apparently divergent claims:

(1)   Interpretation is to be *cognitive* and to give an adequate representation of its subject-matter in a way that subsuming, identifying judgement cannot:

Cognition of the non-identical is also dialectical in that it itself *identifies*, both *beyond* and *differently* from identifying thought. It wishes to say what something *is*, whereas identifying thought says what it falls under.

(*N. D.*, p. 152)

(2)   In dealing with cultural objects it *secularizes* them and 'seeks what is true at the point where thought secularizes the irrecuperable original [*unwiederbringliche Urbild*] of sacred texts'.

(*N. D.*, p. 64)

(3)   Yet, at the same time as dissipating the object's illusory *Schein* it aims to go beyond the object:

The vision which, in interpreting, discovers more in the phenomenon than it merely is, and, only thereby, *what* it is, secularizes metaphysics.

(*N. D.*, p. 39)

Its apprehension is in this fashion both *cognitive* and *utopian*:

Cognition which desires content desires utopia. This, the consciousness of possibility, adheres to the content as the undistorted. It is the possible, never the immediately actual, which blocks the way for utopia.

(*N. D.*, p. 39)

(4) Nevertheless, interpretation is *historical*, aiming to uncover the real processes of development underlying whatever presents itself as immediate:

The indissoluble, in the face of which [philosophy] capitulated, and which Idealism slid away from, is itself a fetish in its 'thus-and-only-thusness' – that of the irrevocability of what is. The fetish dissolves in the face of the insight that it *is* not just the way it is and not otherwise, but that it has *become* under certain conditions. This process of becoming disappears and dwells in the subject-matter [*Sache*], as little to be immobilized in its concept as to be split away from its result and forgotten. Temporal experience takes after it. In reading what *is* as the text of its *becoming*, materialist and Idealist dialectic are contiguous with one another.

(*N. D.*, p. 62)

(5) But, in deciphering the history which the object contains, interpretation does more than record the object's genesis as a natural, causal process. It aims to *reveal* or *release* what is contained:

Such immanent universality of the individual is *objective* as *sedimented history*... To apprehend the constellation in which the subject-matter stands is as much as to decipher the history which, as something which has become [*Gewordenes*], it carries within itself... Knowledge of the object in its constellation is that of the process accumulated within it.

(*N. D.*, pp. 165, 166)

(6) It constructs *models* in order to express the specificity and immanent universality of its objects:

The model captures the specific and more than the specific without evaporating it into its universal concept

(*N. D.*, p. 39)

to do which it brings concepts into *constellations*:

The unifying moment survives without the *negation of negation*, but not by committing itself to abstraction as the supreme principle. It does so not in proceeding by stages from concepts to higher, generic ones, but by setting them in constellation. This illuminates the specific element of the object which the classificatory procedure is indifferent to, or finds burdensome.

(*N. D.*, p. 164)

(7) But interpretation does not just 'point beyond' the object or

'recuperate' its history; it aims to *criticize* it in terms of its own aspirations:

> [Negative dialectic] accepts the unmediated immediacy, the formations which society and its development present to thought, as they come, in order to release their mediations by analysis, according to the standard of the immanent difference of the phenomena from that which they aspire to be in their own right
>
> (N. D., p. 48)

and to *decompose* reified conceptions:

> [Dialectic's] movement does not gravitate towards identity in the difference of every object from its concept. Rather, it treats the identical with suspicion. Its logic is one of the decomposition of the finished and reified form of concepts which the knowing subject is faced with immediately.
>
> (N. D., p. 148)

Now this is an extremely ambitious set of claims. They are strong individually, and, furthermore, they at least appear to be in conflict with one another. To grasp what is specific to an object, to decipher its history, to confront it with its innate aspirations or to place it in the field of a utopian vision, are, at first sight, mutually exclusive projects. Yet Adorno claims all of these things for his materialist practice of interpretation; the rejection of the Idealist conception of *Geist* would hardly appear to have limited the ambitions of his philosophy very seriously.

To understand how Adorno believes these different aims are compatible we must first consider his view of the nature of the meaning-generating process. It is noteworthy that such a process figures in Adorno's philosophy at all, for this is no necessary part of hermeneutic doctrine. As we saw, hermeneutic philosophy believes meaning to be a feature unlike Lockean primary qualities. Although it is sceptical of rooting meaning in the conscious processes of human subjects, this does not oblige the hermeneutic philosopher to find some other origin for meaning. It is perfectly consistent with his programme to refuse the question and to treat the problem of the origin of 'meaning-features' of reality on a par with the question of what gives natural laws their foundation − as misplaced.

But Adorno, like German Idealism, does identify an origin for meaning. It is the real process of society, operating under the division of labour. This thesis forms one of the main points of criticism of phenomenology, whose *Wesensschau* (the 'intuition of essences') fails to incorporate the awareness of the social process, the collective life of *Geist*, which makes it possible:

> On the other side *Wesensschau* denotes the physiognomic eye for [*Blick auf*]
> intellectual circumstances. It is legitimated by the fact that what is intellec-
> tual [*Geistiges*] is not constituted by the consciousness which is cognitively
> turned towards it, but is grounded in itself, far beyond the individual prog-
> enitor, in the collective life of *Geist*, objectively, according to its immanent
> laws.
>
> (*N. D.*, p. 89)

Nor is this collective life historically invariant:

> The more over-socialized [*vergesellschafteter*] the world is, the more tightly
> its objects are knit together with universal determinations... the greater,
> then, is the tendency for the individual state of affairs to be immediately
> transparent in its universal element.
>
> (*N. D.*, p. 90)

In this significant respect, then, Adorno has more in common
with the authors of German Idealism than with modern hermeneutics. Meaning is again to be related to a transcendental process,
although now this is to be comprehended *socially*, and as a source of
antagonism and oppression, rather than a realm of harmony and reconciliation:

> The compulsive order of reality, which Idealism projected into the sphere of
> *subject* and *Geist*, is to be translated back from it... The subjective preforma-
> tion of the material social production process, quite different from theoretic-
> al constitution, is its unresolved element, that which is not reconciled to the
> subjects. Its own *Vernunft* operates unconsciously, like the transcendental
> subject. It founds identity by exchange, remaining incommensurable with
> the subjects it homogenizes: the subject hostile to the subject. The antece-
> dent universality is both true and untrue. It is true because it forms the 'ether'
> that Hegel calls *Geist*; untrue because its *Vernunft* is, as yet, no Reason – its
> universality the product of particular interest.
>
> (*N. D.*, p. 22)

It is important not to misunderstand Adorno's claim that processes of *Geist* are to be 'translated back' into real social processes as if it
were simply a translation from 'mind' to objective, determinate
matter. History is the sum of the social processes constituted by the
alienated labour embodied in them, and this gives historical experience an important double character; inert as it presents itself, but
potentially dynamic. The alienation of labour is such as to make its
products, society, into a falsely naturalized *second nature*. The task of
interpretation is to revivify those products of labour themselves, a
vital and dynamic potentiality, pointing *beyond* reified actuality.

Lukács

We must differentiate Adorno's view of how this reanimation is to take place from that of Georg Lukács, with whom, as a 'left Hegelian' or 'Hegelian Marxist' he is often associated. The Lukácsian would approach the question starting from the idea that labour processes are intrinsically teleological, that they realize goals. Although it may be that these goals cannot be determinately specified in advance of the labour processes performed in pursuit of them, nevertheless, they function as standards by which their realization in processes may be criticized. In a society operating under the division of labour, labour is social, not individual; that is to say the true subject is the collective labourer, striving to realize itself into a total subject against the self-alienation which the division of labour imposes. Theory is only one pole of what is, intrinsically if not in fact, a unified activity, *praxis*; its own role in the struggle for self-realization, therefore, amounts to an aspiration to take on the 'standpoint of totality'. Dialectical thought treats individual phenomena according to a regulative ideal of their completion, which the standpoint of totality legitimates.

It is well known that Adorno was thoroughly pessimistic about the prospects of such a self-realizing collective subject:

History has, until now, had no collective subject, constructible in any way.
(*N. D.*, p. 299)

But we should resist the temptation to read Adorno's philosophy as a *special case* of the Lukácsian picture — theoretical activity which, in the absence of a collective subject, fails to identify itself in political practice. This was certainly how Adorno's New Left critics in Germany mistakenly understood him. Hans-Jürgen Krahl — a former student of Adorno's — put it in the language of the times:

Adorno's dialectical concept of negation distanced itself ever more from the historical necessity of an objective partisanship of thought, contained in Horkheimer's specific differentiation of critical from traditional theory, at least in its programme of the 'dynamic unity' of the theorist with the oppressed class.[5]

But Adorno goes further, in fact, than disputing the existence of one of the conditions for the Lukácsian orientation of thought. He challenges its ideal of interpretation at a more fundamental level. For Lukács the interpreter's orientation to totality is legitimate as an anti-

5   Krahl, 'Der Politische Widerspruch der kritischen Theorie Adornos', p. 286.

cipation of the consciousness of an as yet unrealized collective subject, a materialized version of the Idealist conception of *Geist*. But for
Adorno, as we saw, the concept of *Geist* embodies no ideal of reconciliation. To the contrary it is false insofar as it represents an accurate
image of the totalizing structure of current, oppressive society.
Adorno does not reject the orientation to totality in *default* of a collective subject; he rejects the Lukácsian ideal itself.

The practice of interpretation which Adorno himself proposes instead describes the reading process as *secularizing* and *allegorical*.
Allegory here is to be understood in the sense defended by Adorno's
friend Walter Benjamin. Benjamin, in his *Ursprung des deutschen
Trauerspiels*, had been concerned to rehabilitate allegory from the
depreciation of the late eighteenth century. He rejected the Goethean
account of it as deriving meaning only from an extrinsic, conventional motivation, the polar opposite of the innately meaningful, expressive symbol. For Benjamin allegory is itself an expressive form:

Allegory − the following pages are to serve to demonstrate this − is not a
technique of image-play, but *expression*, as language is expression, indeed, as
script is.[6]

Allegory *does* have a relation to convention, but it is an expressive
one:

The seventeenth century's allegory is not conventional in expression but an
expression of convention.[7]

The expressiveness of the allegorical object is quite unlike that of
the symbol, however. It does not point beyond itself towards a point
of realization and completeness (a theological point for Idealist aesthetics, a political one for Lukács). On the other hand, the allegorist's
secularizing vision is also unlike that of the scientific materialist who
aims to criticize away the anthropomorphic features of the object in
order to open it up for causal, scientific investigation. As Benjamin
puts it, the allegorist *mortifies* the object into yielding its intrinsic
meaning. Where Idealism had taken as its model the harmoniousness
of organic nature, the allegorical sensibility sets against it the *death
mask*, a degraded physiognomy which expresses, but cannot mediate, the gulf between mortality and redemption. Instead of reaching
out for wholeness allegory endeavours to find significance in frag-
ments; instead of the neo-classical ideal of 'unity in diversity' it aims,

6   Benjamin, *Ursprung des deutschen Trauerspiels*, p. 339.
7   Benjamin, *Ursprung des deutschen Trauerspiels*, p. 351.

one might say, at truth without the need for unity. Above all, in contrast to the visual, Neo-Platonist model of meaning as *manifestation*, the expressive unity of allegory is the imageless coherence of *script*.

Adorno's disagreement with Lukács's neo-classical aesthetics of interpretation can be traced back to a basic disagreement as to what supports interpretative practice. Lukács had argued, in *History and Class Consciousness*, that only the identification of theory with an active, historical subject could resolve its antinomies. In the absence of such a subject theory will be *reified* and *undialectical*. But Adorno does not accept this; he believes that dynamism is inherent in language itself, in its capacity to give expression to individual experience. In his view the effects of the division of labour are such that only the separation of theory from practice can preserve conceptual thought as a refuge of the vital and dynamic. Being conceptual, in the specific Adornian sense, it both embodies the abstract structure of a society based on exchange (in its subsuming function) and retains the capacity to think beyond it. Because political practice has capitulated to instrumentalism, the Lukácsian demand for the unity of theory and practice promises only to reduce theory to practice's level:

The demand for the unity of practice and theory has continually degraded theory into practice's handmaiden ... it is in practice's own interest that theory reconquers its independence.

(*N. D.*, pp. 146, 147)

Operating in language, theory retains a power of transcendence, available to the most 'unpolitical' thinker who chooses to resist the instrumentalization of intellectual life. The intellectuals, diminished in stature though they are by their own marginality, are the twentieth century's only culture-heroes.

Theory, for Adorno — this was a point of criticism against Benjamin — is not intuitive. Although he speaks of allegorical *vision* it is one that realizes itself in language and does not, like an intuition, bypass conceptual thought. The conceptual power of language alone can counteract the separation which it itself introduces; having struck the blow it must heal it:

The philosophical concept does not desist from that longing which animates art non-conceptually. But its fulfilment retreats from art's immediacy like a mirage [*Schein*]. The concept — the organon of thought as well as the barrier between thought and what is to be thought — negates this longing. Philosophy can neither avoid nor surrender to such a negation. It must try to get out beyond the concept by conceptual means.

(N. D., p. 27)

Although this 'barrier' corresponds to the Idealist problem of the separation introduced between universal and particular by the subsuming judgement, Adorno's response is neither that of Goethe, for whom intuition (albeit of an elevated sort) yields the innate universality of the particular, nor of Hegel's creative, self-particularizing *Begriff*. For Adorno the task of conceptual thought is one of criticism:

Dialectic alone, in the self-criticism of the concept, can comprehend [*begreifen*] [what is excluded from thought].

(N. D., p. 139)

This stress on the conceptual nature of philosophical activity is a further point of disagreement with Heidegger. Adorno accuses Heidegger's doctrine of the 'revealedness' of truth [*Erschlossenheit*] of irrationalism:

Heidegger has thereby eliminated the rational dimension which Husserl preserved and, with a greater affinity to Bergson, tacitly adopted a procedure which sacrifices an inalienable moment of thought, its relationship to the discursive concept.

(N. D., p. 77)

This is a regression in which Heidegger's philosophy 'creeps into the cave of departed mimesis' (N. D., p. 136). Mimesis itself has long since been displaced in human consciousness by conceptual thought. But, even now, there remains a tension between the mimetic aspiration of knowledge and its discursiveness which only the innate dynamism of the concept when turned against itself can ease:

Secretly the *telos* of identification is non-identity, that which is to be saved in it. The error of traditional thought is in taking identity to be its goal. The power that explodes the illusion [*Schein*] of identity is that of thought itself.

(N. D., p. 152)

Adorno's claim, then, is that language itself has the power to express the contrast between the concept and what is thought by means of it. Adorno draws a contrast between his own and Heidegger's attitudes to language in this respect:

The constitutive participation of language in truth does not produce an identity of the two. The power of language proves itself by the fact that, in reflection, expression [*Ausdruck*] and content [*Sache*] part from one another. Language becomes the deciding instance of truth only in the consciousness of the non-identity [*Unidentität*] of the expression with what is intended [*dem Gemeinten*]. Heidegger refuses this reflection; he calls a halt after the first step of the dialectic of the philosophy of language.

(*N. D.*, p. 117)

The two main features which differentiate Adorno's interpretative conception of philosophical experience from hermeneutic doctrines such as Heidegger's are, then, (1) his aim of giving an account of the source of meaning (and, by identifying that source as a social process, of tying philosophy to social theory) and (2) the aim to operate with a conceptual, discursive form of rationality. In order to illustrate the claim, which I made above, that Adorno draws on Hegel for the distinctive features of his conception of philosophy, I want now to consider lines of objection corresponding to these two features.

Mediation and Reflection

The first line of objection concentrates on how precisely the social meaning process is to be conceived. As we saw, for Adorno, society takes the place of *Geist* in the Idealist schema. Although this is intended as a move away from Idealism, it does not eliminate Idealism's characteristic difficulty, namely, the need to give an account of the relationship between empirical and transcendental realms. The problem is resolved by Hegel's Absolute Idealism because the transcendental subject is, in fact, an absolute one, which itself generates the empirical. Transcendental and empirical, mind and nature, are not heterogeneous but emerge as 'moments' in a unified process; the problem of how one realm is 'constituted on' another is left behind when we operate in the element of Thought. Nor does a thoroughgoing scientific materialism face any such problem. On this view, 'transcendental' questions (if such we may continue to call them) are to be investigated naturalistically. The 'limits of thought' are the subject-matter of an investigation which is, in principle, no different from any other scientific investigation. Yet Adorno, who, as we have seen, rejects both the Absolute Subject, on the one hand, and the reduction of meaning processes to determinate natural processes, on the other, cannot escape Transcendental Idealism's dilemma. It shows itself in his philosophy as the problem of the relation of meaning processes to their material substratum.

The second line of objection concerns the process by which the aims of interpretation are united: the 'sedimented' history of intellectual phenomena released; the direction of the syntheses of conceptual thought reversed; and the constellations, in which the immanent universality of the phenomena is to be expressed, constructed. As Adorno puts it:

The determinable error of all concepts makes it necessary to summon up others. From this there arise *constellations* to which alone something of the hope in the *name* passes on. The language of philosophy approaches it by its negation. What it criticizes in words — their claim to immediate truth — is always, in fact, the ideology of the positive existent identity between word and content.

(N. D.., p. 63)

On the assumptions of Adorno's philosophy the object is only known insofar as it is given through concepts. To determine the 'error' of concepts, therefore, we cannot step outside our cognitive processes in order to compare what is given in them to the object 'as it is in itself'. How, then, can conceptual thought itself provide the standards for its own criticism?

Adorno does not provide satisfactory answers to these questions, although they are vital to his enterprise; without them those features of interpretation, amalgamated by his views on the meaning process and on the nature of cognitive activity, become, once again, disparate. Instead of answers, however, we find Adorno bypassing the problems by *making use* of two concepts which he appropriates from Hegel: *mediation* and *reflection*.

Mediation answers Adorno's need to give conceptual expression to the relationship between transcendental and empirical phenomena: meaning processes and their material substrata. Had he adopted Husserl's distinction of principle between *transcendental-phenomenological* and *empirical-genetic* kinds of investigation then the issue would not have had to be faced in this form. In that case the question of the relationship between transcendental and empirical realms could be treated as a matter of the relationship between two orders of explanation. But Adorno rejects just such a division and so a way must be found of conceiving the relationship between the two spheres within the framework of what is, in principle, a single social process. In particular, he must explain how the two poles of the labour process — meaning-conferring activity and raw material — are related, so that the 'transformation' which the former works upon the latter is more than just the change from one determinate physical disposition to another. Mediation is Adorno's general term for such non-causal relatedness. It forms the object of interpretative investigation, concealed behind the immediately presented appearance which is dialectical philosophy's starting point:

Negative dialectic accepts as it comes mediated immediacy, the formations which society and its development present to thought, in order to release their mediations by analysis.

(N. D., p. 48)

Reflection in its turn is to explain how this 'analysis', recuperating mediations and reversing syntheses, is possible as part of thought's rational progress towards non-subsuming knowledge of its object. Reflection is language's own innate power of determining the effects of its synthetic, conceptual activity. Adorno applies this idea of reflective determination to the beginning of Hegel's *Logic*.

The unfolding of the concept [*Begriff*] is also a reaching back [*Rückgriff*], and synthesis the determination of the difference which was destroyed in the concept – 'disappeared' ... The difference between the self-contradictory moments only reveals itself in the completed synthesis, their unification. Without the step that *being* is the same as *nothing,* each would be – using a favourite expression of Hegel's – 'indifferent' to the other. Only when supposed [*sollen*] to be the same do they become contradictory.

(N. D., p. 160)

Together, then, reflection and mediation express the distinctiveness of Adorno's interpretative conception of philosophy. He himself says as much in criticism of Husserl and Heidegger: 'They hope to cancel *mediations* instead of *reflecting* them'. (N. D., p. 70, my emphasis)

But what entitles Adorno to make use of these two concepts? Evidently they are supposed to constitute the common strand connecting his conception of philosophical experience with Hegel's, and to incorporate the 'experiences ... independent of the Idealistic apparatus' (N. D., p. 19), which the continuation of philosophy was said to depend on. But is he, in fact, justified in making this appropriation?

Referring to Hegel's text, it is apparent that mediation is more than an unspecific (but technical-sounding) word for 'connection'. Mediation, as I argued in Chapter 3, has its place with *immediacy* as part of the unintuitable, apparently paradoxical ontological structure of the Idea, developed and justified in the *Logic*. Adorno, however, in taking the concept over as part of philosophical 'ordinary language', removes it from the context in which the experience of

Thought might give its only rigorous justification.

Nor can reflection, as a term for the subject's reappropriation of its own synthetic activity, be simply adopted to underpin a conception of dialectic. Hegel's speculative dialectic, at least, in raising consciousness to the level of the notion, is beyond *reflection* in that Fichtean-romantic sense. Hegel does not postulate a general capacity of language to redissolve the syntheses of experience; Thought develops its own structures in its own element.

One author who appreciated this quite clearly was Walter Benjamin:

Whilst the concept of reflection forms the foundation of early romantic philosophy, the concept of positing [*Setzens*] only appears in its full development − not without relation to it − in Hegel's dialectic. It is, perhaps, no exaggeration to say that, just because of its combination with the concept of reflection, in Fichte, the dialectical character of positing does not achieve its full and characteristic expression as in Hegel.[8]

Benjamin is quite right; the 'positing' of the movement of Thought goes beyond reflection because it is *creative*. The clarity of Benjamin's perception is somewhat ironic in view of Adorno's own claim that Benjamin 'hardly knew' Hegel and that it was just his failure to adopt 'the thought of universal mediation which founds the totality in Hegel as in Marx' which made him theoretically 'naive'.[9] But Adorno's picture of Benjamin as a philosophical ingenue is misleading, implying as it does that the absence of Hegelian terminology from Benjamin's writings is a matter of ignorance, to be corrected by Adorno's own sophistication. To the contrary, whatever the difficulties in Benjamin's philosophy, he was aware, as Adorno was not, that he could not resolve them by cheques presented against Hegel's account.

Adorno attempts to draw on Hegel to solve the twin problems of Idealism: how the *transcendental* interacts with (or supervenes on) the *empirical*, and how that transcendental activity may be rationally recuperated. But in fact, within Hegel's system, both 'transcendental' and 'empirical' are part of a single world-process emanating from the Idea, a process reproduced by the generative activity of the notion. Adorno, on the other hand, reads Hegel's philosophy as if it undertook (in the manner of Husserl's 'egological reflection') to make the

8 Benjamin, *Der Begriff der Kunstkritik in der deutschen Romantik*, p. 22.
9 Adorno, *Über Walter Benjamin*, pp. 22, 23.

subject's own constituting activity thematic, drawing on language's innate 'reflexive' capacity to do so.

We have in Adorno's philosophy, then, a situation which is just the reverse of that hypothesized at the beginning of this chapter. I suggested there that the value of bringing the reading of Adorno together with that of Hegel could lie in the completion which Hegel's concepts received in Adorno's text. But, although something of the sort can be maintained for *Geist* and *Begriff*, in the case of mediation and reflection it is just the opposite. By means of these concepts Adorno conceals — not least from himself — the difficulties of his own text. So, in this case, it is not the later text which 'completes' the earlier one, but the return to the earlier text which enables us to dispel the 'bewitchment' which its concepts place upon the later. Only when restored to their speculative-mystical shell does the irrational kernel of Hegel's concepts become apparent.

8
Conclusion

Interpreters of Hegel customarily conclude their interpretations by repeating something like Croce's question: *What is Living and What is Dead in the Philosophy of Hegel?* For interpreters who are wedded to a hermeneutic theory of meaning the question, indeed, is inseparable from the practice of interpretation; it is the *vitality* of the text which preserves its meaning and, hence, makes interpretation possible at all. However, I have a short answer to such a question: nothing.

To say this is, of course, to transgress the limitation which I have imposed on interpretation: the distinction between the *experience* of Thought and its characterization. I am now committing myself to an assertion about the self-development of Thought itself. In my view there is no such thing; the content-generating 'hyperintuition' is sheer Neo-Platonic fantasy. But — for reasons I need no longer repeat — this is not something that the interpreter can demonstrate.

But this concession is of no advantage to the established defenders of Hegel; for Adorno, Bubner, Plant, Taylor *et. al.* the possibility of 'saving' something from Hegelianism depends on it being other than speculative Neo-Platonism. This *can* be a matter of argument, and I have tried to give it.

However, I do not want to suggest by my negative judgement that I have a low opinion of Hegel's philosophical ability. To the contrary, he has, in the highest measure, two out of the three cardinal philosophical virtues: he is *rigorous* and he is *original*. But he is *wrong*, and those very virtues ensure that he is thoroughly and consistently so.

Yet, if nothing remains of intrinsic philosophical value, why read Hegel at all? I offer three answers.

First, there is the continuing influence of Hegel's ideas. It is impossible to understand twentieth-century German philosophy without reference to them. Their hold (as I tried to show in the case of

Adorno) is actually *more* effective for being unanalysed. Detached from their context in German Idealism, Hegelian terms like *Geist*, *reflection*, *mediation* have become part of a philosophical 'everyday language' which mystifies those who employ it. The best chance at emancipation from their power is to refer them back to their original context; this is one reason why the interpretation of Hegel is too important to be left to Hegelians.

A second reason is Hegel's wider importance for the history of ideas. This may require some justification — not because that significance could seriously be disputed, but because it is a commonplace of analytical philosophy that philosophy and the history of ideas are separate enterprises. If this separation means to resist the dissolution of philosophy within an all-embracing vision of history — the bogy of *historicism* — then well and good. But philosophy and the history of ideas are connected for the opposite reason. Paradoxical though it may sound, the history of ideas does not deal in *ideas* — determinate entities whose career the detached observer merely traces. This is one of the implications of the arguments of Chapter 1. For this reason a cognitive engagement, such as that traditionally associated with the philosopher, is needed in order to establish the history of ideas' subject matter. Not that the history of ideas should stop there. One hopes that it will go on to investigate why concepts are effective *despite* their incoherence, why their original significance becomes concealed, and how it is that new concepts can actually arise out of misunderstanding. The cognitive interrogation of texts is only a first step towards this. But it is indispensable.

The very difficulty of the Hegelian texts provides a third, final, reason for reading them. I suggested in Chapter 1 that philosophical texts are organized at a fundamental level by concepts which philosophers employ more or less unreflectively to set the standards of their enterprise. If Hegel's writings remain difficult then this is not because their author was inconsistent or obtuse. It is, rather, a measure of the distance which separates his standards from our own. But this distance is a part of the value of reading them. The effort of penetrating their recalcitrant surface is inevitably reflexive; to discover what resists us in the understanding of Hegel is to discover something valuable about ourselves.

Bibliography

Abrams, M. H., *The Mirror and the Lamp* (Oxford: OUP, 1971).

Adorno, Theodor W., *Gesammelte Schriften*, ed. by G. Adorno and R. Tiedemann (Frankfurt: Suhrkamp, 1970–) individual works cited:
Schriften, v, *Drei Studien zu Hegel*.
Schriften, vi, *Negative Dialektik* (translated as *Negative Dialectics*, by E. B. Ashton (New York: Seabury Press, 1973))
(abbreviated as *N. D.*).
Über Walter Benjamin (Frankfurt: Suhrkamp, 1970).

Althusser, Louis, 'Contradiction and Overdetermination', in *For Marx* (Harmondsworth: Penguin, 1969), pp. 89–128.

Saint Augustine, *The Trinity*, trans. by S. McKenna (Washington: Catholic University of America Press, 1963).

Ayers, Michael, 'Analytical Philosophy and the History of Philosophy', in J. Ree, M. Ayers and A. Westoby, *Philosophy and its Past* (Hassocks: Harvester Press, 1978), pp. 41–66.

Benjamin, Walter, *Gesammelte Schriften*, ed. by R. Tiedemann and H. Schweppenhäuser (Frankfurt: Surhkamp, 1974–) individual works cited:
Der Begriff der Kunstkritik in der deutschen Romantik, *Schriften*, i, pp.7–123.
Ursprung des deutschen Trauerspiels, *Schriften*, i, pp. 203–430 (translated as *The Origin of German Tragic Drama* by J. Osborne (London: New Left Books, 1977)).

Blumenberg, Hans, 'Das Licht als Metapher der Wahrheit', *Studium Generale*, 10 (1957), pp. 432–54.

Bubner, Rüdiger, *Dialektik und Wissenschaft* (Frankfurt: Suhrkamp, 1973).
'Strukturprobleme dialektischer Logik', in *Der Idealismus und seine Gegenwart: Festschrift fur Wenner Marx*, ed. by U. Guzzoni,

B. Rang, and L. Siep (Hamburg, 1976), pp. 36−52.

'Die "Sache selbst" in Hegels System', in *Seminar: Dialektik in der Philosophie Hegels*, ed. by R.-P. Horstmann, (Frankfurt: Suhrkamp, 1978) pp. 101−23.

Buchdahl, Gerd, *Metaphysics and the Philosophy of Science* (Oxford: Blackwell, 1969).

Coleridge, S. T., *Biographia Literaria* (London: Dent, 1975).

The Stateman's Manual, in Collected Works, ed. by R. J. White (London: Routledge and Kegan Paul, 1972), vol. vi.

Collingwood, R. G., *An Autobiography* (Oxford: OUP, 1970).

Cook, D. J., *Language in the Philosophy of Hegel* (The Hague: Mouton, 1973).

Culler, Jonathan, 'The Linguistic Basis of Structuralism', in *Structuralism: An Introduction*, ed. by D. Robey (Oxford: OUP, 1973) pp. 20−36.

Dummett, Michael, *Frege: Philosophy of Language* (London: Duckworth, 1973).

Dworkin, Ronald, *Taking Rights Seriously* (London: Duckworth, 1973).

Engels, Friedrich, *Ludwig Feuerbach and the Outcome of Classical German Philosophy*, ed. C. P. Dutt (London: Martin Lawrence, 1934).

Gadamer, Hans-Georg, *Hegels Dialektik* (Tubingen: J. C. B. Mohr, 1971).

Truth and Method (London: Sheed and Ward, 1975).

Goethe, J. W. von, *Werke* (Stuttgart: Cotta, n.d.) individual works cited:

Werke, ii, *Maximen und Reflexionen*.

Werke, xvi, pp. 459−62. 'Über die Gegenstände der bildenden Kunst'.

Werke, xviii, pp. 296−300, 'Analyse und Synthese'.

Haag, Karl-Heinz, *Philosophischer Idealismus* (Frankfurt: EVA, 1967).

Habermas, Jürgen, 'Ein marxistischer Schelling', in *Über Ernst Bloch* (Frankfurt: Suhrkamp, 1971), pp. 61−81.

Knowledge and Human Interests, trans. by J. Shapiro (London: Heinemann, 1972).

Hartmann, Klaus, 'Hegel: A Non-Metaphysical View', in *Hegel: A Collection of Critical Essays*, ed. by A. MacIntyre (Notre Dame, Ind.: University of Notre Dame Press, 1976), pp. 101−24.

Hegel, G. W. F., *Werke in zwanzig Bänden*, ed. by K.-M. Michel and
    E. Moldenhauer (Frankfurt: Suhrkamp, 1971) individual
    works cited:
    Werke, I, *Frühe Schriften*.
    Werke, VII, *Grundlinien der Philosophie des Rechts* (abbreviated as
    Rechtsphil.) (translated as *Philosophy of Right*, by T. M. Knox
    (Oxford: OUP, 1952)).
    Werke, VII–X *Enzyklopädie der Philosophischen Wissenschaften*
    I–III, (abbreviated as *Enz.*) (translated as *Logic, Philosophy of
    Nature*, and *Philosophy of Mind*, by W. Wallace and A. Miller
    (Oxford: OUP, 1971–5)).
    Werke, XII, *Vorlesungen über die Philosophie der Geschichte*
    (abbreviated as *Phil. der Gesch.*) (translated as *Lectures on the
    Philosophy of History*, by J. Sibree (New York: Dover, 1956))
    Werke, XIII–XV, *Vorlesungen über die Ästhetik* I–III, (abbrevi-
    ated as *Ästh.*, I–III) (translated as *Aesthetics*, by T. M. Knox,
    2 volumes (Oxford: OUP, 1975)).
    Werke, XVIII–XX, *Vorlesungen über die Geschichte der Philosophie*
    I–III, (abbreviated as *Gesch. der Phil.*, I–III) (translated by E. S.
    Haldane and F. H. Simson, as *Lectures on the History of Philoso-
    phy*, 3 volumes (London: Kegan Paul, 1892–6)).
Jenenser Realphilosophie, ed. by J. Hoffmeister, 2 volumes (Leip-
    zig: Meiner, 1932).
Phänomenologie des Geistes, ed. by J. Hoffmeister (Hamburg:
    Meiner, 1952) (abbreviated as *P. d. G.*) (translated as *Phe-
    nomenology of Spirit*, by A. V. Miller (Oxford; OUP, 1977)).
Wissenschaft der Logik, ed. by G. Lasson, 2 volumes (Hamburg:
    Meiner, 1971) (abbreviated as *W. d. L.* I,II) (translated as
    Science of Logic, by A. V. Miller (London: George Allen and
    Unwin, 1969)).
Heidegger, Martin, 'The Origin of the Work of Art', in *Philosophies
    of Art and Beauty*, ed. by A. Hofstadter and R. Kuhns (London:
    Chicago University Press, 1976), pp. 650–700.
Henrich, Dieter, 'Anfang und Methode der Logik', in *Hegel im Kon-
    text* (Frankfurt: Suhrkamp, 1971).
Herder, J. G., *Abhandlung über den Ursprung der Sprache* (Stuttgart:
    Reclam, 1966).
Humboldt, Wilhelm von, *Über die Verschiedenheit des mensch-
    lichen Sprachbaus*, in *Werke*, VII (Berlin: De Gruyter, 1968).
Kant, Immanuel, *Werke in zwölf Banden*, ed. by W. Weischedel

(Frankfurt: Suhrkamp, 1977) individual works cited:
Werke, III, IV, Kritik der reinen Vernunft (abbreviated as K. r. V.) (translated as Critique of Pure Reason, by N. Kemp Smith, (London: Macmillan, 1970)).
Werke, X, Kritik der Urteilskraft (abbreviated as K. Uk.) (translated as Critique of Judgement, by J. Bernard (London: Harper, 1968)).

Krahl, Hans-Jürgen, 'Der Politische Widerspruch der kritischen Theorie Adornos', in Konstitution und Klassenkampf (Frankfurt: Neue Kritik, 1971), pp. 285–88.

Kulenkampff, Arend, Antinomie und Dialektik (Stuttgart, Metzler, 1970).

Lakatos, Imre, Proofs and Refutations (Cambridge: CUP, 1976).

Marx, Werner, Heidegger and the Tradition (Evanston, Il: Northwestern University Press, 1971).

Plamenatz, John, Man and Society, 2 volumes (London: Longmans, 1963).

Plant, Raymond, Hegel (London: Allen and Unwin, 1973).

Popper, Karl, 'What is Dialectic?', Mind, 49 (1940), pp. 403–26.

Ricoeur, Paul, Freud and Philosophy (New Haven, Conn.: Yale University Press, 1970).

Ryle, Gilbert, 'Use and Usage', in Philosophy and Linguistics, ed. by C. Lyas, (London: Macmillan, 1971), pp. 45–53.

Simon, Josef, Das Problem der Sprache bei Hegel (Stuttgart: Kohlhammer, 1966).

Skinner, Quentin, 'Meaning and Understanding in the History of Ideas', History and Theory, 8 (1969), pp. 3–53.
    'Motives, Intentions and the Interpretation of Texts', New Literary History, 3 (1971–2), pp. 393–408.

Strawson, P. F., The Bounds of Sense (London: Methuen, 1966).

Taylor, Charles, Hegel (Cambridge: CUP, 1975).
    'Interpretation and the Science of Man', in Critical Sociology, ed. by P. Connerton (Harmondsworth: Penguin, 1976).

Theunissen, Michael, Sein und Schein (Frankfurt: Suhrkamp, 1978).

Tugendhat, Ernst, 'Das Sein und das Nichts', in Durchblicke: Martin Heidegger zum 80. Geburtstag, ed. by V. Klostermann (Frankfurt: Suhrkamp, 1976).
    Traditional and Analytical Philosophy. Lectures on the Philosophy of Language (Cambridge: CUP, 1982).

Wieland, Wolfgang, 'Bemerkungen zum Anfang von Hegels

Logik', in *Wirklichkeit und Reflexion: Walter Schulz zum 60. Geburtstag* (Pfullingen, 1973), pp. 395–414.

Index

DATE DUE			
MAY 0 9 '90			
MAR 1 8 2005			